Practical Approaches to Using Learning Styles in Higher Education

EDITED BY Rita Dunn
AND Shirley A. Griggs

BERGIN & GARVEY
Westport, Connecticut • London

10/2003

Library of Congress Cataloging-in-Publication Data

Practical approaches to using learning styles in higher education /
   edited by Rita Dunn and Shirley A. Griggs.
      p.   cm.
    Includes bibliographical references (p.   ) and index.
    ISBN 0–89789–703–X (alk. paper)
    1. Study skills. 2. Education, Higher. I. Dunn, Rita Stafford,
  1930– . II. Griggs, Shirley A.
    LB2395.P69 2000
    378.1'70281—dc21   99–40321

British Library Cataloguing in Publication Data is available.

Library of Congress Catalog Card Number: 99–40321
ISBN: 0–89789–703–X

First published in 2000

Bergin & Garvey, 88 Post Road West, Westport, CT 06881
An imprint of Greenwood Publishing Group, Inc.
www.greenwood.com

Printed in the United States of America

The paper used in this book complies with the
Permanent Paper Standard issued by the National
Information Standards Organization (Z39.48–1984).

10 9 8 7 6 5 4 3

Contents

Preface

The quality of teaching in many of our colleges and universities is perceived as deplorable and is under attack by many outstanding academicians. Former Harvard University president Derek Bok observed that teaching in academe is one of the few human activities that does not get demonstrably better from one generation to the next (1982). A research report, distributed by the Carnegie Foundation for the Advancement of Teaching, concluded:

In the current climate, students all too often are the losers . . . in glossy brochures they're assured that teaching is important, that a spirit of community pervades the campus, and that general education is the core of the undergraduate experience. But the reality is that on far too many campuses, teaching is not well rewarded and faculty who spend too much time counseling and advising students may diminish their prospects for tenure and promotion. (Boyer, 1990, pp. xi–xii)

Anderson (1992) scathingly asserted that many university intellectuals have betrayed their profession by scorning their students and disdaining teaching. He maintained that the critical problem is not that many professors do not teach *well*, but that so few *teach at all*. This has resulted in a significant part of teaching responsibilities being assumed by teaching assistants. Anderson concluded that "students teaching students," often without training, supervision, or expertise, is so extensive and pervasive that it actually threatens the validity of a university education (1992, p. 61).

Some institutions of higher education have begun to address these criticisms by reordering priorities and linking *teaching effectiveness* to faculty personnel actions for tenure and promotion. Additionally, on selected college campuses, learning and teaching centers have been instituted to help college faculty and their teaching assistants move away from the exclusive use of lectures to more creative and innovative approaches to learning. For too long, faculty have focused on the *content* of what is to be learned while ignoring the individual learning-style characteristics of their students—which should dictate the *process* of learning.

Within this book, the initial two chapters by Rita Dunn and Shirley Griggs describe the theory, practice, and research on learning styles and provide step-by-step practical approaches to capitalizing on students' strengths in higher education. The contributors to this text have a commitment to identifying and accommodating their students' individual learning styles. They command faculty positions in higher education, representing multiple disciplines and varied professional schools, including business, education, the health professions, the humanities, and law. Almost all the authors in this book begin to respond to students' learning styles through assessment (Stage 1). Other authors describe additional alternatives for complementing individual differences (Stages 2–5). Thus, readers will be exposed to the various ways in which different professors have implemented a process for accommodating their students' unique learning and processing styles. Those approaches reflect stages in an implementation process and include:

Stage 1: Assess students using the *Productivity Environmental Preference Survey* (PEPS) (Dunn, Dunn, & Price, 1974–1996b). Subsequently, PEPS is used to:

• identify individual and group patterns among students' learning-style preferences and then develop teaching strategies to respond to those patterns. For example, Ralph Terregrossa and Valerie Englander (Chapter 22) used Cooperative Learning strategies to teach their peer-oriented students.

• interpret PEPS results so that each student becomes aware of his/her own learning-style strengths—as almost all the contributors do.

• obtain results for empowering students to study through their learning-style strengths. Some actually assign computer-generated prescriptions for studying and doing homework (Dunn & Klavas, 1990), as described by Joyce Miller and Rose Lefkowitz (Chapter 16) and Sue Ellen Read (Chapter 3).

• suggest instructional approaches that respond to individual, rather than group learning-styles—which is what Barbara Thomson does (Chapter 14).

Stage 2: Design instruction to respond to both global and analytic students' processing styles, as illustrated by Robin Boyle, Karen Burke, Shirley Griggs, and Nancy Montgomery (Chapters 17, 9, 12, and 4).

Stage 3: Develop course content to accommodate a variety of perceptual preferences—auditory, visual, tactual, and kinesthetic—as addressed by Robin Boyle, Ann Braio, Karen Burke, Katy Lux, and Barbara Thomson (Chapters 17, 10, 9, 13, and 14).

Stage 4: Create special materials to individualize instruction based on students' need for choices, environmental variations, mobility, structure, and peer-versus-authority orientations, such as:

- Contract Activity Packages, as addressed by Heather Dunham and Barbara Lewthwaite, Bernadyn Suh, and Janet Whitley and Pam Littleton (Chapters 20, 8, and 5);

- Multisensory Instructional Packages, as contained in the chapter by Janet Whitley and Pam Littleton (Chapter 5); and

- Programmed Learning Sequences, as discussed by Miller and Lefkowitz, Sue Ellen Read, and Janet Whitley and Pam Littleton (Chapters 16, 3, and 5).

Stage 5: Totally implement learning-styles-based instructional strategies as found in:

- academic skills seminars conducted by Joanne Ingham (Chapter 18);

- consortium training for preservice and inservice teachers as conducted by Barbara Thomson (Chapter 14); and

- inservice workshops for college faculty as presented by Katy Lux (Chapter 13).

The chapters included in this book provide university faculty and administrators with a totally new approach to teaching in higher education. This approach, based on three decades of prize-winning research and lauded by international practitioners, is the logical and practical response to the many respected critics cited in the introduction to this Preface.

Part I

Introduction to Learning Styles
in Higher Education

Chapter 1

Capitalizing on College Students' Learning Styles: Theory, Practice, and Research

Rita Dunn

PROBLEMS CONCERNED WITH TEACHING IN HIGHER EDUCATION

Problem #1. It is logical to believe that college students know how to study. Without that ability, how could they have succeeded well enough in high school to warrant admission into college?

Response: High school teachers tend to *spoon feed* their students. They feel that if they "don't cover the curriculum," their students won't learn it! One outcome appears to be that at least 25 percent of freshmen fail or are placed on probation when, for the first time, they need to:

- listen to a lecture and *intuit* "what is important";
- listen to a lecture and take notes for studying for the test;
- listen to a lecture and remember three-quarters of what they hear;
- read and *intuit* what is important;
- *read* and take notes for studying for the test; and
- remember three-quarters of what they read.

And, if the freshman lives in an on-campus dormitory, there are additional problems that get in the way of studying, such as concentrating with:

- someone else in the room;
- someone else's need for music—or quiet—while concentrating;
- someone else talking to friends in person, on the telephone, or on a cell phone;
- vastly different lighting needs;

• a roommate who requires different study hours;

• a roommate who handles food or drinks differently.

Problem #2. Minority student enrollment in higher education increased steadily throughout the 1980s and into the early 1990s (Carter & Wilson, 1992). Minority freshmen often are somewhat deficient in English and appear to be less prepared academically than former students on American campuses (Mentzer, 1993).

American institutions of higher education also have been enrolling more foreign students and mid-life adults preparing for new careers (Dunn, Ingham, & Deckinger, 1995). The differences in age, culture, experience, and language skills among traditional high school graduates, minority and foreign students, and career-changing adults in their forties and fifties suggest a diversity that is unlikely to find any single teaching style effective (Bovell, in progress). Furthermore, although professors' teaching styles may differ, each tends to teach in one unique pattern with only infrequent variations (Dunn & Stevenson, 1997).

Response: Whereas at least 20 institutions of higher education have adopted learning-style strategies (Dunn, Given, Thomson, & Brunner, 1997), many others have failed to integrate any of these strategies with conventional instructional approaches. Many college instructors appear to be unaware that prize-winning research (see Appendix A), often published in some of the best refereed research journals in the United States, has verified that:

• Practitioners who have used Dunn and Dunn learning-styles approaches reported statistically higher standardized achievement and attitude test scores among average, poorly achieving, and special education students at every academic level in urban as well as suburban and rural schools (*Research on the Dunn and Dunn Model*, 1999).

• Researchers at more than 115 institutions of higher education have published studies with the Dunn and Dunn Model (*Research on the Dunn and Dunn Model*, 1999).

• A meta-analysis of 42 experimental studies conducted with the Dunn and Dunn Learning-Style Model between 1980 and 1990 at 13 different universities revealed that eight variables coded for each study produced 65 individual effect sizes (Dunn, Griggs, Olson, Gorman, & Beasley, 1995). The overall, unweighted group effect size value (r) was .384 and the weighted effect size value was .353 with a mean difference (d) of .755. Referring to the standard normal curve, this suggests that students whose learning styles were accommodated with compatible instructional interventions could be expected to achieve 75 percent of a standard deviation higher than students who have not had their learning styles accommodated. This indicates that matching students' learning-style preferences with educational interventions compatible with those preferences is beneficial to their academic achievement.

- According to the Center for Research in Education, the 20-year period of extensive federal funding (1970–1990) produced very few programs that consistently resulted in statistically higher standardized achievement test scores for special education students (Alberg, Cook, Fiore, Friend, & Sano et al., 1992). Prominent among those programs that *did* consistently increase standardized achievement test scores was implementation of the Dunn and Dunn Learning-Style Model.
- In a profession in which many community colleges lose almost 70 percent of their entering freshman class, and in which only 30 percent of entering candidates graduate, teaching at the college level requires sober examination—and revision.
- When previous researchers addressed the learning styles of college students, they did so to assist non-conventional or at-risk students in danger of becoming dropouts (Clark-Thayer, 1987, 1988; Clay, 1984; Cook, 1989; Dunn, Bruno, Sklar, & Beaudry, 1990; Mickler & Zippert, 1987; Nelson, Dunn, Griggs, Primavera, Fitzpatrick, Bacilious, & Miller, 1993; Williams, 1994). Therefore, early studies focused on samples comprised of college students with academic problems.

That initial focus on underachievers was re-directed when the emotional fears of nursing majors were addressed. Those undergraduate students were required to master a mandated science curriculum in Anatomy and Physiology (n = 134) and Bacteriology (n = 69) in the same classes with science majors whom they perceived as extremely proficient in the science content (Lenehan, Dunn, Ingham, Murray, & Signer, 1994). The nursing students (n = 203) in the control group were provided with conventional study-skill guidelines, tutoring, and advisement assistance. An experimental group was provided with homework prescriptions for how to study based on their learning-style preferences identified with the *Learning Style Inventory* (LSI) (Dunn, Dunn, & Price, 1990). Both groups were administered the *State-Trait Anxiety Inventory* to examine the differences in their levels of anxiety, curiosity, and anger.

Students in the experimental group achieved statistically higher (a) science test grades, (b) grade-point averages, (c) lower anxiety and anger scores, and (d) higher curiosity about science than students in the control group who were not given learning-styles-based how-to-study prescriptions (*Homework Disc*, 1992).

A meta-analysis of research conducted at 13 different universities revealed that college students evidenced the largest effect-size gains when instructional strategies or resources were complementary to their learning-style strengths. Eight experimental studies of 894 students revealed the highest weighted effect size of .413 in comparison to 23 studies of 1,914 elementary school students with a weighted effect size of .364 and five studies of 373 secondary students with a weighted effect size of .155. Therefore, the meta-analytic study found that school level was an accepted moderator for the quality set with the subset of college level attaining the greatest gain in academic improvement, resulting from learning-styles-based instruction is beneficial to their academic achievement (Sullivan, 1993).

Subsequently, the effects of learning-styles-based instruction on the achievement and attitudes of allied health college students who consistently performed well in their college courses were examined. Once again, results demonstrated that, when the instructional approach capitalized on their learning styles, achieving students performed statistically better than when it did not (Miller, 1997; Miller & Dunn, 1997).

Finally, two studies of staff development conducted for teachers with master's degrees through both traditional and learning-styles approaches revealed significantly higher knowledge gains with the learning-style methods (Raupers, in press; Taylor, Dunn, Dunn, Klavas, & Montgomery, 1999/2000). The Raupers study yielded significantly higher long-term gains over time and Taylor's results yielded statistically higher attitudinal scores with learning-styles versus traditional instruction.

Problem #3. Although college and university professors have experimented with instructional approaches such as case studies, cooperative learning, independent studies, role playing, and simulations to enable their students to improve academically, for the most part these strategies have proven no more effective than lectures or readings—particularly with at-risk students (Boyle & Dunn, 1998; Jones & Watson, 1991).

Response: In contrast, strategies designed to complement individuals' learning styles have reversed underachievement among many at-risk and achieving college students (*Research on the Dunn and Dunn Model*, 1999). Chapter 2 describes successful learning-style practices for improving college students' achievement and retention. However, each strategy may be effective with only certain students! Will *you* be able to identify for which students each approach is likely to be successful?

HOW CAN WE TEACH THEM IF WE DON'T KNOW HOW THEY LEARN?

Several theorists have generated concepts related to learning differences (Cronbach, 1957; Glasser, 1966; Skinner, 1983). Although each contributed to an understanding of how learning generally occurs, their research did not reveal what made the identical instruction effective for some students and ineffective for others.

What Are the Differences Among the Various Learning-Style Models?

Eight researchers' definitions of learning style suggest that, although there are similarities among models, there also are important differences (Dunn, DeBello, Brennan, Krimsky, & Murrain, 1981). For example, Canfield and Lafferty (1976) were the only ones to address goal setting, whereas, almost three decades ago, the Dunns (1972) were the first to reveal individuals' requirements for alternative environments when concentrating. The value of providing environmental variations is internationally recognized today (Brunner & Dunn, 1996; DiSebastian, 1994; Dunn & Brunner, 1997; Jadid, 1998). However, three decades ago only limited research was available on individuals' diverse preferences for warmth versus cool, intake (snacks), music, or conversation versus background silence, soft versus bright illumination, or informal versus formal seating arrangements while concentrating (Dunn & Dunn, 1992, 1993; Dunn, Dunn, & Perrin, 1994). In addition, the Dunns differentiated among six sociological possibilities— learning alone, in pairs, as part of a team, with peers, with a collegial versus an authoritative adult, and with variety versus with routines and patterns.

Well in advance of the current interest in multiculturalism, both Hill's (1971) and Ramirez' and Castenada's (1974) models included culture as a crucial aspect of learning style. When, during the mid-1980s, the National Association of Secondary School Principals (NASSP) released its learning-style model (Keefe, Letteri, Languis, & Dunn 1986), that paradigm paralleled many of the Dunns' 21 elements, but also included study skills. Then, in contrast with Dunn, Dunn, and Price's *Learning Style Inventory* (LSI, 1974–1996a) identification of global versus analytic "strengths" (Dunn & Dunn, 1993, p. 40), the National NASSP's *Learning Style Profile* (LSP) (Keefe et al., 1986) identified students' processing styles as either *high* or *low analytic.*

DeBello (1990) described some models as narrow in focus with only one or two variables on a bipolar continuum. He cited the Dunn and Dunn (1972), Hill (1971), and NASSP (1986) models as the only three that were comprehensive; each requires analysis of many variables. DeBello (1990) also challenged the learning-style nomenclature of other models. He perceived the *Myers-Briggs Type Indicator* (Lawrence, 1982) as a *personality index* rather than a learning-style identifier.

DeBello (1990) and Tendy and Geiser (1998/1999) analyzed McCarthy's 4 MAT model (1990) as a *lesson-plan design* that prescribed teaching all students in the same class with identical resources, in the same sequence, at the same time, and in the same amount of time. In addition, all three reviewers reported that the quality of learning-styles research varied from model to model and from study to study (DeBello, 1990; Tendy & Geiser, 1998/1999).

Each of the learning-style models has been evaluated extensively (Curry, 1987; DeBello, 1990; Dunn, DeBello, Brennan, Krimsky, & Murrain, 1981; Tendy & Geiser, 1998/1999). One important outcome has been that the focus on instructional strategies gradually shifted from identification of suitable approaches for *all* learners to identification of strategies responsive to students with selected characteristics—particularly when they were confronted with challenging academic tasks.

Comprehensive Versus Single- or Dual-Dimensional Models

Learning-styles theory recognizes that learners' cognitive, affective, physiological, and sociological patterns determine their academic outcomes. Those patterns, according to Keefe (1982), serve as relatively stable "indicators of how learners perceive, interact with, and respond to the learning environment" (p. 4). Several learning-styles theorists focus on only one or two variables—often on a bipolar continuum (Gregorc, 1982; Hunt, 1982; Kolb, 1976; McCarthy, 1990). The complex nature of learning suggests that a multidimensional model is required to reflect the many individual differences resulting from each person's biological, developmental, and psychological experiences. A multidimensional concept of learning style is the basis of the three comprehensive models—Dunn and Dunn (1972, 1992, 1993, 1998, 1999), NASSP (Keefe et al., 1986), and Hill (1971).

Most people are affected by between 6 and 14 learning-style variables. Some learners are impacted by many variables and others by only a few. When using only a single- or dual-dimensional model, the very variable that might produce the most achievement gains for one individual could be the variable *not* included in that model. Both the NASSP and Hill models were designed for secondary students. The Dunns' model and various versions of its related instrumentation were designed for, and have been applied to, primary (Dunn, Dunn, & Perrin, 1994), elementary (Dunn & Dunn, 1972, 1978, 1992), secondary (Dunn & Dunn, 1978, 1993), and adult (Dunn & Dunn, 1998, 1999) populations. Therefore, this book focuses on the multidimensional model that has reported extensive research with adults—the Dunn and Dunn Learning Style Model.

WHAT *IS* LEARNING STYLE?

According to Dunn and Dunn (1993), learning style is the way students begin to concentrate on, process, internalize, and remember new and difficult academic information. Restak (1979), Thies (1979, 1999/2000), and the Dunns (1992, 1993) theorize that learning style is comprised of both biological and developmental characteristics that make the identical instructional environments, methods, and resources effective for some learners and ineffective for others. Most people have learning-style *preferences*, but individuals' preferences differ significantly.

Educators in primary school through college across the United States have increased students' academic performances significantly by responding to their diverse learning styles (Dunn & DeBello, 1999). And, at both the elementary (Schiering, 1999) and middle school (P. H. Roberts, 1999) levels, students have capitalized on their style strengths to teach themselves complex science units. Moreover, the less well students perform with traditional instruction, the more important it is to accommodate their learning-style preferences (Braio, Dunn, Beasley, Quinn, & Buchanan, 1997; Mitchell, Dunn, Klavas, Lynch, Montgomery, & Murray, in press; Roberts, 1998/1999; Roberts, Dunn, Holtschneider, Klavas, Miles, & Quinn, in press).

THE DUNN AND DUNN LEARNING-STYLE MODEL

Rita and Ken Dunn describe learning style as individuals' personal reactions to each of 21 elements when concentrating on new and difficult academic knowledge or skills (1992, 1993, 1998, 1999). To capitalize on their learning style, students need to be made aware of their:

- reactions to the immediate instructional environment—sound versus silence, bright versus soft lighting, warm versus cool temperatures, and formal versus informal seating;
- own emotionality—motivation, persistence, responsibility (conformity versus non-conformity), and preference for structure versus choices;
- sociological preferences for learning—alone, with peers, with either a collegial or authoritative adult, and/or in a variety of ways as opposed to patterns or routines;
- physiological characteristics—perceptual strengths (auditory, visual, tactual, and/or kinesthetic strengths), time-of-day energy levels, intake (snacking while concentrating), and/or mobility needs; and
- global versus analytic processing as determined through correlations among sound, light, design, persistence, sociological preference, and intake (Dunn, Bruno et al. 1990; Dunn, Cavanaugh, Eberle, & Zenhausern, 1982; Guastello & Burke, 1998/1999) (see Figure 1.1).

THEORETICAL CORNERSTONE OF THE DUNN AND DUNN LEARNING-STYLE MODEL

Learning style is a biologically and developmentally determined set of personal characteristics that make the identical instruction effective for some students and ineffective for others (Dunn & Dunn, 1972, 1992, 1993; Dunn, Dunn, & Perrin, 1994; Restak, 1979; Thies, 1979, 1999/2000). Although initially conceived as an outgrowth of practitioners' observations, this learning-style model traces its roots to two distinct learning theories—cognitive-style theory and brain-lateralization theory.

Cognitive-style theory suggests that individuals process information differently on the basis of learned or inherent traits. Many previous researchers investigated the variables of field dependence/independence, global/analytic, simultaneous/successive, and/or left- or right-preferenced processing. As they conducted studies to determine whether relationships existed among these cognitive dimensions and students' characteristics that appeared to be more or less responsive to environmental, emotional, sociological, and phys-

Figure 1.1
The Dunn and Dunn Learning-Style Model

ELEMENTS

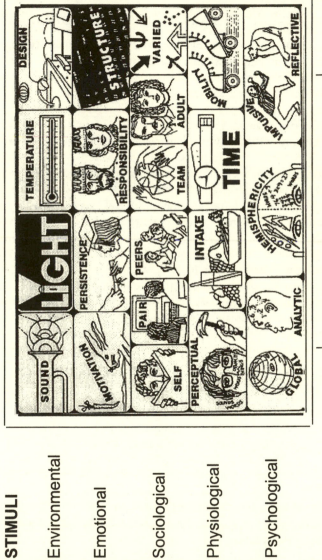

STIMULI

Environmental

Emotional

Sociological

Physiological

Psychological

Simultaneous or Successive Processing

Source: Dunn, R., & Griggs, S. A. (1995). *Multiculturalism and learning style: Teaching and counseling adolescents.* Westport, CT: Praeger, p. 83. Copyright © 1995 by Rita Dunn and Shirley A. Griggs. Reproduced with permission of Greenwood Publishing Group, Inc., Westport, CT.

iological stimuli, we found that selected variables often clustered together. Indeed, relationships appeared to exist between learning persistently (with few or no interspersed relaxation periods), in a quiet, well-lit environment, in a formal seating arrangement and with little or no intake, and analytic left processing. Similarly, students with comparatively short attention spans who learned easily in soft illumination, with breaks, informal seating, and snacks, often revealed high scores as global right processors (Dunn, Bruno et al., 1990; Dunn, Cavanaugh et al., 1982; Guastello & Burke, 1998/ 1999). Furthermore, field dependence/field independence correlated in many ways with global/analytic cognitive style and elicited the same clustering as right- and left-preferenced students did (Brennan, 1984; Burke, Guastello, Dunn Griggs, Beasley, Gemake, Sinatra, & Lewthwaite, 1999/ 2000; Douglas, 1979; Levy, 1982; Trautman, 1979).

In some cases, more attributes allied themselves with global/right tendencies than with their counterparts. Thus, although global/rights often enjoyed working with peers and using their tactual strengths, analytic/lefts did not reveal the reverse preference, nor were their sociological or perceptual characteristics similar (Dunn, Cavanaugh et al. 1982).

As the relationships among various cognitive-style theories became evident, brain-lateralization theory emerged based, to a large extent, on the writing of Paul Braco, whose research led him to propose that the two hemispheres of the human brain have different functions. Subsequent research by the Russian scientist Alexander Luria (1973) and the American scientist Roger Sperry (1968) demonstrated that the left hemisphere appeared to be associated with verbal and sequential abilities, whereas the right hemisphere appeared to be associated with emotions and spatial, holistic processing. Those conclusions, however, continue to be challenged. Nevertheless, it is clear that people begin to concentrate, process, and remember new and difficult information under very different conditions.

Thus, the Dunn and Dunn Learning-Style Model is based on the theory that:

1. most individuals can learn;

2. instructional environments, resources, and approaches respond to diverse learning-style strengths;

3. everyone has strengths, but different people have very different strengths;

4. individual instructional preferences exist and can be measured reliably (Burke, Guastello et al., 1999/2000);

5. given responsive environments, resources, and approaches, students attain statistically higher achievement and attitude test scores in congruent, rather than in incongruent treatments (Dunn & Dunn, 1992, 1993; Dunn, Dunn, & Perrin, 1994; Dunn, Griggs et al., 1995); they also behave better in style-responsive environments (Oberer, 1999);

6. teachers can learn to use learning styles as a cornerstone of their instruction (Dunn & DeBello, 1999);

7. students can learn to capitalize on their learning-style strengths when concentrating on new and difficult information (P. Roberts, 1999; Schiering, 1999).

During the past 30 years, this model has been developed, researched, refined, revised, and used to examine many instructional practices as they affected students with diverse learning styles. Age-compatible versions of its related instruments identify the learning-style profiles of students in kindergarten through adulthood (Burke, Guastello et al., 1999/2000; Dunn & Dunn, 1992, 1993, 1998, 1999; Dunn, Dunn, & Perrin, 1994; Guastello & Burke, 1998/1999).

Identifying College Students' Learning Styles

College students' learning styles can be identified within 30–45 minutes with only minimal cost and effort. Table 1.1 describes several adult learning-style instruments. Choose the appropriate tool for the students you teach. Directions for administration accompany each assessment and are easy to follow.

EXPERIMENTAL RESEARCH WITH COLLEGE STUDENTS' LEARNING STYLES

The experimental research with college students' learning styles is replete with significantly higher results. Gains were evidenced in anatomy (Cook, 1989; Lenehan et al., 1994), bacteriology (Lenehan et al., 1994), marketing (Dunn, Deckinger, Withers, & Katzenstein, 1990), legal writing (Dolle, in progress), mathematics (Dunn, Bruno et al., 1990), physiology (Lenehan et al., 1994), sonography (Miller, 1997; Miller & Dunn, 1997), across subjects (Clark-Thayer, 1987, 1988; Mickler & Zippert, 1987), and for overall grade-point averages (Nelson, Dunn et al., 1993).

For example, Clark-Thayer (1987) identified underachieving college freshmens' learning styles with the *Productivity Environmental Preference Survey* (PEPS) (Dunn, Dunn, & Price, 1982). Trained tutors were assigned to teach them with instructional approaches that complemented their learning-style strengths. Students' achievement scores were significantly higher ($p < .01$) when they studied with strategies congruent, rather than incongruent, with their learning-style preferences. In a subsequent study, Clark-Thayer (1988) described students' statistically higher attitude scores toward course content after they had studied with congruent rather than incongruent strategies.

Later, Dunn and others (1990) identified the processing styles of 1,000 minority college students in remedial mathematics classes with the PEPS.

Table 1.1
Instruments for Identifying College Students' Learning Styles

Instrument	Authors	Appropriate for	Cost per Person	Research History
Learning Style Inventory (LSI)	Dunn, Dunn, & Price (Price Systems, Lawrence, KS)	Non-traditional college students and freshmen	About $1.00	Valid, reliable. * Used by researchers at 115 institutions of higher education.+
Productivity Environmental Preference Survey (PEPS)	Dunn, Dunn, & Price (Price Systems, Lawrence, KS)	Post–high school working adults	About $1.00	Valid, reliable. * Used extensively in published studies that examined adults' learning styles.+
Building Excellence (BE)	Rundle & Dunn	Adults in business or corporate positions	About $6.00	Beginning data are now available.++

*Curry, 1987; DeBello, 1990; Tendy & Geiser, 1998/1999.
+ *Research on the Dunn & Dunn Model,* 1999.
++Dunham, 1999; Lewthwaite, 1999; *Performance Concepts,* 1999.

Most of these students were global processors. The textbook assigned to the classes had been written in a step-by-step analytic style in which procedures were itemized, but no direct applications relating the content to the user's experiences were provided. The researchers re-wrote alternate textbook chapters in a global processing style—with stories, applications, examples, illustrations, and humor; the alternate analytic chapters remained intact.

Students were required to study all the revised global chapters and all the intact analytic chapters by themselves—with no direct teacher instruction. Requiring students to teach themselves (a) eliminated the possible intervention of different teachers' teaching styles and (b) resulted in significantly higher test scores ($p < .001$) on each of the chapters that matched, rather than mismatched, individuals' global learning styles.

Nelson and others (1993) identified individual freshmen's overall learning styles with the PEPS and provided directions for studying with complementary strategies. The matched prescriptions impacted significantly on student achievement ($p < .01$) to the point where the college's annual dropout rate was reduced from 39 percent to 20 percent. Those results were particularly meaningful in light of Demitroff's (1974) earlier findings that poor study habits resulted in inadequate student scholastic performance and led to either voluntary or involuntary withdrawal from college.

HOW DOES LEARNING STYLE DIFFER AMONG STUDENTS?

Dunn and Griggs (1995) reviewed studies of multiculturally diverse students in the United States and reported that so many varied styles existed within each group that there were more *within-group* than *between-group* differences. In the same family, mothers and fathers usually have diametrically *opposite* learning styles; their first two offspring rarely learn like each other.

Four learning-style traits significantly differentiate between groups and among individuals within the same group. They differ by (a) achievement level (Milgram, Dunn, & Price, 1993), (b) gender (Greb, 1999; Mitchell et al., in press; Pizzo, Dunn, & Dunn, 1990), (c) age (Dunn & Griggs, 1995; Price, 1980), (d) culture (Dunn & Griggs, 1995; Milgram et al., 1993), and (e) global versus analytic brain processing (Dunn, Bruno et al., 1990; Dunn, Cavanaugh et al., 1982).

Differences by Achievement

Individuals' learning styles differ based on their high versus low academic achievement. Although many gifted students learn differently from each other, and underachievers have many different learning-style variations, gifted and underachieving students have significantly different learning styles and do not perform well with the same methods (Dunn, 1989). Conversely, gifted students in nine diverse cultures, with talents in either athletics, art, dance, leadership, literature, mathematics, or music, evidenced essentially similar learning-style characteristics to other students with the same talent (Milgram et al., 1993).

Differences by Gender

Individuals differ by gender (Greb, 1999; Mitchell et al., in press; Pizzo et al., 1990). Males and females frequently learn differently from each other. Males tend to be more kinesthetic and tactual, and if they have a third modality strength, it often is visual. Males also need more mobility in a more informal environment than females. They are more non-conforming and peer motivated than their female classmates, who tend to be relatively conforming and either self- , parent- , or teacher-motivated (Dunn & Griggs, 1995).

Females, more than males, tend to be auditory, conforming, authority-oriented, and better able to sit passively in conventional classroom desks and chairs. Females also tend to (a) need significantly more quiet while learning (Pizzo et al., 1990), (b) be more self- and adult-motivated, and (c) conform more than males (Marcus, 1977).

Differences by Age

Learning styles change as individuals grow older (Dunn & Griggs, 1995). Students' learning styles undergo transition between elementary and middle school, and between middle school and secondary school. They continue to change in college and during adulthood (Dunn & Griggs, 1995; Price, 1980) and the styles of older adults in the 65–85-year-old range differ in many ways from those of younger people (Van Wynen, 1999). Nevertheless, individuals change uniquely and, although many change patterns do exist, some people hardly change at all and others experience rapid and multiple changes. Interestingly, it is possible to anticipate approximate achievement and behavioral patterns by merely knowing the age, gender, and learning styles of students in an incoming class.

Sociological Preferences. Sociological preferences for learning (a) alone, (b) with peers, (c) with an authoritative versus a collegial teacher, and (d) with routines and patterns—as opposed to in a variety of social groupings, develop over time, change with age and maturity, and are developmental (Dunn & Griggs, 1995; Thies, 1979). Young children tend to begin school highly parent- , teacher- , and/or adult-motivated. Many become peer-motivated by fifth or sixth grade and remain that way until approximately ninth grade, when they become self-motivated. Gifted children tend to become self-motivated early—frequently by first or second grade—and rarely experience a peer-motivated stage. Underachievers become peer-motivated earlier than average students and tend to remain that way longer—often well past adolescence.

Emotional Preferences. Motivation, responsibility (conformity versus non-conformity), and the need for internal versus external structure are perceived as being developmental (Thies, 1979). Motivation fluctuates day to day, class to class, and teacher to teacher. Many humans appear to experience at least three stages of non-conformity, which correlate with high and low "responsibility" levels (Dunn, White, & Zenhausern, 1982).

The first period of non-conformity occurs for many between the first and second years of life. In the United States, that stage euphemistically is called "the terrible twos" and coincides with children beginning the pattern of saying "no!" It lasts, for most children, for less than a year. The second period of non-conformity often begins at about sixth grade and tends to last until ninth or tenth grade for many average children. Some remain non-conforming until well past high school and others into adulthood. Gifted students often are among the most non-conforming youth; they invariably perceive things in their own way.

Perceptual Preferences. The younger the children, the more tactual (learning by handling and manipulating instructional resources) and/or kinesthetic (learning by active involvement and experience) their perceptual strengths are likely to be. Less than 12 percent of elementary school children are "auditory" learners; few children *or adults* are capable of remembering approximately 75 percent of academic information they listen to for between 30 and 40 minutes. Less than 40 percent are "visual" learners; few children *or adults* are capable of remembering approximately 75 percent of academic information they read for between 30 and 40 minutes. The older the children become, the more their auditory and visual modalities develop. However, many adult males are neither auditory nor visual learners and some remain essentially tactual or kinesthetic all their lives. Poorly achieving and average-achieving students earn statistically higher achievement and attitude test scores when taught through tactual/visual and kinesthetic/visual instructional resources, as opposed to when taught through auditory/visual approaches (Dunn, Bauer, Gemake, Gregory, Primavera, & Signer, 1994; Ingham, 1991; Jarsonbeck, 1984; Mitchell et al., in press; Roberts, 1998/1999; Roberts, et al., in press). Adult teachers learned more, more quickly, and retained it better in learning-style-responsive, than in traditional, staff development (Raupers, in press; Taylor et al., 1999/2000).

Differences by Culture

Correlational studies of the five major cultural groups within the United States revealed significant differences in learning-style preferences among the groups, including Native Americans (n = 11 studies), Hispanic Americans (n = 12 studies), African Americans (n = 13 studies), Asian Americans (n = 6 studies), and European Americans (n = 15 studies). Although each cultural group encompassed multiple styles, patterns emerged that suggested that there were greater-than-average preferences for selected learning-style elements within each cultural group (Dunn & Griggs, 1995).

Analyzing these differences on a continuum revealed the following learning-style patterns within each of the five stimulus areas:

- *Cognitive style.* African and Hispanic Americans were significantly more field dependent, whereas European Americans were significantly more field independent. Asian Americans tended to have higher analytic skills than Native Americans. European Americans were higher in sequential processing skills than African Americans, whereas Native Americans were higher in simultaneous processing skills than European Americans.

- *Emotional stimulus.* Asian Americans tended to be significantly more persistent and motivated than Native Americans. Asian Americans preferred highly structured learning activities, whereas African Americans preferred minimum structure.

- *Environmental stimulus.* African Americans preferred quiet and dim lighting whereas European Americans preferred sound and bright light. Asian Americans required a formal design, whereas European Americans preferred an informal design. African Americans concentrated better in a warm environment, whereas Native and Hispanic Americans preferred cooler temperatures.

- *Sociological stimulus.* European Americans were more likely to prefer learning alone, whereas Native Americans were more peer oriented.

- *Physiological stimulus.* European Americans were significantly higher in auditory learning than Native and Hispanic Americans, who tended to be visual learners. African Americans were more likely than European Americans to prefer kinesthetic or experiential learning activities. Asian Americans learned best in the morning and had low mobility needs, whereas African Americans preferred learning in the afternoon (Dunn & Griggs, 1995).

As stated previously, there was great diversity within each cultural group. Research indicates that the differences *within* each cultural group were greater than the differences *between* cultural groups. Therefore, teaching college students cannot be approached with a cultural mind-set. Instead, the learning-style strengths of each student must be assessed and interventions must be designed that are compatible with these preferences.

Differences by Processing Styles

Individuals differ in how they absorb and process new and difficult information (Restak, 1979; Thies, 1979, 1999/2000). Comparisons of global and analytic and left- or right-preferenced processing revealed that: (a) relationships exist among these cognitive dimensions and many students' environmental, emotional, sociological, and/or physiological learning-style traits; and (b) these cognitive dimensions and specific learning-style traits often cluster together. For example, learning persistently (with few or no intermissions), in a quiet, well-lit, formal setting with little or no intake, often correlates with being an analytic or left processor. Conversely, learning with intermittent periods of concentration and relaxation, in soft lighting and with sound (music or voices), while seated informally and snacking correlates with high-global or right-processing styles (Cody, 1983; Dunn, Bruno et al., 1990; Dunn, Cavanaugh et al., 1982). In some cases, more attributes allied themselves with one processing style than another. Although global and right-preferred students often preferred learning tactually and with peers (Jarsonbeck, 1984), no clear perceptual or social pattern was revealed by analytic or left-preferred students.

Many experimental studies have been conducted to determine the effects of specific sequential versus simultaneous instructional approaches on identified analytic and global students (Brennan, 1984; Douglas, 1979; Dunn, Bruno et al., 1990; Dunn, Cavanaugh et al., 1982; Orazio, 1999; Tanenbaum, 1982; Trautman, 1979). Early researchers found that analytic students who were taught analytically and global students who were taught globally achieved statistically higher achievement test scores with complementary, rather than with dissonant, instructional strategies. That occurred in high school biology (Douglas, 1979), mathematics (Brennan, 1984), and nutrition (Tanenbaum, 1982), in junior high school social studies (Trautman, 1979) and in community college mathematics (Dunn, Bruno et al., 1990). More recently, however, Orazio (1999) reported different data. Almost all average- and well-achieving seventh-grade adolescents performed statistically ($p < .001$) better on mathematics achievement tests with global, rather than with analytic, teaching approaches. Only the extreme analytics (approximately 10–12 percent of the population) performed better ($p < .001$) with analytic than with global strategies. Similarly, Burke (1998) reported that most of the middle school populations she examined preferred a global to an analytic learning-styles identification inventory significantly more—except for the extreme analytics who preferred the analytic assessment.

USING LEARNING-STYLE STRATEGIES IN HIGHER EDUCATION

College professors, who normally engage in teaching-by-talking, questioning, student presentations, and the use of small-group strategies such as brainstorming, case studies, Cooperative Learning, and Simulations, may appreciate guidelines for using learning-styles approaches in their courses. Chapter 2 overviews many of the available strategies and describes for whom each is likely to be effective.

Chapter 2

Practical Approaches to Using Learning Styles in Higher Education: The How-to Steps

Rita Dunn and Shirley A. Griggs

Knowledge about learning styles and brain behavior is a fundamental new tool at the service of teachers . . . It clearly is not the latest educational fad. It provides a deeper and more profound view of the learner than previously. (Keefe, 1982: v)

Individuals have such unique patterns for learning new and difficult information that it is hard to judge accurately how to teach anything academically challenging without first identifying how each student learns. Once learning styles have been identified, instructors can estimate the processing approach(es), method(s), and sequence(s) of perceptual exposures to resources that are likely to make learning relatively comfortable for each person. Contrary to traditional practice, however, teachers are neither expected nor required to teach directly to the entire class. All students may elect to attend each lesson but, as indicated in Chapter 1, some progress more rapidly when learning alone than in a class presentation and others learn better with peers. It becomes the students' responsibility to follow their own computer-generated prescriptions for mastering the course content itemized in the course module.

TEACHING TO STUDENTS' LEARNING STYLES

Step One: Course Modules

For independent students to learn independently and for peer-oriented students to learn in pairs or in small groups, both types need to be made aware of the objectives that must be mastered for each course. Clearly stated objectives also are required by students who need structure and/or may be either authority- or teacher-oriented. Therefore, just as has always been the case, instructors need to develop an outline for each course taught that clearly indicates the:

- course number and title;
- professor's name, office number, telephone, e-mail, and or fax numbers;
- objectives to be mastered by all or, in some cases, by individuals who may have (a) previously mastered specific objectives, or (b) special interests in a specific topic or curriculum;
- units of study;
- available resources;
- assignments to demonstrate mastery;
- due dates and test dates;
- additional requirements that may be necessary; and
- level of mastery required for an A.

Step Two: Individual Prescriptions for Studying with Learning-Style Strengths

Once a person's learning style has been identified, a simple computer package (Dunn & Klavas, 1990):

- analyzes that individual's strengths;
- determines the most complementary instructional methods or resources for that person to master what needs to be learned;
- examines the person's perceptual preferences and suggests the sequence through which difficult information initially should be attacked and then reinforced; and
- based on processing inclinations, suggests environmental alternatives that are likely to prove comfortable.

Instructors need to overview learning styles and explain any items in the personalized homework prescriptions that individuals might not understand. Few adults require extensive explanations. The printed directions that accompany the how-to-study guides for different students suffice for most elementary school students and should be "a piece of cake" for young adults.

Step Three: Exposing Students to Alternative Methods for Learning Challenging Material

Many non-traditional students achieve poorly because how they have been taught does not complement ("match") how they learn. There are at least five different ways—other than lectures and discussions that require auditory strength—to master new and difficult information. This chapter briefly describes each of those ways. All are not necessary, but each is responsive to how diverse populations learn.

A. *The Contract Activity Package Method.* A Contract Activity Package (CAP) is an instructional strategy that allows motivated people to learn at their own speed. A CAP consists of several components:

- simply stated objectives;
- multisensory resources that permit choices of resources that match individuals' perceptual preferences;
- Activity Alternatives in which students apply their newly mastered information by creating original resources to show that they have learned what was required or selected;
- Reporting Alternatives so that the completed Activity Alternatives can be shared with others who are studying the same material;
- at least three small-group techniques to permit persons who enjoy working or learning with colleagues to do so; and
- a performance or written test so that students can show their working knowledge of the material they have mastered.

Van Wynen (1997) used a CAP in a managed-care project for training nurses in New York (see Figure 2.1). Based on each nurse's PEPS profile, she issued study guides that capitalized on each participant's unique learning style (see Figure 2.2). At first, the participants were surprised that they were permitted such choices; they had never experienced similar assignments during their entire college career. Van Wynen, director of nursing education at Dominican College, reported that the nurses "loved having the choice of how to proceed with an assignment. Their grades were equally positive. In addition, they reflected critical-thinking skills, quality written work, and creativity" (p. 48). She concluded that "one size doesn't fit all!" (p. 44).

For Whom Are CAPs Effective?

CAPs are most effective with *independent* and *motivated* students because they provide self-pacing for individuals who want to achieve, improve, or be among the best in their field. They also are effective for *non-conformists* because CAPs provide multiple options and allow creative individuals to

Figure 2.1
Course Assignment: Patient Care Delivery Models/Managed Care Project

---

Change Project

You may select one of the following suggested activities for submission of your change project to *Liz Van Wynen on of before March 11, 1996:*

CHOICE 1: Learning Exercise (textbook, page 90, #4.6):
Based on a given scenario, this exercise requires the learner to assume the role of the change agent at the organizational level. Driving and restraining forces for change must be identified and strategies created to overcome resistance. Learner analysis should include the roles and responsibilities of the change agent during the unfreezing, movement, and refreezing phases of the planned changes.

CHOICE 2: Case Study:
You are a 24-year-old, unmarried female RN and you have returned to your hometown to work in the local rural 55-bed hospital. Your only working experience has been on a general medical/surgical unit in a large city where you attended college. At that inner-city hospital, they have recently switched from team leading to primary care nursing. At your present place of employment, the nurses use task-oriented nursing-care management and you find that this type of organization fragments patient care and, in addition, affords you little personal satisfaction. Your Director of Nursing seems open to new ideas and you decide that you would like to be the change agent, suggesting a newer method of patient care assignment. One evening after working the 3–11 P.M. shift you return to your parents' home and you spend the rest of the night working on your planned change.

Assignment:
1. Is there a need for change?
2. What do you feel your approach should be in this case? Why?
3. Outline your plan.
4. How would you summarize your chances for success?
5. What are some risks that you should guard against?

CHOICE 3: You must complete both "a" and "b":

*Refer to your handout on "Mindmapping" distributed in class.
a. Create a mindmap of Chapter 4 in your textbook.
b. Brainstorm a list of ways to cope with great amounts of change in rapid succession in the healthcare fields, using the mindmapping technique.

CHOICE 4: If you work/learn better in a group, arrange for three of your classmates to work together with you on this case study:
Many organizations undergo so much change that people in the organization cannot keep track of all that is changing. It is important to notice change so that we don't become desensitized to it. If we become desensitized, we take change for granted and fail to plan carefully for change initiatives. Identify the changes that have taken place in the healthcare organizations where you have worked or have had a clinical experience during the last one or two years or in general, the healthcare

(continued)

Figure 2.1 (continued)

industry. Think of what the organization, department, or work unit was trying to move away from and trying to move toward. An example might be moving away from centralized control and moving toward departmental control, or completing various quality improvement projects. Perhaps you could interview a staff nurse and/or manager. Write down as specifically as possible for each situation what people were moving away from and what they were moving toward. Then complete the following:

Assignment:

Select one of the changes from your list and analyze the change in terms of how it was presented to the potential adopters by answering the following questions:

1. Was a credible change agent used?
2. Was it introduced on a trial basis?
3. Was the relative advantage (to the adopters) clearly explained?
4. Was there an attempt to make the benefits visible?
5. Was the change compatible with the beliefs and values of the adopters?
6. Was there an attempt to reduce the apparent complexity?
7. Was the change introduced during relative stability?
8. With the benefit of hindsight, which of the above is most amenable to improvement?
9. What actions would your group recommend to make the improvement?

Source: Van Wynen, E. A. (1997, September/October). Information processing styles: One size doesn't fit all. *Nurse Educator, 22*(5). Used with permission.

demonstrate mastery of the inservice requirements *their* way. CAPs can be used by the *learning-alone* preferents, who enjoy working by themselves, and by *peer-oriented* preferents in a team. This approach reduces much of the frustration and anxiety often experienced during inservice by *motivated* and very competent teachers who are required to progress at the larger group's pace. CAPs can be used flexibly to accommodate a variety of learning-style characteristics. For example:

Sound. When *quiet* is important to an individual, ear plugs can be used to block out unwanted noises. Conversely, when *sound* is desired, ear plugs can be used to provide recorded music to block out the environmental noise distractions that disturb certain adults. Such sounds often may not be noticed by others; not only do they not *hear* them, sometimes they unconsciously *make* them—as when breathing loudly, speaking to themselves, tapping their fingers or pencils, and/or humming to themselves while thinking!

When discussion and interaction are important to one group of individuals, a work area, similar to a classroom Learning Station or Interest Center, can be established in a corner of the facility—whether that be a room, cor-

Figure 2.2
Excerpts from Nurses' Homework Study Prescriptions

Learning Style Inventory Homework Guides

Name: SENIOR #1 (ANALYTIC PROCESSOR)
Occupation: STUDENT NURSE Date: 02/17/96
Affiliation: NURSING

SOUND–37; LIGHT–28; TEMPERATURE–76; DESIGN–55; MOTIVATION–60; PERSISTENCE–56; RESPONSIBLE–64; STRUCTURE–57; ALONE–32; AUTHORITY–44; VARIETY–51; AUDITORY–35; VISUAL–59; TACTILE–57; KINESTHETIC–50; INTAKE–34; TIME OF DAY–64; LATE MORNING–60; AFTERNOON–38; and MOBILITY–39.

SOUND: You often need quiet when learning something new or difficult and when working on a challenging project. It would be productive for you to find a quiet area at home or at the office where you can concentrate on your work.

LEARNING ALONE: You often prefer to work and learn new and difficult information by yourself. You are usually more productive when you alone are responsible for specific tasks. When working on a committee or team, assume specific responsibilities to complete by yourself and then contribute the product to the group.

INTAKE: You usually do not eat, drink, smoke, chew or require intake while you are learning something new or difficult and when working on a challenging task.

Name: SENIOR #2 (GLOBAL PROCESSOR)
Occupation: STUDENT NURSE Date: 02/17/96
Affiliation: NURSING

SOUND–70; LIGHT–66; TEMPERATURE–37; DESIGN–34; MOTIVATION–44; PERSISTENCE–61; RESPONSIBLE–54; STRUCTURE–57; ALONE–67; AUTHORITY–57; VARIETY–30; AUDITORY–76; VISUAL–48; TACTILE–57; KINESTHETIC–47; INTAKE–70; TIME OF DAY–28; LATE MORNING–40; AFTERNOON–79; and MOBILITY–69.

SOUND: You usually work with some type of sound present in your office or study, whether it is the radio, TV, or tapes. You find it disconcerting to learn something new or difficult and concentrate on a demanding project when it is too quiet in your environment.

DESIGN: You often concentrate most efficiently in an informal work area. Your office or workspace should be relaxing and might include a soft chair or couch. When learning something new or difficult and when working on a challenging task, an informal work or study space will maximize your productivity.

PEER ORIENTED: You often prefer working on challenging projects and learning new and difficult information with someone else, rather than alone. Working and learning as a team or with a colleague enhances your ability to concentrate.

INTAKE: You usually have some kind of intake, such as something to drink or snack on while learning something new or difficult or when working on a challenging task. Intake enhances your ability to concentrate.

Source: Van Wynen, E. A. (1997, September/October). Information processing styles: One size doesn't fit all. *Nurse Educator, 22*(5). Used with permission.

ridor, or office. Cardboard or available furniture, such as tables, file cabinets, or bookcases, can be used perpendicularly to the wall to serve as dividers and to form a sanctuary for its occupants. Simultaneously, these created spaces, "offices," or "dens" protect classmates who require quiet to avoid distraction because of the movement or conversation that occurs when others are actively engaged and interacting.

Rules for participants' discussions need to be posted on a large oak-tag surface mounted to the wall within that area so that no one, either inside or outside the instructional area, is distracted from concentrating and doing his or her work. These rules could include the following:

- Your learning style may not distract anyone with a different learning style.
- No student either inside or outside this room should be able to repeat the exact words being used by anyone in this group.
- Each student needs to master the objectives for this lesson.
- Evidence of the creative application of whatever was mastered during this period should be submitted to the professor within one week.

Light, Temperature, Seating, Intake, and *Sociological Preferences*. Participants who elect to use a CAP are encouraged to work on it anywhere in the immediate environment as long as they do not interfere with anyone else's learning style and they respect the rules that have been established for that area. Therefore, they can adapt the available *illumination, temperature*, and *seating* to their personal learning-style preferences. In addition, participants may work *alone* or with a *classmate* or two and either snack or not as they choose.

Structure, Mobility, and *Responsibility* (Conformity/Non-Conformity). The CAP system itself provides a great deal of structure through the itemization of specific Objectives, Activity and Reporting Alternatives, Small-Group Techniques, and a related Self-Test assessment. By permitting these choices, CAPs provide "breathing room" for non-conformists, who often resist direction or structure from others in authority.

Processing Style. As indicated previously, a CAP is essentially an outline of specifically what needs to be learned and how to learn it while, simultaneously, providing options for those with different learning-style preferences and *non-conformists*. As such, CAPs tend to respond to *analytic* processors. However, through multiple illustrations, graphics, and Activity Alternatives, CAPs also respond to both *perceptual* and *sociological* preferences in addition to individual interests. To that extent, they can respond to the preferences of *global* users.

B. *The Programmed Learning Sequence Method*. Another method for responding to students' learning styles is to program the course content so that it can be learned in small, simple steps without the direct instruction of a presenter. Like any other method, programmed instruction responds to only certain learning-style characteristics and should not be prescribed for all students. The special type of programming adopted by professors whose chapters you will read in this book is called Programmed Learning Sequences (PLSs) (Dunn & Dunn, 1993, 1998, 1999).

Translate into clearly stated objectives the specific information or skills that you require the students enrolled in your course to master. It should be made clear that the PLS has been designed to teach to those objectives and that you expect each student to master all of them.

Objectives can range from simple to complex. All students who use the PLS proceed through the identical sequence. However, they may pace themselves and study in the section of the classroom, library, resource, or computer room that is most responsive to their unique preferences for sound, light, temperature, seating, and intake (whichever elements you decide to permit). In the past, programmed learning resources that were commercially produced often yielded uneven results because they were:

• used with everyone;
• solely *visual*—similar to a textbook and, therefore, had only limited appeal to adults who neither enjoyed reading nor retained information easily through their visual modality; or
• used too frequently; students who required *variety* or did not appreciate *structure* quickly tired of them.

Students are given copies of the PLS and, as the various objectives and their related questions are completed, they gradually master the content. Unless they need and seek assistance, individuals work through the material by themselves without much peer or professor interaction.

However, there are at least several students in each college course who function better with a *colleague* or *two* than they do *alone*. Therefore, if you are able to test students with the PEPS or the LSI, the information concerning their individual preferences for learning *alone*, with a *colleague*, or with you—the *teacher*—will allow you to encourage them to work with the PLS in ways that respond to their sociological preferences.

Learning-Style Characteristics Responsive to Programmed Learning Sequences (PLSs)

Because PLSs originally were designed to be used by students who enjoyed learning *alone*, participants who used this resource needed to be *persistent*; they were required to continue working with it until they completed the entire program. If they found the content difficult, they were advised either to review each frame until they had mastered the material or to seek assistance from an appropriate source, such as the *teacher* or a *peer*.

Today, everything in a PLS that should be learned is organized so that only one item at a time is presented. Therefore, the sequenced materials in each PLS provide extensive *structure*. Participants cannot proceed to the next PLS "frame" (page) until the content included on the previous frames has been understood, as demonstrated by correct answers to the questions included in a brief quiz at the bottom of each frame. Adults who are *self-structured* and prefer to avoid external direction may find the PLS less challenging and somewhat irritating with repeated usage. However, PLSs remain an excellent alternative for students who:

- lack *independence;*
- thrive with *variety;*
- prefer learning either *alone* or in *a pair;*
- enjoy reading text supported by illustrations, *tactual* resources, and an accompanying tape recording for those who prefer *hearing* the material read to them;
- do not read well because the accompanying tape familiarizes them with the content that must be mastered;
- function best with *structure* and small steps followed by periodic, game-like reinforcements; and because a PLS should always have a short-story beginning; that part also appeals to
- *global* processors.

A PLS can be used in any facility—a classroom, a library, a corridor, or an office; thus, it accommodates each person's environmental and physiological preferences. For example, it can be taken to a silent area if *quiet* is desired, or to the center of classroom activity if the participant either prefers *sound* or wishes to be with a friend or two and can block out *noise*. The PLS can be taken to either a *warm* section of a facility and used near a sunny window or radiator, or to a *cool* area. It can be studied at a desk or in an easy chair; in either a well-illuminated space or away from *bright light*. A person may snack—or not—as he or she works, and can use the PLS at any time of day. In addition, participants can "take a break" whenever mobility is necessary.

Components of a Programmed Learning Sequence

Developing a PLS is not difficult, but it *does* require organization of the topic to be taught in a logical, easy-to-follow sequence and includes each of the following:

- a series of individual frames that permit self-pacing and provide space for direct student feedback;
- a cover and all frames in a shape related to the topic rather than in a rectangular book shape (to attract tactual/visual students);
- clear identification of the topic, concept, or skill that students are required to learn;

- a short, beginning humorous or dramatic story that relates the content to learners' interests and lives to attract global learners' attention;
- clearly stated objectives that make it easy to focus after the story has attracted interest;
- periodic, built-in tactual games (an Electroboard, Pic-A-Hole, or set of Task Cards) to reinforce what was taught in print and on tape to help tactual learners;
- printed and illustrated explanations to help visual learners;
- tapes that *read* the information and can be used repeatedly to hold the attention of both auditory and low-auditory learners;
- the option of students working together to appeal to peer-oriented adults; and
- a portable book that can be used anywhere the learner feels comfortable.

Miller and Lefkowitz (1998) analyzed the effects of PLSs on the achievement and attitudes of students enrolled in Sonography and Cross Sectional Anatomy courses in a college of health-related professions. Students were administered the PEPS to identify their learning-style strengths, and alternately were presented with lessons using a PLS in a book format and traditional lectures. The Sonography class also was exposed to a PLS in a CD-ROM format. The *Semantic Differential Survey* (SDS) compared students' attitudes toward learning via lecture versus PLS versus CD-ROM.

In both classes, achievement and attitude test scores were statistically higher with the PLS than with traditional lectures. In Sonography, achievement was significantly higher with the book PLS than with the CD-ROM PLS (effect size 1.11). Significant correlations emerged between learning-style elements and achievement: students who preferred learning with the book PLS required more *quiet* than those who preferred the computer. Students who preferred learning traditionally and with the computer PLS required more *light* than those who preferred learning with the book PLS. Students who preferred learning with an *authority* favored the traditional method. Many other correlations were revealed.

C: *Tactual Manipulatives.* These easy-to-make and easy-to-use instructional resources teach basic facts to essentially tactual learners who cannot remember three-quarters of what they hear (*low-auditory*) or read (*low-visual*). They *can*, however, remember 75 percent of what they focus on while "playing" with these specific tactual manipulatives—Electroboards, Flip Chutes, Pic-A-Holes, and Task Cards (Dunn & Dunn, 1992, 1993). Heretofore, college instructors have thought that students who cannot learn by listening or reading are "not college material." Many studies have shown that, to the contrary, students who prefer to absorb and retain new and difficult academic information tactually become good students when taught that way (Billings & Cobb, 1992; Clark-Thayer, 1987; Cook, 1991; Dunn, Bruno, Sklar, & Beaudry, 1990; Dunn, Ingham, & Deckinger, 1995).

D. *Kinesthetic Floor Games.* An interesting alternative for teaching many college students—particularly athletes—involves continuing body movements combined with printed words that are supplemented with colored illustrations. Three decades ago, many teachers believed that students who appeared hyperactive, inattentive, or unfocused were unable to achieve well academically—and indeed they were not with traditional methods! However, increasing knowledge of the brain led to Restak's (1979) revelation that many males needed to learn through active body participation rather than through passive acquisition. Initially, it was thought that people's tactual proclivities necessarily were related to their kinesthetic preferences. Today we know that some students have both tactual and kinesthetic strengths, but many students—particularly males—have only one or the other of those two perceptual strengths.

Academically gifted students often have multiple perceptual strengths; they learn easily by listening, reading, or using manipulatives and/or kinesthetic approaches. Others, however, are only kinesthetic. For these, Floor Games or huge, oversized tactual resources that require students to stand and move while they are learning are the best way to master complicated facts and information.

"Real-life" learning experiences are not new to college professors, but often they are equated with trips, independent or career-related studies, internships, or residencies. Those often require students to leave the college campus and vary as either excellent or poor, dependent on their design, the persons involved, and the events included. In contrast, Floor Games easily are constructed with a minimum of effort and time, produce similar results, and tend to be under the professor's control as far as the content and the quality of the incorporated activities are concerned. Samples of adult Floor Games are available in Dunn and Dunn (1998, 1999).

E. *Multisensory Instructional Packages* (MIPs). An MIP is an instructional package designed to individualize learning through direct appeal to personal learning styles. Because students work either *independently* or in a *pair*, and the materials are self-corrective, the packages can meet the needs of learners on several academic levels, including college students with a learning disability and advanced students capable of progressing faster than their peers.

Because of their multisensory components, MIPs are very motivating to slow learners, who usually require repetition and a variety of approaches through several senses before they can acquire and retain complex knowledge and skills.

Learning-Style Characteristics Responsive to MIPs

Instructional packages are especially appropriate for students who require a high degree of structure when learning. The step-by-step procedures provide clear, sequenced directions that are repeated in a *variety* of ways until mastery is achieved. Students who prefer to learn alone usually enjoy multisensory resources because they can take the resources to an area that is compatible with their environmental and sociological preferences. Therefore, they could study in a library carrel, the local coffee shop, or the residence hall and pursue their work *alone*, with a *peer*, or in a *small group*.

All perceptual strengths are accommodated. By definition, MIPs include *visual*, *auditory*, *tactual*, and *kinesthetic* activities. Activities can be sequenced so that each student starts learning through his/her strengths and then is reinforced through different senses. Students who are extremely self-structured will not enjoy MIP as a routine, unless the content is challenging to them. *Conforming* students will find them interesting; *non-conformists* will enjoy the choices and *variety* of activities.

An MIP is comprised of each of the following items:

• Each package focuses on a single concept.
• At least four senses are used to master the content.
• Feedback and evaluation are built into the package.
• Learning is private and aimed at a accommodating individual learning styles (Dunn & Dunn, 1999).

Step Four: Responding to Individuals' Sociological Strengths

Faddish instructors adopt each new method currently being focused on in the literature of professional associations and adopt it carte blanche for everyone—as so many educators did when requiring Cooperative Learning practices for everyone. Less than 30 percent of the school-age population learns best in groups. Among adults, dependent on their achievement and age levels, the percentage is substantially lower. Small-group instructional strategies often may be effective with the peer-oriented, but most college students vary in their sociological preferences. Many profit from the structure provided by authoritative adults; others perform better alone and some work best in pairs rather than in groups. Furthermore, selected Cooperative Learning strategies require students to assume roles for which they may not be well suited. Learning-styles approaches include a series of small-group instructional strategies that students elect to use based on their individual learning-style profiles. Among these strategies are:

• Team Learning for introducing new and difficult material;
• Circle of Knowledge for reinforcing material to which students previously have been exposed;
• Brainstorming—a form of problem solving;
• Case Studies that may be used for any of these above-cited, small-group approaches; and

• Simulations, a dramatic application of Case Studies that often require creativity and a willingness to actively participate, rather than observe.

Step Five: Re-designing the Instructional Environment

Given the variety of instructional environments in which individuals function well and either commit to memory or internalize new or difficult information, no single classroom design is *best* for all students. These are some of the environmental changes you may care to permit.

• Comfortable seating; students may bring a pillow for their backs or seats; they may even sit on the floor—as long as they do not distract anyone else.
• Varied lighting—with brighter and dimmer sections of the room available. Turning off some of the classroom lighting may disturb you, but strongly global students will tell you how appreciative they are. Also, visors or hats with brims will be helpful to certain students (Studd, 1995).
• Sweaters and shawls for those who need them.
• Healthful snacks may be brought to class—but discarded at the end of the period.
• Earphones may be used during tests (to increase concentration).

RELATING LEARNING-STYLES APPROACHES TO HIGHER EDUCATION TEACHING

As you read the chapters that have been contributed by various professors across the United States who have adopted selected learning-styles approaches for their courses, consider the implementation guidelines recommended by Klavas (1993) (see Figure 2.3). None of the authors use *all* the methods; many use only a few. What and how many of the methods actually are used depends on the type of students in that class and the willingness of that particular professor to stretch, adapt, experiment, and/or "play with" alternative approaches. Many of the authors merely explained learning styles to their classes, tested students to identify their learning-style preferences, provided homework prescriptions (Dunn & Klavas, 1990), and suggested ways in which they could teach themselves and/or each other (Van Wynen, 1997). Read on to develop insights into how this system worked for them and their students.

Figure 2.3
Learning-Style Process of Implementation with the Dunn and Dunn Model

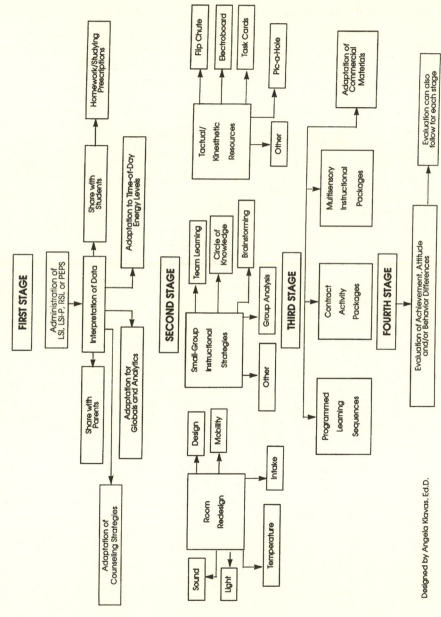

Designed by Angela Klavas, Ed.D.

Part II

Applications in Education

Chapter 3

Learning Styles in Graduate Education Classes: The River of No Return

Sue Ellen Read

DIVING IN

After a career in public and private schools, followed by a stint as an adult educator, I settled in to teach at a regional university in Tahlequah, Oklahoma, the capital of the Cherokee Nation. Northeastern State University (NSU) has an enrollment of approximately 9,000 students on three campuses and graduates more Native American students than any other institution of higher education. The NSU College of Education has long enjoyed a reputation of excellence. Both the Secretary of Education and the Superintendent of Schools for the State of Oklahoma are NSU alumni.

During most of the years in which I taught, I thought I considered myself a good teacher. This belief was reinforced by flattering evaluations from students, peers, and supervisors. I was in great demand; my classes were always full, and I frequently was recruited to teach at other institutions. I worked hard because I loved teaching and because I was determined to prevent the Oklahoma hills surrounding us to become a barrier that prevented the arrival of state-of-the-art education.

Two courses that I teach, Cognitive Learning Styles and Instructional Strategies, are required for all Masters of Administration and Masters of Teaching candidates. A few of my students began to truly soar as a result of information they learned in those classes. In particular, students in my Cognitive Learning Styles classes began to change the way they taught. They were doing what I had been advocating. When another professor asked for a list of former students who were using learning styles in their own classrooms, I was delighted. That colleague had wanted to make a film for her undergraduates to demonstrate what the Dunn and Dunn Model looked like in practice.

As I watched the first few minutes of the completed video, I was proud of what these teachers had accomplished. Then, as I continued to watch, I felt something tearing away in my mind. By the end of the film, I felt suffocated by an overwhelming conclusion: *they* were the great teachers, not I! At best, I was a grand illusionist who could rival Houdini or Copperfield.

These teachers had crossed the treacherous river of *disequilibrium*. They had graduated from theory to practice; all I had done was stand on the bank and holler "Swim!" They proved to be the geniuses upon whom professors are so dependent. They were the ones who practiced what was preached, even if the preacher couldn't. They were the ones we offered up as proof that although the majority of students rarely attempted to swim—or drowned while trying—the fault was not the teacher's; it had to be the learner's. Could I be as good as the students I'd taught? Fifty-something and scared to death, I jumped into the water and began to swim for that distant shore.

That crossing stretched muscles I hadn't even known I had! The work required for implementing the Dunn and Dunn Learning-style Model seemed overwhelming. The exasperation of transporting all the teaching tools from campus to campus was, and still is, daunting. When I first began teaching this new way, I sometimes felt superfluous in my own classroom. Shifting control models was, at best, excruciating. The patience required to wait for the learning atmosphere to become firmly rooted would have strained even the saintly. Although I am still evolving in my efforts to teach my graduate students through their individual learning styles, I am more than willing to proclaim, "Come on in! The water's fine."

THE CROSSING

For the first two weeks of the semester, my Cognitive Learning Styles class resembles a traditional classroom. After collecting student data cards, taking Polaroid snapshots of the registrants to tape onto the cards (for visual professors who need a way to match names with faces), and distributing the class syllabus, the first order of business is to administer the Dunn, Dunn, and Price *Productivity Environmental Preference Survey* (PEPS). When these tasks have been completed, my lecture commences and the setup begins. I make every effort to relate the content of the lecture to the context of the students' lives, to generate class discussions as we begin to explore the basics of cognitive learning styles. As the first class session ends, I assign pages of the text to be read by the next session.

The second week, all students receive an individual PEPS profile deline-ating their preferences on each of the learning-style variables. In addition, I give each student an individual learning prescription that is generated by the *St. John's University Homework Disc* (Dunn & Klavas, 1990).

With a sample learning-style profile projected on the overhead, the entire two-and-one-half hour session is spent teaching the students to read learning-style profiles. Each student uses his or her individual profile as a learning tool in this interactive process. Definitions and a brief impact statement are provided for each of the variables. The students ask questions and always answer in the affirmative when I ask if the information being provided is clear to them. At the end of the second class, I remind them of their previous text assignment (one chapter) and emphasize the importance of mastering this material because it forms the cornerstone of the course.

By the third class session, the stage is set for the sting. When class commences, I ask a series of questions regarding the materials that had been covered in the two previous classes and in the first chapter of the text. The questions are addressed to the class as a whole and the students are encouraged to abandon the hand-raising ceremony and answer at will. Silence abounds.

Finally, a single tentative voice proffers an answer that usually ends with an implied question mark. After approximately five minutes of this exercise which, to both them and me, seems to turn into eternity and exposes the true nature of the implied contract delineating the roles of the teacher and the taught, I cease this line of questioning and begin another.

I now ask them why they don't know this material. Now the silence remains uninterrupted; they are hoping that the question is rhetorical. I tell the class that I don't know what else to do. I plead with them, telling them I have taught with as much humor, relevance, and context as I know how and have extended myself in an effort to create meaning for them. "What's wrong?" There is still no response, but always many downcast eyes signaling fear, anger, frustration and, sometimes, embarrassment. I remind them that they are supposed to be the best and the brightest and that entering graduate school is voluntary; and, after all, this is their education. The sting is in.

I next ask how many of them have felt what I am feeling? How many of them have known the frustration of preparing lessons, working as hard as they can, and teaching with all their might—only to be rewarded by the teaching muse repeating that old refrain, "Why bother?" My students' expressions begin to register their first inkling that, perhaps, the past 10 minutes of discomfort have not been about them at all.

Changing direction and tone, I state that I am not paid to teach them. I am paid for them to learn and that, thus far in this class, I have done almost nothing to promote learning. At this point the class is totally lost because most of them think that I am a better-than-average professor and because, truth be told, even though most of them spend every day teaching, they aren't sure what learning is.

I then offer my adaptation of the work of brain-based educators by suggesting that there are six questions that the brain asks before it will learn anything. I invite them to analyze whether all six of the questions can be answered affirmatively with regard to the content and process of this class to date:

1. Are conditions right for me to make connections?
2. How can I connect this to what I already know?
3. How can I connect this to the world I live in *now*?
4. Can I connect to this material intellectually, emotionally, and physically?
5. Whose brain is making the connection?
6. Do I regularly reconnect to this—refreshing and refining it?

After a brief introduction to the questions, I state my hypothesis that learning will occur only if I can provide a setting in which these six questions can be answered affirmatively by each learner. I believe that this occurs only in the context of each learner's individual learning style. I tell my students that they will spend the next 13 weeks of class testing this hypothesis for themselves.

Each semester, students are introduced to a variety of tools that are available for *them* to actually *learn* those constructs deemed necessary for mastery of the goals and objectives of this course. I briefly explain the use of Flip Chutes, Task Cards, Pick-an-Answer, a plethora of games, Electroboards, films, audiotapes and Programmed Learning Sequences (PLSs). Then I tell the students that they will use the next hour, as well as the first hour of most subsequent classes, to explore these tools in groups, with peers, alone, or as team members when the activity provides for team competition. They may go to a "silence zone" which has been provided and can sit where and how they like according to their own design, light, and temperature requirements. Students are assured that I will be available to any and all who want me to work with them. I remind them that instructions are available with all the learning strategies, both in writing and on audiotape. Then I simply say, *Go!*

The hesitancy of some of the students is at first palpable. Filled with skepticism or, perhaps, assuming that if they go along with my silly strategies the sting ultimately will be on me, they rise from their chairs and commence the process. When the students first begin taking charge of their own learning, a great deal of reassurance is required from me. Many want to know if they are doing everything correctly. By the end of the hour, most students are getting on track.

After a break, we begin processing the experience. I ask the students what they liked and didn't like. Predictably, the dislikes are few or non-existent, either because the methods worked for them or because the courage to

Figure 3.1
Suggestion List for Creating Your Own Knowledge Base: Learning-Style
Overview and Elements

Activity Alternatives	Reporting Alternatives
1. Find, copy, and summarize three (3) research articles cited in Chapter One of our required text (Dunn & Dunn, 1992, 1993).	1. Submit the articles and a one-page summary of each.
2. Develop a cassette tape of an original jingle for remembering the five (5) domains for learning style.	2. Submit the cassette tape of the jingle and play it for a small group of peers.
3. Read and record on tape pages 1, 2, 3, 4, and 6.	3. Submit the cassette tape and allow it to be checked out by classmates who would like to hear the book read to them.
4. Make and color Task Cards of all the elements with pictures on one side and one or more words naming the element on the other side.	4. Submit the Task Cards for class use.
5. Create a pictorial representation of each stimulus.	5. Display the pictorial representations in the classroom.
6. Create a game for remembering the elements of the Dunn and Dunn Model.	6. Include printed instructions and demonstrate how to play the game for a small group of classmates.

speak out is still negligible. As the discussion progresses, however, a subtle change in the quality and nature of the questions asked by the students begins to emerge. They abandon "Would you repeat that?", "What number are we on?", and "Define that please" and begin to substitute "Okay, so does this really mean . . .", and "Could this be the explanation for . . . ". They often offer suggestions for improving the activities they experienced.

Inevitably, questions of how much time it takes to produce the learning tools take center stage. I explain the amount of time and money that I initially invested and inform them that the majority of the instructional technology was produced by their peers in prior classes. It is at this point that I introduce the "Suggestions List for Creating Your Own Knowledge Base" (see Figure 3.1) that I have modified from Contract Activity Packets (CAPs) (Dunn & Dunn, 1992, 1993, 1999).

A list is developed for each of the knowledge-based units and class members are assigned to each of the various units. Students select an activity, or substitute one of their own from an instructor-approved list, and report in the format suggested. The main objective of this assignment is to have students interact creatively with course content to facilitate memory retention and to use higher-order thinking skills. Students consistently report that these assignments promote their peak learning experiences in this class. The lists also provide a vehicle for addressing students' absences. For each class session missed during a unit, an additional activity must be submitted. This insures that students interact with the content, as opposed to simply borrowing someone's notes.

By the fourth session of class, students take charge, commencing work the minute that they enter the classroom, helping each other, explaining, verifying, and gleefully pointing out misinformation that might be unintentionally contained in the learning materials. They are actively engaged for the full 60 minutes.

After our break, I introduce the students to the mastery test concept. Beginning with week five, mastery tests are available for them to assess their own level of learning and decide how their time best can be spent. A list of students' names is mounted in the room with the objectives to be mastered in each unit. As they master each objective, they check it off on the chart. A quick glance at the chart alerts me to problem areas that need to be addressed in group sessions.

The class progresses in this format for the rest of the semester, interspersed with guest presenters and various assessment devices (including traditional tests) and projects. Invariably, a learning community emerges that always surprises the students and never fails to please me.

IS IT ANY BETTER ON THE OTHER SIDE?

I expected (hoped for?) more and better content mastery. That happened quickly. What I did not expect was the realization of how little must have been mastered beyond test-taking requirements in my previous classes. A comparison of the quantity and nature of the students' questions makes this an inescapable conclusion. The ratio of student-initiated questions greatly exceeded professor-initiated questions and the lion's share of the students' questions are now generated by higher-order thinking skills.

At first, I was amazed by the number of students who began to incorporate what they were learning into their own professional and personal lives. Now, I expect it. By the fifth class session, the vast majority of my students have jumped into the river and are swimming with all their might. Granted, their proficiency levels are different and some are gulping and treading, but they are in the water. Because they are immersed in the model, it no longer seems abstract or quite so dangerous.

It was not unexpected that students in my learning-styles class would ultimately appreciate learning through their own individual learning styles. What caught me off guard was how quickly students who also were enrolled in my other courses began to inquire why I wasn't using similar techniques in all my classes. It was with mixed feelings that I heard them explain to other students, "If she taught this class the way she teaches in learning styles, *everybody* could understand this stuff." I knew then what I would be doing the next semester.

Is my students' perspective of the Dunn and Dunn Model different from my own? I'll let them speak for themselves. In the sixth week of class, I distribute a survey with one question: "Would you prefer this class return to a traditional lecture/discussion format? Why or why not?" To date, only one student of 65 has revealed a preference for the traditional method. The following is a sample of the comments from the other students.

- I can grasp things better in the learning centers because I teach myself and assess my own strengths and weaknesses.
- The actual hands-on materials we are using add variety to studying what we need to know; it helps put the content into a much more usable format.
- Great and interesting class! I feel as though in a traditional classroom format I only skim the surface of what there actually is. In this format, I feel as though learning is much deeper and more meaningful.
- This is one of the first times that I have learned things without frustration. It has been so much easier to get those pictures of words or phrases and retain the ideas. It has been easy to remember information longer. It makes such sense.
- You are not just telling us how to teach, you are showing us *how* to teach.
- Although the current structure confused me at first, I now understand how and why it is used and believe it to be very helpful in the learning process.
- Although I do like the lecture/discussion format, I very much like the mix. I like having half the time to work at my own pace. That way I can spend more or less time as needed in a specific area. Then, after a brief break, we come back together and discuss what we have learned, experienced, or discovered!
- This suits me, as I like to learn by doing. The lecture/discussion then is like a clarification, reinforcement and closure time for what we have done during the first half.

CONCLUSION

For me, there is no going back. I could never, in good conscience, return to my old paradigm of what teaching entails. I began this journey to rid myself of the burden of being a pedagogical illusionist. In the process, I found a way for my students to answer in the affirmative all six of the questions that the brain asks before it will learn.

Recently, I was talking with my daughter and lamenting the years when I really hadn't understood my role in the classroom. She paraphrased something Maya Angelou had once said: "You did then what you knew how to do. When you knew better, you did better."

I now pass this on to my students every semester.

Chapter 4

Educating Secondary Teachers to Work with Students' Diverse Styles

Nancy Montgomery

This description of how global and tactual students might *follow* directions for assembling some new gadget makes my skin crawl:

> They merely empty the box, let every piece fall where it may, and then proceed to pick up each interesting part, one by one—and sometimes several at a time—and push, pull, jab, alter, cajole, threaten, and eventually make each piece fit somewhere. When they are finished, leftover parts may still be lying on the floor or on the table, but the "mechanic" views them as not really necessary because the gadget works without them. (Dunn & Dunn, 1993, p. 102)

Rita and Kenneth Dunn proceed to explain that whatever strategies are used to put together anything new that comes with parts, all adults generally "will get the job done. How they do it depends on their processing style and perceptual strengths" (p. 402). Over 500 research studies at more than 115 universities confirm the reliability and validity of the Learning-Style Model (*Research on the Dunn & Dunn Model*, 1999). As strong a believer as I am in the authority of expert opinion, I still need to repeat these findings over and over to myself. It is difficult to understand how some people could live with leftover parts and how, for global processors, this simultaneous rather than sequential approach to solving a problem or completing a task is not only all right (p. 410), but also necessary—in fact, the *only* way they can do it!

I am one of the prototypical analytic/visual and auditory learners. Although it was 30 years ago, I still remember with amazement how my sister could claim to have "read" a 600-page novel and not recall the names of key characters. To me, not absorbing every word—skimming—was an injustice toward the sanctified process of reading. (She is now a wildly successful computer entrepreneur in Silicon Valley.) Of course, "the first two offspring seldom learn similarly" (Dunn & Griggs, 1998, p. 16). Earlier this year, a strongly preferenced global/tactual and kinesthetic ex-boyfriend (opposite processing styles attract . . . supposedly) tried to show me how to use a new cellular phone. He started with an overview and a hands-on demonstration: "Try this; do that." Finally, I couldn't stand it. Getting out a piece of paper and a pencil, I implored him, "Tell me exactly what to do first, so I can write down the steps."

Another global ex set me up with an entire new IBM computer system at home, though both he and I had previous experience only with Macs. He put the hardware together through trial and error without reading the directions! I laid them out in front of him discreetly. I reminded him that these pages explained how to position the woofers and cable up the printer. But he wouldn't take the hint. To be polite, because he was helping me, I choked back my impulse to make him follow the directions. Incredulously, the configuration worked beautifully. Still, I have carefully saved all the directions for future reference. (I never had the heart to look around on the floor to see if there were any dreaded leftover parts.)

A similar experience happened in Lord & Taylor's when a 19-year-old cosmetic maven tried to teach me how to give myself a makeover. Finally, at my insistence, she said that yes, she would jot down the brands and steps on a little brochure. After 15 minutes, I couldn't take it any more. I had to get a big, blank piece of paper and write down for myself, in my own words, exactly what to do in which order to have a chance at replication. My mother—who was accompanying me, the salesgirl, and even her colleagues at other stations, could barely hold back their amusement that somebody would be so intent on "taking notes," like when in school.

But that's how I learn; indeed, I have no choice. Like the global gadget-assemblers referred to above, I can only learn well and easily in the way that is natural for me; natural because almost four-fifths of learning style is biologically imposed (Restak, 1979; Thies, 1979). What matters is that, as a learner, I know *how* I learn best and have taught myself to learn independently in both personal and professional contexts. The revelation for me is that as magnificently as I feel I can master new and difficult material analytically and through my preferred modalities, I now know that it is just as necessary that my global/tactual or kinesthetic students be introduced to challenging academic content through *their* strengths—not through mine! I have been guilty of "naturalizing" my own learning and teaching styles because they work well for me, and because I have been exposed to analytic/auditory and visual teaching styles throughout my educational career in traditional classrooms—as have most of us. But all my untested assumptions were shaken the first time Dr. Rita Dunn visited my teacher education course as a guest speaker.

THE CONTEXT FOR PROSPECTIVE TEACHERS EXPERIMENTING WITH LEARNING STYLES

A former teacher of secondary English and psychology, I graduated from schools of education at Indiana University and New York University. An English professor for 17 years, I directed the Writing Center at Long Island University in Brooklyn and the writing and speech communications program at Sacred Heart University (Fairfield, CT), where I taught professors how to use online networked instruction across the curriculum. However, it was not until I joined the faculty in Instructional Leadership at St. John's University in 1997 that I began to hear much about learning styles. I only regret now how many hundreds of students and teachers I might have influenced more positively had I understood that learners have their own individual strengths and that teachers need to help them identify and use them independently.

I taught a class this spring for secondary education minors, majoring in a variety of subjects in the liberal arts and sciences. As future teachers of English, foreign languages, mathematics, diverse sciences, art, and social studies, these students take a mandatory combined six–credit practicum and methods course. Just prior to their associate-teaching experience, these students study general methods, including topics such as selecting content; preparing objectives and lesson plans; maintaining a safe, supportive classroom learning environment; student- and teacher-centered instructional strategies; media aids; and resources. They also learn how to assess and report student achievement and the importance of continuing their professional development. Once a week, students are in middle schools and high schools observing a variety of teachers in their disciplines—taking detailed qualitative field notes; critiquing and evaluating teaching styles; and constructively and concretely explaining which approaches they personally would take in similar circumstances and why. Many are fortunate to be able to tutor students on a one-on-one basis, facilitate small-group work, and conduct whole-class sessions. During alternate meetings, students do micro-peer-teaching, which requires presenting lessons for our college class with classmates taking the role of secondary pupils.

This semester, these prospective teachers did their observations at a special education site in East New York, Brooklyn and at a high school in Jamaica, Queens. The former is a self-contained special education school for students from 14.9 years to 21 years old. A learning-styles school, it offers a specialized instructional environment with programs for youngsters who are severely handicapped, autistic, severely emotionally disturbed, deaf, and blind. The latter is a typical New York City public high school, with a diverse student population of about 3,500. Both East New York and Jamaica are economically depressed inner-city locations. Students are predominantly from minority groups, mostly African American or Latino. According to administrators, these adolescents face an array of academic and personal problems.

LEARNING ABOUT LEARNING STYLES IN THE COLLEGE CLASSROOM

In addition to a general methods textbook, my students were assigned the Dunn and Dunn (1993) book, *Teaching Secondary Students through Their Individual Learning Styles: Practical Approaches for Grades 7–12*, as well as a special edition of *Inter-Ed* entitled *Everything You Need to Successfully Implement a Learning-Styles Instructional Program: Materials and Methods* (The Association for the Advancement of International Education, 1997). We were honored to have both Dr. Rita Dunn and Dr. Angela Klavas talk with us about learning styles during the semester, and guide our observations and applications in the field. (Dr. Klavas is the Assistant Director for the Center for the Study of Learning and Teaching Styles at St. John's.) We held numerous discussions about these readings and lectures. We also experimented with the creative applications of what we learned by actively integrating a variety of teaching- and learning-style elements into our team-taught, interdisciplinary, thematic lessons that groups of students presented to their peers (Dunn & Dunn, 1993, p. 409).

Also critical was the introduction and manipulation of real tactual and kinesthetic materials into our sessions. While the required texts are thankfully replete with pictures, diagrams, samples, extensive illustrations, PLSs, CAPs, and MIPs, it is only true to the *spirit* of learning-styles theory that we examine firsthand an array of actual materials for students to manipulate and experience. After understanding the need to reach tactual and kinesthetic students through these resources, the typical analytically inclined and analytically educated future teacher says, "What in the world would devices like this look like? How would a student actually use them?" Twenty years of testing thousands of people have demonstrated that 65 percent of teachers are strongly analytic and 50–60 percent of secondary students are strongly global (p. 410). Therefore, prospective teachers need to see manipulatives and whole-body activities modeled for teaching global students and to learn, through guided practice, how to reach these too-often ignored learners.

EVALUATING THE USE OF LEARNING-STYLE PRACTICE IN THE SCHOOLS

Having observed secondary teaching styles with my students, and having conferred with them as they wrote their final analyses of, and recommendations for, classroom dynamics, I next read my 30 students' papers and categorized the major thematic strands of learning-styles theory that seemed most important to them. I noted how many students mentioned certain topics, how much of their papers were devoted to these issues, and how vehemently they professed their beliefs and pedagogical intentions. Focusing on these subjects then, I interviewed the prospective teachers who represented common viewpoints and questioned them for clarification of their perspectives. I found that their interests lay particularly in the following aspects: (1) how to be successful with global students, and (2) how to capitalize on tactual and kinesthetic strengths. This is where they perceived the greatest need and was also what they didn't know before attending my class. Let's examine their assessments of learning-style applications in their own words.

PLANNING LESSONS TO INCLUDE GLOBAL LEARNERS

In the introduction to his paper, Chris modeled the kind of opening paragraphs that engaged global learners. He used a concrete, dialogue-rich, subjective, personal anecdote relating his topic to real-life situations and the interests of his readers. He told the story of two high school buddies with a great deal in common, except that one was failing miserably in math while the other was excelling. He led up to the information he wanted to present on learning styles by stating that perhaps Sammy didn't fare well in math because of his global need to understand *why*, for example, the Chain Rule made sense.

P implies Q
Q implies R
Therefore, P implies R

Sammy's need to have a real-life analogy was met, Chris asserted, when the teacher Mr. Haberman provided the following comparison: "James, a Republican, gets (implied) John to be a Republican. Then John gets (implies) Sara to become one also. Therefore, James got (implied) Sara to be a Republican."

Most training is designed to teach analytic learners, while the global learners' needs are not addressed (Dunn, 1996). But Chris's point that globals require additional encouragement, short, varied tasks, and constant connections between content and real life, like the above example, reminded me that many of my students at least imply—if not state outright—that addressing learning style takes time, experience, creativity, and a firm control of classroom management. Chris believes that global students are seen by teachers as distracters who necessitate the use of "every single environmental element that teachers don't normally use" because they often require a different learning environment—soft illumination, informal seating, sound, and occasional mobility. No wonder these fledgling teachers are unsure of how soon or how well they will be able to implement these approaches. They fear that, as beginning teachers, their classes will be noisy and appear chaotic or that parents, colleagues, and administrators will question their tactics. All the more reason that, next semester, I will address their doubts more directly because these questions and concerns are all dealt with thoroughly in their text, *Teaching Secondary Students*. I have learned that if we don't confront and teach specific ways to overcome perceived obstacles, learning-styles theory will be remain just that.

Noel cited attempts by instructors to engage global learners with humor. A chemistry teacher reminded his class that "tomorrow we'll be going fission in a nuclear lake!" And when one student put her head down to sleep, he said jokingly, "Will somebody please activate Lucy?" Aneil discussed how a ninth-grade biology teacher included globals by vividly recounting her own childhood explorations in nature; by facilitating groups in creating DNA helix models and leading students to deduce the facts and details for themselves; and by illustrating information with colored chalk and three-dimensional visual aids. Identifying himself as a global learner, Aneil appreciated this lesson and intended to emulate it. Usually, globals find it less threatening and more fun to discover information and details; they solve problems for themselves through group learning rather than by being given information directly by their teacher (Dunn & Dunn, 1993, pp. 102–103).

Diane suggested an educational game, such as the $25,000 Pyramid, to help a ninth-grade social studies class review for a quiz rather than the straight lecture the teacher presented. She also remarked about a civil law class concerning filing claims for faulty merchandise. When students' attention drifted, Ms. Levi "reeled them right back in by telling them a story that happened to her last week." This elicited questions like, "For whom were you buying the dresser?" Another class featured a guest speaker, an administrator from a school that specializes in helping students find employment after high school graduation. Mr. Hemmings reached students with practical advice, such as good interview manners, and with references students found relevant, such as one song by the Spice Girls. In an American history class, Diane admired the way Mr. Caban told stories connecting to his students' racial and ethnic backgrounds. He included African American, Hispanic American, and Native American tales and "even the role of women in war—especially interesting to Diane, who was surprised that students in her all-girl high school had never raised the subject.

Observing at this high school, Chris, Noel, Aneil, and Diane cited numerous instances of lesson plans that reached out to both analytic and global processors. However, all observers conceded that relatively few teachers incorporated global approaches. Diane concluded, "The majority of teachers had little if any contact with students. I do not remember one teacher asking how a pupil's day was going or why the homework was not done." She echoed Chris's concerns for beginning teachers: how many of the elements can I address initially and what if some strategies actually "disrupt" learning? "I do not believe in my students sitting on the floor or allowing them such freedom as moving around the class while I am trying to teach." Although she attests to a belief in the principles of learning-styles theory and recounted enthusiastically all these examples, these kinds of comments tell me that in future classes we need frank discussions of how to practically design, monitor, and evaluate these innovative classrooms. Here is just one sample of how the research already has documented answers to practitioners' dilemmas: by redesigning the educational environment, which takes one class period per semester, the teacher is automatically responding to 12 elements (Dunn, 1997, p. 4).

These potential problems are dealt with completely and satisfactorily in learning-styles literature. However, my students, having internalized the hidden curriculum of the conventional classroom and the traditional "banking" concept of education (Freire, 1970), need to voice their fears and doubts and learn more of the *why* behind the suggested changes, as well as more of the practical how-tos. I also need to work harder to identify productive learning-styles teachers in all disciplines in our affiliated schools, those who are eager to model and discuss their style with prospective teachers.

TEACHING TO ALL STUDENTS' PERCEPTUAL STRENGTHS

Most teachers are analytic, while most secondary students are global. Furthermore, as many as 85 percent of underachievers are global (Dunn & Dunn, 1993, pp. 102–103). Thus, it becomes imperative that prospective teachers learn how to counteract the all-too-common occurrence of tactual/kinesthetic learners becoming poor learners because their teachers lecture or require readings as the basic source of introductory learning (p. 151). Instructors need to help these learners toward one of our most important educational goals: to teach students to teach themselves independently as adults (p. 197). Unfortunately, that is a skill to which they seldom aspire (p. 151). Let's see what our student-teachers observed in the field and how learning-styles theory influences how they accommodate all students' perceptual strengths in their own future classrooms.

Chris noted that, at the East New York school, learning style is automatically incorporated "as a necessity for special education." (This is one of the many reasons why all future teachers in regular education should observe some special education classes.) Students saw many lively, real-life examples of students learning by doing and experiencing. This happened on two levels for us, as Glenn, a prospective teacher, said that "the experience that I gained from watching these children could never be learned in a classroom at any university."

Antonia had participated at the Jamaica site in a science class where students worked together to grow vegetables from seeds they had chosen. They demonstrated their mastery of objectives through their choice of projects, such as charts for growth rate and games to teach measurement. At the special education school too, Jed, a future teacher, found that in the concrete world of East New York, students were "disconnected from nature." "Transforming a rundown vacant lot into a vibrant garden" symbolized a revitalization in the community, a grassroots movement initiated by students and empowering them as active change agents in their school neighborhood. Jed also was intrigued with learning reading skills through Task Cards and the local newspaper want ads, in addition to making key chains in shop class. Glenn enjoyed baking and cooking in the kitchen, the "hands-on experience of working with the food and utensils," the room "full of life and laughter" as students were taught nutrition, science, social studies, math, and language skills through making treats for Easter.

Cindy discussed one class's visit to the aquarium, where each student selected one "denizen of the deep" on which to gather information. Of course, "globals tend to draw meaning from . . . visual representations; they respond less well to words and numbers" (Dunn & Dunn, 1993, p. 103). Thus, using multisensory materials, students researched their creatures, and the bulletin boards and tables displayed diaramas, pictures, photographs, symbols, drawings, charts, and graphs, as well as their written summaries about habitat, feeding habits, and degree of endangerment. Using computers, students then created text, selected audio and graphics, and drew on-screen illustrations to synthesize a multimedia presentation of the whole aquarium adventure to be given for the entire school at the end of the year. Many of my young "teachers" wanted to go back and see the presentation— not because they had to, but because they had created it with the students. My students also volunteered to work in East New York during their spring break due to their enthusiasm for visiting a learning-styles school.

Since the level of participation at the site became intense and enveloping, and since our group developed a cohesive camaraderie and a commonality of purpose, both my students and I felt this was the most valuable teaching experience we had all year. And what we had done was to learn about teaching tactually and kinesthetically by actually doing and experiencing for ourselves.

With a class of non-verbal, non-ambulatory students with multiple handicaps, many quadriplegics, we all had a wonderful time participating in the dying of Easter eggs, the making of Jell-O molds and Easter-bunny sandwiches. Even though these students could not feed themselves or manage bathroom skills—let alone talk, read, write, or manipulate objects—inventive teachers and paraprofessionals walked among them to ask their preferences of color and flavor for the Jell-O. For many, it was an accomplishment to indicate their choices by blinking or head movements; for others, isolating a finger to try to point was an achievement. My students and I discussed later how, after observing these teachers' creativity, we had no excuse for not coming up with ideas for tactual/kinesthetic activities in regular education. These teachers modeled profoundly for us the attitude that all students "do have valuable strengths, are capable, can learn, and are worthy" (Dunn & Dunn, 1993, p. 197).

Primarily because I observed this class, I was later able to counter a "low" third-grade teacher's claim that she couldn't really let her students read and write much in class (this at an inservice workshop in Bushwick, Brooklyn): their handwriting often looked like chicken-scratch; their spelling was atrocious; they stumbled when they read aloud. Several teachers echoed that they dared not allow students to use language until their skills were good enough. I described the class I had seen in East New York and my own burgeoning awareness of how we could immerse students through multisensory resources and collaborate on generating techniques to help them learn through all their senses. We then discovered through group learning (modeling teaching for globals) a substantial list of concrete ideas for creating manipulatives and using body actions to help students read and write. I elicited from peer groups (another strategy for globals) specific examples of what had worked for them.

Although visual and auditory myself, I had learned by doing and experiencing in the kitchen, the shop class, the garden, and the multimedia presentation on the aquarium field trip at this special education school. It is most valuable for prospective teachers to have experience firsthand with the acquiring of new information tactually and kinesthetically. Auditory and visual learners like myself can reinforce classroom lectures and reading about the use of multisensory materials with secondary exposure through manipulatives, floor games, field trips, and so on. Interestingly, the tactual/kinesthetic reinforcement was what really reached me about the value of teaching through these strengths. It also was what made me commit myself to training teachers about and through these methods.

Lastly, my student-teachers remarked on the sometimes nearly painful need for mobility that many students at both schools exhibited. In regular education in Jamaica, Aneil saw "students getting up and walking around without permission." In special education, Cindy suggested that one student, Joyce, obviously "disinterested in the written word" and long ago having "tuned out Ms. Miller's lesson," be offered the opportunity to walk around and manipulate objects to learn the rules for subtracting fractions. I noticed too that Joyce actually could not sit still and found reason—whether to get her breakfast together or go to her locker—to be up and down constantly. Admonished frequently to get her books out, sit up straight, and pay attention, she didn't appear to listen or look at the teacher.

Much to our surprise then, as observers, when Joyce was called on for some rather difficult problems and put on the spot to explain the steps she used to find her answers, she did an outstanding job. Perhaps this was because, even though she "got in trouble," she found a way to express her need to be constantly moving while Ms. Miller was lecturing; she had the intake of breakfast and juice as she was listening; and she knitted (!) and doodled and drew throughout the lesson. She instinctively knew what she had to do to learn the day's objectives in math.

It is critical that teacher preparation programs instruct future educators in incorporating hands-on, real-life experiences and whole-body games and activities so that we do not consign 55 percent of our adult population (Dunn, 1999, p. 87) to low self-image and lack of confidence in their ability to learn independently. But this cannot be accomplished if we continue to teach only to students who learn best by listening, discussing, reading, and hearing explanations of information written on the chalkboard (Dunn & Dunn, 1993, p. 143). Underachieving and at-risk students are motivated when we introduce new material through their perceptual strengths (p. 199).

IMPLICATIONS FOR TEACHER EDUCATION

One elementary school principal asserted that "it is not the child who bears the responsibility for learning; it is the teacher who bears the responsibility for identifying each child's learning-style strengths and then for matching those with responsive environments and approaches (Andrews, 1997, p. 58). Thinking about her role as a prospective math teacher, the majority being analytic (Dunn & Dunn, 1993, p. 410), Anne emphasized the importance of a teacher understanding her own teaching style. Our class took *The Teaching Style Inventory* (Dunn & Dunn, 1993, pp. 411–425) and then learned how to plan lessons that incorporated both processing styles. I agree that if we learn about styles different from our own, we will gain the same perspective on what is natural and comfortable for us as we do when we study a foreign language or culture.

As another student-teacher, Keri, quoted from Dr. Klavas's presentation, "Learning-style is an awareness and an appreciation of different ways of learning; it reflects an attitude, a willingness to be flexible and adjust our teaching to accommodate our students" (Oral Communication, March 1998). Noel stressed the importance of garnering continuous feedback from students on how well a teacher is "connecting." He recommended teachers explore and experiment with working with style elements (Dunn & Griggs, 1998) and making learning enjoyable "so that a sense of accomplishment will drive students toward higher plateaus as independent lifelong learners: It all starts with us!"

IMPLICATIONS FOR HIGHER EDUCATION

Ingham (1991) reported that "less than 25% of college students are auditory learners—able to remember approximately 75% of the new and difficult information they listen to during a 40- to 50-minute period. Less than 40% are visual learners—able to remember approximately 75% of what they read during a 40- to 50-minute period (Dunn & Griggs, 1998, pp. 16–17). Claxton and Murrell (1987) attested that college students claim improved performance if they understand their own learning style. Dunn, Griggs, and others (1995) undertook a meta-analytic evaluation of the Learning-Style Model by analyzing 36 experimental studies conducted at 13 universities during the 1980s. Their conclusion was that, for college students whose styles were accommodated, achievement was at least 75 percent of a standard deviation higher than for others whose styles were not addressed.

This substantial body of research provides evidence for the matching of teaching and learning styles. With the success of learning-styles approaches in classrooms I have described, I know that my undergraduate student-teachers will continue to profit personally as independent learners who capitalize on their own strengths. They also will benefit as educators trained and practiced in accommodating each unique student's most natural and effective ways of acquiring and retaining new knowledge.

I am (a) a competent facilitator of Cooperative Learning who doesn't much care to do it myself, (b) a professor who secretly was surprised that my "best" student-teacher professed himself to be a global/tactual learner, and (c) a former doctoral candidate whose dissertation committee had to chant, "Flow chart, flow chart" to get me to add something other than words to my thesis. However, I, too, have become aware and appreciate, both personally and professionally, that there is no one right way for everyone to learn. In fact, what works for me and probably for most professors in higher education is the opposite of what works for the majority of our students.

My son, a 20-year-old undergraduate in business, studies with earphones, intake, soft lighting, and air conditioning blasting in the dead of winter. He lounges casually on the couch or bed, takes frequent breaks, and sometimes paces across the floor while reading. He sets his alarm for 4:00 A.M., his self-proclaimed time-of-day preference for his highest energy peak. With a 4.0 average at a prestigious research institution, he did nothing but struggle with academics, and thus self-esteem, through six years of secondary school and ended up in Resource Room. Why? Neither his award-winning Greenwich, Connecticut school system nor his family knew anything about his learning style.

While preparing middle school students in a low-performing district in Brooklyn for the annual standardized reading test this spring, it irritated me to no end that one seventh-grader was always drawing pictures instead of looking at me as I conducted the drill. He could have at least been writing down words from my lesson! I invariably asked him to stop; but the drawings were superb—of musclemen, Superman, giants—and the boy *was* seemingly alert and attentive with as many right answers as anybody in the class. I believe that next year I'll progress to finally being able to leave globals alone to learn the way they have to learn. I think back to Joyce, the special education student whose apparent attention was on everything *but* the teacher's lesson; however, when it came to demonstrating mastery over fractions, she was a crackerjack. And isn't that what it's all about?

Chapter 5

One Texas University's Approach to Integrating Learning Styles in Teacher Education: Talking the Talk and Walking the Walk

Janet Whitley and Pam Littleton

"The proficiencies are in!" we were all told one day while having lunch. We eagerly examined the new Texas *Learner-Centered Proficiencies* recently issued. These are, in essence, the vision that Texas administrators have for classrooms. As we read through and discussed each of the five proficiencies, we became excited thinking about preparing teachers to teach in learner-centered classrooms. But we also began to examine what these proficiencies meant for teacher preparation at the university level. Our question, it seemed, was: could we prepare university students for teaching in learner-centered schools if our own classrooms were not learner-centered? Can you talk the talk without walking the walk? As we continued our discussion, we began to plan.

SAGE ON THE STAGE OR GUIDE ON THE SIDE?

The Learner-Centered Proficiencies are clearly written to communicate to present and future teachers in Texas that curriculum and instruction must be student-centered rather than teacher-centered (see Figure 5.1). As we read through the proficiencies, the images that came to mind were that those strategies were active, hands-on, and experiential. Instruction needed to become meaningful, relevant, and constructivist in nature—quite the opposite of the images of the teacher as a "sage on the stage." Rather, the teacher now was to become a facilitator, a guide, and a coach.

How could university professors help develop future teachers as facilitators, guides, and coaches? Following a constructivist philosophy at the university level seemed to make sense—especially if we believed the adage that we teach as we were taught. That seemed to say to us that we ourselves

Figure 5.1
Learner-Centered Schools for Texas: A Vision of Texas Educators

Learner-Centered Knowledge

The teacher possesses and draws on a rich knowledge base of content, pedagogy, and technology to provide relevant and meaningful learning experiences for all students. The teacher exhibits a strong working knowledge of subject matter and enables students to better understand patterns of thinking specific to a discipline. The teacher stays abreast of current knowledge and practice within the content area, related disciplines, and technology; participates in professional development activities; and collaborates with other professionals. Moreover, the teacher contributes to the knowledge base and understands the pedagogy of the discipline.

As the teacher guides learners to construct knowledge through experiences, they learn about relationships among and within the central themes of various disciplines while also learning how to learn. Recognizing the dynamic nature of knowledge, the teacher selects and organizes topics so students make clear connections between what is taught in the classroom and what they experience outside the classroom. As students probe these relationships, the teacher encourages discussion in which both the teacher's and the students' opinions are valued. To further develop multiple perspectives, the teacher integrates other disciplines, learners' interests, and technological resources so that learners consider the central themes of the subject matter from as many different cultural and intellectual viewpoints as possible.

Learner-Centered Instruction

To create a learner-centered community, the teacher collaboratively identifies needs; and plans, implements, and assesses instruction using technology and other resources. The teacher is a leader of a learner-centered community, in which an atmosphere of trust and openness produces a stimulating exchange of ideas and mutual respect. The teacher is a critical thinker and problem solver who plays a variety of roles when teaching. As a coach, the teacher observes, evaluates, and changes directions and strategies whenever necessary. As a facilitator, the teacher helps students link ideas in the content area to familiar ideas, to prior experiences, and to relevant problems. As a manager, the teacher effectively acquires, allocates, and conserves resources. By encouraging self-directed learning and by modeling respectful behavior, the teacher effectively manages the learning environment so that optimal learning occurs.

Assessment is used to guide the learner community. By using assessment as an integral part of instruction, the teacher responds to the needs of all learners. In addition, the teacher guides learners to develop personally meaningful forms of self-assessment.

The teacher selects materials, technology, activities, and space that are developmentally appropriate and designed to engage interest in learning. As a result, learners work independently and cooperatively in a positive and stimulating learning climate fueled by self-discipline and motivation.

Although the teacher has a vision for the destination of learning, students set

(continued)

Figure 5.1 (continued)

individual goals and plan how to reach the destination. As a result, they take responsibility for their own learning, develop a sense of the importance of learning for understanding, and begin to understand themselves as learners. The teacher's plans integrate learning experiences and various forms of assessment that take into consideration the unique characteristics of the learner community. The teacher shares responsibility for the results of this process with all members of the learning community.

Together, learners and teachers take risks in trying out innovative ideas for learning. To facilitate learning, the teacher encourages various types of learners to shape their own learning through active engagement, manipulation, and examination of ideas and materials. Critical thinking, creativity, and problem solving spark further learning. Consequently there is an appreciation of learning as a life-long process that builds a greater understanding of the world and a feeling of responsibility toward it.

Equity in Excellence for All Learners

The teacher responds appropriately to diverse groups of learners. The teacher not only respects and is sensitive to all learners but also encourages the use of all their skills and talents. As the facilitator of learning, the teacher models and encourages appreciation for students' cultural heritage, unique endowments, learning styles, interests, and needs. The teacher also designs learning experiences that show consideration for these student characteristics.

Because the teacher views differences as opportunities for learning, cross-cultural experiences are an integral part of the learner-centered community. In addition, the teacher establishes a relationship between the curriculum and community cultures. While making this connection, the teacher and students explore attitudes that foster unity. As a result, the teacher creates an environment in which learners work cooperatively and purposefully using a variety of resources to understand themselves, their immediate community, and the global society in which they live.

Learner-Centered Communication

While acting as an advocate for all students and the school, the teacher demonstrates effective professional and interpersonal communication skills. As a learner, the teacher communicates the mission of the school with learners, professionals, families, and community members. With colleagues, the teacher works to create an environment in which taking risks, sharing new ideas, and innovative problem solving are supported and encouraged. With citizens, the teacher works to establish strong and positive ties between the school and the community.

Because the teacher is a compelling communicator, students begin to appreciate the importance of expressing their views clearly. The teacher uses verbal, nonverbal, and media techniques so that students explore ideas collaboratively, pose questions, and support one another in their learning. The teacher and students listen, speak, read, and write in a variety of contexts; give multimedia and artistic presen-

(continued)

Figure 5.1 (continued)

tations; and use technology as a resource for building communication skills. The teacher incorporates techniques of inquiry that enable students to use different levels of thinking.

The teacher also communicates effectively as an advocate for each learner. The teacher is sensitive to concerns that affect learners and takes advantage of community strengths and resources for the learners' welfare.

Learner-Centered Professional Development

The teacher, as a reflective practitioner dedicated to all students' success demonstrates a commitment to learn, to improve the profession, and to maintain professional ethics and personal integrity. As a learner, the teacher works within a framework of clearly defined professional goals to plan for and profit from a wide variety of relevant learning opportunities. The teacher develops an identity as a professional, interacts effectively with colleagues, and takes a role in setting standards for teacher accountability. In addition, the teacher uses technological and other resources to facilitate continual professional growth.

To strengthen the effectiveness and quality of teaching, the teacher actively engages in an exchange of ideas with colleagues, observes peers, and encourages feedback from learners to establish a successful learning community. As a member of a collaborative team, the teacher identifies and uses group processes to make decisions and solve problems.

The teacher exhibits the highest standard of professionalism and bases daily decisions on ethical principles. To support the needs of learners, the teacher knows and uses community resources, school services, and laws relating to teacher responsibilities and student rights. Through these activities, the teacher contributes to the improvement of comprehensive educational programs as well as programs within specific disciplines.

needed to be facilitators, guides, and coaches. We recognized that we needed to adjust some of the things we were doing so that our classrooms became learner-centered. We reasoned that if our students had opportunities to personally experience learner-centered classrooms during their teacher preparation, they would be better able to set up and implement learner-centered classrooms for their own students.

EXAMINING HIGHER EDUCATION PROGRAMS

In Texas, the last set of state standards (1989) did away with degrees in education; teacher preparation programs were limited to 12 semester hours in education coursework plus six hours of student teaching. In response to these restrictions, the scope and sequence of the teacher preparation program across the state, and in particular at Tarleton State University, were changed. The first set of changes responded to the 12 semester-hour limit on education courses. The scope and sequence of that program was fairly traditional—the first class focused on educational philosophy and history, the second on educational psychology, and the last two covered teaching methods and classroom management. The Tarleton program changed again in the fall of 1996 (see Figure 5.2). That change brought a new scope and sequence to the program and we began to teach courses we called Professional Development I (PD I), PD II, PD III, and PD IV. These new courses included content similar to what was offered previously in the old sequence but provided depth and complexity as well as a spiraling curriculum. We moved toward a more student-centered program including field-basing some of the courses and requiring students to spend more time in public school classrooms with "hands-on" experiences rather than just observations. Students also now completed a full semester of student teaching. We found, however, that even in the public schools, students were not always exposed to true learner-centered classrooms. As field-based programs became more prevalent, there were fewer restrictions from the state regarding the total number of education hours; however, some universities, including Tarleton, maintained those original requirements that limited the number of education hours.

At the same time the teacher preparation program was undergoing changes, Tarleton faculty became interested in learning styles. This led to a visit from Dr. Rita Dunn, who presented an overview of learning styles to local teachers and administrators and provided follow-up training with Dr. Ken Dunn during the summer of 1995. In 1996, Tarleton created the Tarleton Institute for Research on Teaching and Learning and applied to become a member of the International Learning Styles Network (Dunn, Given, Thomson, & Brunner, 1997). Three faculty members attended the summer St. John's University Annual Learning-Styles Certification Institute in New York and two have become certified trainers.

In the current program, elementary, secondary, and all-level students are combined in the first two professional development courses. They are divided by secondary, all-level, and elementary classifications during the last two professional development courses. This split occurs during the last two courses because of the laboratory requirement of from one-half to one day a week in the public schools. The second course in the professional development sequence is titled "The Learner and the Learning Environment" and is called PD II. As seen in Figure 5.2, the content of PD II centers around effective planning and instructional strategies for diverse learners. A key component of the course includes instruction on learning styles. The Dunn and Dunn Learning-Style Model is used. The following is a description of the implementation of a learner-centered classroom in PD II.

Using Learning Styles in Higher Education

Because learning style is an integral part of the second professional development course, the instructors of that class utilize learning-styles concepts and strategies throughout the course. When one examines the research on adult learning, this makes very good sense. For example, Arcieri (1998) states that adults learn more effectively when actively involved in learning through their learning-style strengths and that they often want to acquire practical knowledge and skills they can use in their teaching. However, implementing all of the elements of learning styles can be a problem at the university level. A college classroom that is used by many professors from various disciplines throughout the day does not lend itself to implementing some of the elements (especially those in the environmental domain), and professors often use several different classrooms a day. There are, however, some elements that lend themselves for implementation on the university campus. For instance, intake is available for those students that prefer it and students generally may choose to work by themselves, in pairs, or in small groups for many of the assignments. Perceptual preferences also are addressed; students are given visual and auditory information simultaneously (through lecture and overhead transparencies and/or handouts) and are generally given tactual and kinesthetic tasks to do during each period. In addition, the students in the teacher preparation program at Tarleton have all taken the *Productivity Environmental Preference Survey* (PEPS) (Dunn, Dunn, & Price, 1982) and have received instruction in interpretation of the PEPS profile. On a personal level, students are encouraged to learn as much about themselves as possible. They are encouraged to study in an environment that is conducive to their own learning and to begin understanding what their learning style means to them—not only when they study, but in interactions in and out of the classroom. For example, students discuss what it means in and out of the classroom if one is intrinsically versus extrinsically motivated, or global versus analytic, or persistent versus non-persistent. Later, students are asked what their learning style will mean to them as a teacher.

However, while these activities make some basic attempts to use learning styles at the post-secondary level, we feel that we need to make a real commitment to "walking the walk" if we truly expect students to create learner-centered environments in their classrooms. We continue to examine the Learner-Centered Proficiencies Standards to find other ways to make classrooms at the university level learner-centered. We have collaboratively analyzed what the proficiencies might mean to a professor of a university class—can these proficiencies be a vision for the university classroom as well as the public school classroom? Can learning-style strategies be a key component to understanding, on an experiential level, what a learner-centered classroom at the post-secondary level would look like? Below, the proficiency domains

Figure 5.2
Professional Development Program—Department of Curriculum and
Instruction—Tarleton State University

FIRST SEMESTER	SECOND SEMESTER
EDU 3303	**EDU 3353**
Introduction to Teaching	*Learners and the Learning Environment*
Professional Development I (3)	**Professional Development II (3)**
*Curriculum Design	*Modifying the Curriculum
*Developmentally Appropriate Practices—*Instruction*	*Developmentally Appropriate Practices—*Learners*

*Models of Instruction
  Effective Teaching Practices
   Direct Instruction
	*Models of Instruction
	  Effective Teaching Practices
	   Cooperative Learning

*Code of Ethics/Professionalism	*Modifying Instruction for Diverse Learners
	  Learning Styles
	   Multiple Intelligences
	   Exceptional Learners
	   Cultural Diversity

*Correlates of Effective Schools
  Instructor Leader
	*Correlates of Effective Schools
	  Opportunity to Learn
	   Time on Task

*Middle School Concept	*Middle School *Adolescent Behavior*
*Intro to Classroom Management	*Classroom Management *Social Skills*
	*Assessment & Evaluation
*Instructional Technology & Lab	*Instructional Technology *Materials Development*
*Field Experiences	*Field Experiences

*Demonstration of Competencies
  Micro Teach
	*Demonstration of Competencies
	  Micro Teach

*Professional Portfolio
  Professional Development Plan
	*Professional Portfolio
	  Professional Development Plan
	   Self-Analysis of Personal Learning Style

THIRD SEMESTER	FINAL SEMESTER

THIRD SEMESTER

EDU 4303
*Application of Effective
Teaching Practices*

Professional Development III (3)

* Integrating the Curriculum

* Developmentally Appropriate
Practices—*Curriculum*

* Models of Instruction
  * *Effective Teaching Practices*
    * *Inquiry/Discovery*
    * *Critical Thinking*
    * *Problem Solving*
    * *Creative Thinking*

* Correlates of Effective Schools
  * *High Expectations*

* Middle School Instruction
  * *Interdisciplinary Planning*

* Classroom Management
  * *Conflict Resolution*

* Evaluating Instruction

* Instructional Technology
  * *Multi-Media Development*

* Field Experiences

* Demonstration of Competencies
  * *Micro Teach*

* Professional Portfolio
  * *Professional Development Plan*

FINAL SEMESTER

EDU 4353
Issues in Professional Development

Professional Development IV (3)

* History

* School Functions

* School Administration

* Classroom Management

* Law/Ethics

* Parent Conferencing

* Assessment & Evaluation

* Correlates of Effective Schools
  * *Parent & Community Involvement*
    * *Safe & Orderly Environment*

* Case Studies

EDU 4906
*Professional Practicum in
Teaching* (6)

* Full Semester Student Teaching
  * *Multi-Media Presentation*

61

are examined and strategies discussed that integrate learning styles into a learner-centered university classroom, in particular in Tarleton's Professional Development II course.

Learner-Centered Proficiencies for Teachers

Learner-Centered Knowledge: the teacher possesses and draws on a rich knowledge base of content, pedagogy, and technology to provide relevant and meaningful learning experiences for all students. As one reads the description in the first paragraph from Figure 5.1, it seems ready-made for a college classroom; most professors stay abreast of current knowledge and practice and participate in professional development activities. Many also contribute to the knowledge base. Certainly, professors in teacher preparation programs would understand the pedagogy of the discipline. But do professors guide learners to construct knowledge through experiences so that students understand relationships within the various disciplines while they are also learning how to learn? How do college instructors help students make clear connections between what is taught in the classroom and what they experience outside the classroom? For students in a teacher preparation program, that means the real world—the public school classroom. Certainly, programs that are focusing on field-based instruction and experience are working toward that goal and, at the very least, students should be able to apply learning from the college or field-based classroom while working with public school students. But the idea of a learner-centered classroom implies that content-specific instruction in teacher preparation needs to be active and constructivist in nature. At Tarleton, our students learn about Cooperative Learning through direct experience in cooperative groups. Then, by comparing and contrasting those cooperative experiences with other types of learning experiences (for example, group work without those cooperative experiences built in) the students and the instructor discuss the elements of Cooperative Learning. This activity involves several of the learning-style elements. It addresses the perceptual preferences by offering activities using the auditory, visual, tactile, and kinesthetic modalities. The activity also offers students the opportunity to work in groups for part of the assignment and then to have a choice of working alone, in pairs, or in groups for other parts of the assignment.

Learner-Centered Instruction: To create a learner-centered community, the teacher collaboratively identifies needs; and plans, implements, and assesses instruction using technology and other resources. This proficiency identifies the roles of the teacher as, among others, a facilitator, coach, and manager. The teacher is also required to effectively manage the learning environment by encouraging self-directed learning. These ideals do not evoke images of the "sage on the stage" where the teacher is involved in primarily lecturing to the class. Often, university classes are lecture-based and many students attended high schools where lecture was the major mode of presentation. It is often difficult, therefore, for students in teacher preparation classes (especially, it seems, secondary education students) to visualize other ways of teaching. We assist our students to engage in active learning by offering classroom experiences that are designed to address perceptual preferences and by offering differentiated levels of structure as required by students.

When working with auditory learners, we give verbal clues with a visual presentation, use colored chalk to separate chalkboard assignments, use colored pens on the overhead, give both oral and written directions for completing class tests or assignments, and sometimes offer opportunities for students to give auditory responses to tests. For visual learners, we may write the problems and examples or directions on the chalkboard or overhead while explaining the process. We also use charts, graphs, cartoons, and/or maps to show information and help students visualize abstract ideas. For tactile/kinesthetic learners, students are allowed to work on the chalkboard or overhead, plan and make games to demonstrate certain skills or knowledge, use paper-folding activities to depict mathematical ideas, or use task cards or other playing card activities to engage in learning.

In addition, allowing students to choose whether to engage in some of the activities alone, in a pair, or in a group meets students' sociological needs. Elements such as persistence and motivation are met on an individual basis. Persistence can be addressed by offering the option for students to work on two or three projects at a time or to work on only one until that one is completed. Need for low or high structure is met by providing differentiated sets of directions for students.

This proficiency also addresses assessment as an integral part of instruction—especially self-assessment. One way to engage university students in a form of self-assessment is to encourage reflective thinking and writing by asking them to think about their activities with public school students; for example, asking them which activities were the most successful and why is the key to reflective thinking and writing. Which activities were not as successful and why? What would they do differently if they were going to do that activity again? In fact, this form of self-assessment encourages students to strengthen their intrapersonal skills and assists them in developing one of the characteristics of effective teachers—reflective thinking. If public school teachers are to help their students take responsibility for their own learning and to understand themselves as learners, then that process must begin with them while they are still students. Hopefully, this process will begin while they are still in school; they need to understand themselves as learners and reflect on what that will mean to them as teachers.

Equity in Excellence for All Learners: The teacher responds appropriately to diverse groups of learners. This proficiency specifies that teachers are to design learning experiences appropriate for students' cultural heritage, unique endowments, learning styles, interests, and needs. In assuring equity for all learners, teachers need to know how to plan and implement Cooperative Learning activities. The use of Cooperative Learning facilitates understanding and acceptance of differences among ethnic groups at different socio-economic levels. While we know from the learning-styles research that not all students learn best in cooperative groups, it would be hard to argue that not all learners need to be able to work cooperatively. Using cooperative groups at the university level allows learners to experience the effects of the different sociological elements. Cooperative Learning activities require active learner participation and can certainly help students engage in relative, meaningful activities. Cooperative Learning also allows many opportunities for visual, auditory, tactile, and kinesthetic needs to be met.

Another way to help students learn through their preferred learning style is to adapt the concept of learning centers to the university-level classroom. For some content concerning learning styles, Cooperative Learning, and lesson planning, we plan activities that are center-styled and students choose the activity they participate in first. Sample activities include directions for participating in a Cooperative Learning activity called *Three-Step Interview*, where students take turns interviewing each other on two questions: "What do you know about learning styles?" and "What do you *want* to know about learning styles?" Some groups of students then will take the PEPS and others learn about themselves in different ways (for example, completing checklists on global versus analytic characteristics, etc.). Others will read several articles and complete a Team Learning (Dunn & Dunn, 1992, 1993, 1999) for each article. Examples of articles often used include "Rita Dunn Answers Questions on Learning Styles" (Dunn, 1990), "Mildly Handicapped Students Can Succeed with Learning Styles" (Brunner & Majewski, 1990), and "Teaching Young Children To Read: Matching Methods to Learning Styles Perceptual and Processing Strengths" (Dunn, 1990). Still other students may sit with the instructor and listen to an explanation of learning styles. At some point, all students will examine samples of learning-styles materials including CAPs, PLSs, tactile materials, and so forth. Students in each group compare and contrast CAPs and PLSs and begin to define the attributes of each. Then they determine the type of student that would benefit most from each of the materials. Afterwards, all students meet with the instructor to discuss their knowledge base of learning styles and to ask questions and have information clarified for them. It is at this same time that the elementary and secondary objectives from the state criterion-referenced assessment instrument, the *Texas Assessment of Academic Skills* (TAAS) are examined.

All teachers in Texas, regardless of the grade level or the content they teach, are required annually to show how they support student achievement on the TAAS in their classroom. To show preservice teachers how to do this, we require them to write two objectives from their content area at a grade level of their choice. Then, as a group, they write a mini-CAP and a mini-PLS. They then compare the objectives and activities of the CAP and

PLS to the objectives of the TAAS. Subsequently, they are able to understand that by utilizing good teaching strategies, active experiences, and teaching to learning styles they cover the objectives in the TAAS. This is one of the most valuable experiences of the class because it gives preservice teachers a framework for covering the curriculum but not directly "teaching the test."

Learner-Centered Communication: While acting as an advocate for all students and the school, the teacher demonstrates effective professional and interpersonal communication skills. This proficiency describes the environment to be created by the teacher as one where taking risks, sharing new ideas, and innovative problem solving are supported and encouraged. Certainly, meeting students' learning-style needs is an integral part of this proficiency. Understanding whether or not they are persistent in approaching tasks and then responding to their need—or lack of need—for authority and structure all help create an environment for risk taking. To help teacher-preparation students understand the impact of these variables in their own classrooms, our university programs address them in a number of ways. Flexibility may be the most crucial skill needed by the university professor to enhance an appreciation of the importance of the elements of persistence, motivation, and structure. Understanding that some students need little structure whereas others need a great deal of structure, and then trying to be responsive to each student opens many possibilities in terms of the types of assignments professors require in their classes. In addition, if we hope that our students can develop self-directed learners when they become teachers, we need to help them become more self-directed learners themselves. One place we start is by helping students learn to add their own structure to assignments rather than imposing so much structure at our level.

Learner-Centered Professional Development: The teacher, as a reflective practitioner dedicated to all students' success, demonstrates a commitment to learn, to improve the profession, and to maintain professional ethics and personal integrity. It is important for students to realize that the teacher is also a learner—that we all learn new things every day. We can model for students how to learn from our experiences and help them to understand that one must renew oneself professionally to remain an effective teacher and to avoid burnout. One of the activities that faculty at Tarleton State University engage in is peer reading groups. We choose a professional book and all of us read and discuss that book. To encourage this same type of professional growth in preservice teachers, we ask that they form book share groups, choose a professional book from a list, and share that book in their group. Class time is available once a week for about half of the semester to give students time to discuss their books. They also take some time to personally reflect on the meaning the book has for them. To assist students in learning how to work in groups and in building skills to work collaboratively, students often are given items to discuss in groups, make a group decision, and then report back to the class. The process of collaboration also is discussed.

The semester begins and ends with a discussion of the Learner-Centered Proficiencies. At the beginning of the semester, students can see where they are going during the semester and why—they come to understand the vision Texas has for its classrooms. At the end of the semester, they are asked how they will plan instruction for the diverse learners they will have, and how they plan to create and maintain a learner-centered classroom. By the end of the course, students are able to see that teaching to learning styles is one critical piece to creating learner-centered classrooms. They see this because they have had direct experiences during the semester in a class that is learner-centered and have had their own learning-style preferences addressed. They have learned through direct experiences with learning styles that learner-centered classrooms make sense.

Other University Support

While individual learning styles and different approaches to teaching are an integral part of Professional Development II, other faculty members also incorporate learning styles into their teacher preparation courses. In the College of Arts and Sciences, and specifically in the Mathematics and Physics Department, an effort is made to support and reinforce the tenets of PD II. All students seeking secondary certification in mathematics, or those who are interdisciplinary studies majors with a middle school emphasis, are required to take MATH 3043, Survey of Mathematical Ideas. It is recommended that students take this course as close to the student teaching semester as possible. This course is designed to bring together and supplement the technical material of other mathematics courses to communicate mathematics effectively. To teach and thus communicate mathematics effectively is where learning styles comes in. Students are required to prepare instructional materials that address different perceptual strengths. They may work alone on either a CAP or a PLS or they may work in groups of three to put together a Multisensory Instructional Package (MIP) (Dunn & Dunn, 1992, 1993, 1999). Students are graded on accuracy of content, creativity, and implementation of learning styles.

Responses from students are very positive. First, they appreciate that something they were taught in their education courses is used elsewhere. Second, they like preparing materials that are relevant to the area of specialization they choose. In the education classes, there is a heterogeneous mixture of students and each group decides what content area will be used for material development. Frankly, mathematics is not the most popular content area. Using this project in a mathematics class forces students to think about the diversity of learners in the specific content area chosen for specialization. This project has "opened" students' eyes to multiple ways of thinking about and doing mathematics.

Tarleton State University's faculty engage in joint writing projects, co-operative strategy development with colleagues at other institutions of higher education who use learning styles as a basis for teaching future teachers, and in shared research projects. Our emphasis on learning-styles-based instruction has extended our own understanding of what constitutes effective teaching and appears to assist our students in applying the Texas Standards efficiently in the classrooms they enter during their preservice experiences.

Chapter 6

Hannibal "Lecture" Changes His Oral Menu

Kenneth J. Dunn

In the film *The Silence of the Lambs*, Anthony Hopkins delivered a remarkably focused and horrifying portrayal of Hannibal Lecter, the criminal genius who cannibalized his victims. Somewhat analogous is the way many higher education professors, including myself, have devoured or blocked student thinking ability by lecturing for hours on end, sometimes from old notes we had prepared.

Indeed, college students enjoy telling the decades-old story of the renowned professor of anthropology at a leading university who was so in demand around the world that he resorted to tape recording his lectures for his classes; a student assistant would dutifully play them at the right time and his students signed in for each session. One day, his travel schedule permitted him to visit his reduced-teaching-load class. There he found tape recorders absorbing his lecture in each of the 38 seats. Listening, taking notes, and then responding to test questions could hardly be described as active learning.

I'm certain that most of us in higher education have started moving toward aiding students in accepting the burden of learning and teaching at much higher levels of brain activity. There are many successful strategies that you may have tried, but I'd like to share five techniques that have worked very well for me in teaching advanced courses in administration and supervision. They involve students in the direct participation in, and practice of, what they need to learn, apply, and evaluate. Further, the brain receptors of tactual, kinesthetic, oral, and visual communication are engaged; not just the passive-auditory mode. Only 20 to 22 percent of adults learn best by listening and can remember only 75 percent of what is taught through the lecture method.

SIMULATIONS

Simulations may include case study materials, scenarios, role playing, resolution of problems, decision making, debate, negotiation to success, positive interpersonal relations as an end goal, and creativity.

Example: Planning an Integrated Curriculum

Begin with a description of the need to relate content, learning, and global needs in the new millennium. List some of the general change problems a grade, department, or school will face, and the specific goals and timelines. The entire class of adult students is divided into groups around meeting tables.

Round 1 Warm-up (10–15 minutes). During this period, the purposes of the Simulation will be discussed and questions will be answered by the instructor.

Round 2 (30–40 minutes). Roles will be assigned and realistic attitude scenarios will be distributed as well as place cards visible to all, with the names implying the personality and predictable behavior of each participant (e.g., Dan Innovator, Bur O'Kaat, Ace Yourkall, Merit Myway, and Noble Goodness to represent a collaborative leader, a bureaucrat, a great compromiser, an autocrat, a country club manager, and others as needed for a particular project situation). Each member of the Simulation receives the overall outline, but only his own "attitude scenario." The group members discuss the project from their own viewpoint as described in the scenario and attempt to list possible approaches to meeting the final objectives of the project. Consensus is not reached at this stage. Usually, all of the problems, blockages, and typical types of resistance will be expressed and should be noted.

Round 3 (30 minutes). A series of national conferences has been called by the U.S. Office of Education to discuss the various issues that confront your group. Those with similar views are to meet in subsections to develop strategies to bring back to each local meeting. Your group members (those with similar views) are to meet at the following locations:

- Innovators—Hawaii;
- Bureaucrats—Washington, DC;
- Mediators—St. Louis, Missouri;
- Autocrats—Las Vegas, Nevada;
- Country Club Managers—Miami Beach, Florida, and so forth for others.

As a group, develop a set of guidelines that realistically will meet the Simulation assignment. The final version should be based on total agreement, if possible, or consensus at the very least.

Round 4 (30 to 45 minutes). All members report back to their original groups and bring perspectives from their "national" conferences to aid in resolving a final set of guidelines and procedures to meet the goal of an integrated curriculum (or other set of objectives for the course being taught). The class then evaluates all potential solutions or approaches and decides which will have the best chances of succeeding and why.

This approach appeals to those learners who prefer to work in groups and who require verbal interaction in order to engage cognitive activity in the brain. Further, many will take notes, correct them, and engage visual and tactual strengths at a higher level than they do when merely listening to lectures and taking notes.

FILMS

1. Portions of Hollywood films offer stimulating examples of situations that can teach object lessons, initiate energetic discussions, begin small-group evaluations, and promote creative applications.

Examples

Amadeus. This outstanding award-winning movie can be used to contrast global, holistic genius versus plodding, mediocre analytic music composition. Mozart could create entire musical compositions in his head; the rest was just "scribbling," as if he were just taking dictation, as noted by Salieri. Indeed, most historical accounts of Mozart's work report that he recorded one copy of originals without changes or errors. Salieri, on the other hand, plunked out notes, one at a time, through slow, laborious effort with constant review of each new portion. Mozart demonstrates his genius by improvising brilliant variations on Salieri's charming but simple march of welcome.

Several other scenes at the court of the emperor realistically display manipulation and intrigue among the director of the opera, Salieri, and other advisors to the ruler. This dialogue and the attitudes of various leaders repeat throughout history in all types of organizations.

Dead Poets' Society. Robin Williams gives an excellent performance as a global, innovative instructor in a very conservative, analytic, lecture-oriented private school.

When Harry Met Sally. Billy Crystal and Meg Ryan portray opposite types of personalities and processing styles. Crystal is holistic (he orders a number 3 on the menu) while Sally is extremely analytic and takes several minutes ordering something prepared "exactly the way she wants it." Their attitudes and ways of behaving are maintained throughout until they realize that opposites can, and often do, result in great, loving partnerships.

Portions of films that students see or know make excellent motivating examples for lesson objectives.

2. Adult student-made films often release creativity and aid students in planning, organizing, and creating examples to demonstrate their knowledge and to use in their own schools and organizations.

Examples

One graduate student created a film designed to build pride and motivate his students to achieve at higher levels. Individual students, teachers, groups, and past great instructors were flattered. This "feel good" film was artistic, colorful, and used at the school and within the community for several years before updates were needed. A group of adult students elected to write and act out a typical set of morale problems in a school required to embrace inclusion as a total concept without appropriate involvement, planning, tryouts, evaluation, and acceptance by the staff. Spirited discussions and potential solutions followed.

Between 30 and 38 percent of the population respond best to visual stimuli. Moreover, 55 percent of adults are global and respond to pictures, films, color, diagrams, graphics, and print. Professional films bring art, creativity, and stimulation to mature learners that lecture could not match.

In addition, films created by students appeal to kinesthetic learners through positive, motivating challenges to their visual strengths, movement requirements, scenario development, and totally kinesthetic activities during filming. Editing can be tactual and cooperative as well, and teams involved in a film project must work together to assemble the best possible product.

BRAINWRITING

Most of us have used Brainstorming techniques for decades and they do aid in solving problems, planning, setting objectives, and so forth. They are useful, too, for instruction, training, and setting priorities. For variety, however, brainwriting is very efficient and productive for groups of four or five sitting in tight circles. Here are two versions that involve adults in associative and planning processes that stimulate and achieve results far beyond those that are obtained by question-and-answer sessions. Try it and compare the multiple interactions of all the students with the usual raising of hands by those few who answer our questions.

Card Passing. Post a typical problem or mini project to each group of four or five adult students seated in closely knit circles of chairs or desks. Give two participants who face each other two 5 × 8-inch blank cards. The two with cards initiate the process by writing the first solution, idea, suggestion, or criterion related to the proposed problem, for example, "How should we begin a program on inclusion?"; or, "How can we break down division boundaries?" The responses are limited to one or two sentences and passed clockwise to the right by the first initiator and counterclockwise by the second initiator. Within three to five minutes the cards are filled after three or four "rounds." The group then organizes the results into a logical sequence or set of procedures. This highly productive process is the first step in jointly attacking a problem or initiating a project for positive change.

Card Tossing. Each of the four or five participants, again sitting in a tight circle, is given five minutes to respond to the problem or project question on 5 × 8-inch blank cards, but they do not pass them. Instead they toss them into a pile in the center of the table around which they sit. Short questions or discussions between or among some of the group are permitted, but all are expected to contribute three or four cards to the collection point. The group then jointly sorts the responses, organizes them, and prioritizes the entire set.

Both of these brainwriting techniques respond to adults who are group oriented and who require active tactual and visual stimuli through reading other participants' thoughts and then creating their own suggestions.

Further, organization and decision making are achieved through oral interaction, debate, and negotiating to consensus. All these activities appeal to diverse learning-style strengths and supplant the usual lecture, note-taking approach which is responsive to the learning styles of perhaps that 20 to 25 percent of the students who learn by listening and note-taking.

ROLE PLAYING

Mock Interviews

Six to eight participants assume roles (with large place cards identifying them to all in the room) such as principal, board members, assistant superintendent, union leader, teacher, and so forth with a set of prepared questions and clues to follow-up responses. The "candidate" is expected to respond extemporaneously, and does not know which questions will be asked. Those not involved directly watch and take notes on style, voice, confidence, posture, appropriateness and focus of the response, the successful answers, those responses that could be improved, reactions, use of "uh," "o.k.," and other negative speech flaws, fillers, and so forth.

Usually, the interviewee is asked to evaluate herself or himself in several categories. Next the "role players" evaluate the interview, including their own parts. Finally, the class and then the professor make suggestions. Sometimes it is worthwhile to reassume roles for certain questions that were difficult for the interviewee. Candidates always report that repetitions of these sessions, even informally with friends, aid in building confidence and ease in responding to the real thing.

Mock Difficult Situations on the Job

Again participants assume roles (wearing place cards) to discuss a difficult problem, for example, parents demanding to have a child changed from one teacher to another; unfounded complaints about an assistant principal; a board member attempting to administer a building on his own initiative, and so forth.

Unlike Simulations, which combine case study scenarios, attitude, and belief cards, role playing can be initiated with spontaneity and enthusiasm based on events that are immediate and very timely.

Again, learning-style strengths, including team or group discussion preferences, kinesthetic acting, and oral interaction, planning, decision making, and consensus building improve adult instruction.

TEAM LEARNING (DUNN & DUNN, 1992, 1993, 1999)

Team Learning is an excellent strategy to involve all adult students in learning and applying new and difficult material. Prepared written material is given to each participant to read. It may include diagrams, photos, cartoons, graphs, and all that is necessary to meet the objectives of a difficult topic, for example, writing a successful proposal, learning a complex schedule, using multiple-budget formulas, negotiating with success, and so forth.

The hand-outs should not exceed one to two pages plus three types of questions:

1. *Factual*: answers may be found directly in the prepared material.
2. *Inferential*: answers vary and must be discussed and thought through.
3. *Creative*: applications are designed by the group and may include games, drawings, poetry, songs, and so forth.

The group responds to these activities together through consensus. As the teams work, the instructor may visit each circle three or four times, ask questions, challenge, intervene, require them to add questions, and to improve the material. Have each group report answers, compare responses, and applaud creative efforts. They will remember and you will know how all of them think and what they know by joining each group several times and by listening to their reports.

Learning-style preferences for group interaction and stimulation supplant lectures. Moreover, creative applications may involve tactual, kinesthetic, and visual strengths as adult students develop responses to the inventive assignments. Creative power is released and the boredom too often prevalent during lectures and "chalk talk" is replaced by high energy involvement and successful products.

Invent other approaches that do away with Hannibal *Lecture* approaches such as case studies, power-point presentations, interactive video and television games, simulated conference calls, and so forth. Oral presentations should be brief and used to introduce topics, begin planning, and respond to general questions. The variety will stimulate many students to participate and learn, including all of us ex-lecturers. Success will be achieved through the use of the various learning-style strengths in the adult classroom and the weakest learning approach—listening—will be eliminated except for those who learn best that way and for those who require oral reinforcement through a secondary or tertiary strength.

Hannibal Lecture *can* become Hannibal the Enabler of Learning by accommodating individual learning-style strengths.

Chapter 7

Distance Education: Reaching Beyond the Walls

Jody Taylor

"Terrific article! I would really like to use this in my Distance Education Class; but how can I?"

TEAM LEARNING: A SUCCESSFUL WAY TO *USE* ARTICLES IN DISTANCE EDUCATION

You have a great article you want to share with your students. The information in it complements your upcoming lecture and emphasizes the views of others in the field. Because there are several important technical points in the article, you have used it in two on-campus classes and the interactions and dialogues were both interesting and challenging to the students. The question you have is how to use this article in your distance course. Because you broadcast to multiple sites by one-way video and two-way audio, you know you can't hear or lead the discussions at each site. Can you use the article and facilitate a discussion in a broadcast class? The answer is *yes*! The dilemma you now face is how to keep students focused, engaged, and lead discussions at a distance. The answer to these dilemmas and engaging students is structuring for success. The bottom line is pre-planning.

To prevent distance education courses from becoming a static medium, the instructor must engage the students in active involvement with each other, with the material, and with the instructor. Vertecchi (1993) infers that the quality of distance education depends, to a large extent, on the frequency and quality of interaction. Marland and Store (1993) suggest a need to structure materials in a way that provides students with greater access to the content. James and Gardner (1995) recommend enhancing distance education with variety and interactive opportunities. Egan, Welch, Sebastian, and Lacey (1992) advocate involving students to maximize instructional effectiveness and prevent boredom and feelings of isolation. They encourage instructors to use participatory instructional techniques. To use articles and discussions as participatory techniques in distance education, instructors must pre-plan, structure, and coordinate.

One structured participatory approach that I have found to be highly successful in my distance education classes for the past five years is Team Learning. Team Learning is a peer-oriented, small-group technique introduced by Dunn and Dunn (1996). This small-group technique introduces new and/or difficult material to students in elementary through college classrooms. The structured approach of Team Learning transitions easily from the traditional face-to-face teaching to distance education classes. This approach allows for planned interaction and gives students access to content. It is the pre-planning that allows for orchestration at a distance.

The Basics of Team Learning

To implement the Team Learning strategy in distance education, select an article or reading of between three and six pages. I also write short, one- to three-page readings for Team Learning exercises. After selecting the article, structure the in-class discussion by writing three different types of questions directly related to the content for students to discuss.

The first type of question is factual and based directly on information found in the reading. Students easily find the answers in the text by re-reading, underlining, or discussing. These factual questions allow students to seek and find specific information. These questions also set a tone for success and focus the group on working together. For a distance education broadcast, limit the number of factual questions to no more than three. This limited number of questions emphasizes important factual information while limiting the amount of time required to answer the questions. It is essential to focus on the important factual information.

The second type of question incorporated into the Team Learning is higher-level thinking questions that require students to consider, discuss questions, and formulate answers. These questions promote reasoning and group decision making while structuring discussion among the participants. By focusing participant interactions through the structure of these questions, the distance instructor oversees discussions without being at each site. The organization of the Team Learning questions and structured discussion on the same questions at each site then allow for interaction and involvement among sites. In our inter-site discussions, we have found both similarities and differences in the answers leading to further involvement and discussion.

The third type of question for Team Learning requires learners to take the new information and use it in a creative way. Students must translate the essence of the article into a pictorial representation, a graphic, a rap, an outline, a chart, a poem, a three-dimensional puzzle, a tactual resource, a pantomime, a case study, a quiz, and so forth. Creative application requires students to select important information and re-frame it into their own words or pictures analyzing or synthesizing the material. Dunn and Dunn (1992) research findings emphasize that creative application of information increases retention. The Dunns point out that when students can transfer what they are learning into another medium, they retain it.

Team Learning at a Distance

The instructor sends the articles and questions to the participants at each site with directions for working with Team Learning. Directions indicate that the students should organize into small groups of four to five students and select a group leader and recorder. Allow two to three minutes for students to organize into groups and select roles. Because the instructor is separated by distance, group leaders play an important role in the delivery of Team Learning at receiving sites. The group leaders are responsible for keeping the groups on task, monitoring time, and assuring that their teams complete all parts of the Team Learning activity. The recorders write the groups' responses. Only the recorders are responsible for writing answers that are sent to the instructor. However, others may write if they believe they will remember the material by note-taking. Dunn and Dunn (1992) emphasize it is important to write short, succinct answers and to keep the discussion process moving. The leaders or the recorders answer for the groups if on-air answers are required or requested by the instructor. In our distance classes, we have had fun with selecting the leader and recorders' roles with humor and creativity.

After allowing time for groups to organize, the instructor introduces the Team Learning activity, gives the title of the article, outlines the procedures, and sets specific time limits for completing the exercise. In distance education, I suggest a maximum of 12 to 18 minutes for working on a Team Learning exercise. You may allot time for reading short articles as part of the exercise or you may assign longer articles to students to read prior to the broadcast in which they engage in the Team Learning. Reading prior to class saves on-air time. During the small-group work, keep graphics on the screen reminding learners of the group process, showing the questions, and displaying a clock that counts off the time. The visual graphics support the auditory instructions given by the instructor prior to the exercise and also provide reinforcement and a visual reminder of the procedures. Instructors should announce a three-minute warning prior to the end of the work time.

Team Learning requires small-group skills. My classes are comprised of college students and, thus, small-group procedures and courtesies normally expected from learners as team members are understood. I make only brief comments about group processing and encourage learners to meet and talk with each other during class breaks. To reinforce and encourage the importance of the small-group work, I send a copy of the Team Learning guidelines for team leaders at the receiving sites. Setting and maintaining time limits, asking for feedback, and interacting with the sites are critical factors in adapting this technique and bridging the distance. The teams' group leaders at each of the sites monitor the time along with the instructor. To assist in facilitation, you may want to ask designated sites to contact you when they have completed the exercise. This helps gauge the time students need to complete the work. Students may fax, call, or answer on the air for immediate feedback and interaction, or the recorders can fax answers at the end of the session. It is important for the instructor to see and/or hear answers generated by the students at the different sites. This provides ongoing interaction between the instructor and the students and allows for feedback. The instructor can summarize and highlight the Team Learning by sharing the comments and answers of individual teams at remote sites. Setting and maintaining time limits, asking for feedback, and interacting with the sites are critical factors in adapting this technique and bridging the distance.

Team Learning may be used with or without an on-site facilitator. If a facilitator is part of your distance education course, send him or her the articles, guidelines for conducting the Team Learning small-group activity, answers to the factual questions, and share potential points for discussion in Type Two questions. In my training seminars with facilitators prior to the course, I ask them to participate in a Team Learning exercise on the topic of Team Learning. This gives the facilitators an opportunity to practice the process and to clarify the procedures prior to facilitating in class.

After completing several Team Learning exercises, I give students opportunities to design their own Team Learning questions and answers for articles. This extension of Team Learning involves students in analyzing and synthesizing new or difficult material and encourages active participation with the content. I often share their Team Learning exercises by asking students to answer colleagues' questions from different sites.

In summary, Team Learning, a powerful traditional strategy, is adaptable for distance education. Using a brief article or reading, the distance instructor involves students with the material and with each other (see Figure 7.1). The structure of the three types of questions focuses and directs the learners' discussions. The interaction allows the adult learner to actively participate rather than just see and hear the material via the broadcast. They assume responsibility for their own learning and participation and, through interaction, feel connected to the content, discussion, and process.

Is it a waste of time for students to work with an article when you have so much to tell them? The answer is *no!* Through structured Team Learning

Figure 7.1
Sample Team Learning Exercise

Take the opportunity now to answer the following questions on this sample Team Learning exercise: *Team Learning Assignment on Team Learning in Distance Education.*

Please record the names of the Team Members.

Recorder, please write your team's responses to the questions on Team Learning in Distance Education. Write short, succinct answers. Keep the discussion moving. If you need more space, use the back of this sheet.

1. What is *Team Learning*?

2. What are the three types of questions required for a Team Learning?
   (a) _____
   (b) _____
   (c) _____

3. Based on your experience and this Team Learning article, compare and contrast the differences between using Team Learning in traditional and distance classes.

4. Review these five questions and decide which is Type One, Two, and Three. Based on the information in the article, draft at least one new question for each question type.

5. Create a draft of an outline, a graphic, an organizer, and/or a set of instructions explaining Team Learning to a student in your distance education course. (This may be given as an outside assignment to be presented in the next class.)

Self-Evaluation
I would rate my participation in this Team Learning exercise as (circle one):

Active/Involved   Interested/But Not Involved   My Mind Wasn't with It

Other: _____

exercises students investigate, discuss, draw conclusions, and create, using material important to the instruction of the course. In my experience, students enthusiastically take part in Team Learning exercises. Facilitators and students at multiple receiving sites consistently report 100 percent active participation when Team Learning is part of the class. Students report enjoying the interaction among and with colleagues, and state that it assists in clarifying points and issues made during lectures. It is pre-planning and the structure of Team Learning that allow for successful orchestration at a distance.

Chapter 8

Learning Styles in a Suburban College

Bernadyn Kim Suh

Learning Styles has been infused into many education courses at Dowling College, a private, suburban institution on Long Island, New York. Various aspects of the Dunn and Dunn Learning-Style Model have been taught to prospective teachers in a number of ways. This chapter: (a) describes the graduate and undergraduate courses that address learning-styles theory and practice; (b) cites examples of master's-level research on learning styles; and (c) briefly discusses the International Learning Styles Network and the Center for Learning and Teaching Strategies at Dowling College.

GRADUATE COURSES UTILIZING LEARNING STYLES

In a course entitled, Graduate Social Studies Methods, students are asked to develop social studies unit plans, using the CAP approach (Dunn & Dunn, 1992, 1993, 1999). Students select a social studies topic appropriate to the grade level in which they will do their student teaching. They develop a comprehensive unit of study by identifying the concepts, skills, and attitudes they want to present to their students. The social studies standards for New York State also are included in this unit of study. The format for developing a CAP is used and Activity Alternatives and Reporting Alternatives are presented to give students choices in activities to help them achieve the behavioral objectives. The initial and final assessments also are developed and presented to the students in the CAP. In those social studies CAPs, students develop small-group techniques, such as Circle of Knowledge, Team Learning, Group Analysis, Role Playing, and Case Studies. Students are asked to incorporate at least two small-group techniques into their social studies CAP.

In addition to the CAP, students are instructed to develop tactual and kinesthetic resources such as: Electroboards, Flip Chutes, Pic-A-Holes, and MIPs that relate to the social studies topic. By the end of the course, when all the assignments are completed, student teachers are ready to present the CAP and the tactual and kinesthetic teaching materials to their pupils. The beauty of the Dunn and Dunn Learning-Style Model is that it relates individuals' styles to classroom applications and the theoretical paradigm has direct implications for all types of children in a variety of curriculum areas.

Another graduate course in the Dowling College education sequence that uses aspects of the Dunn and Dunn Model is the Creative Arts class. Students are taught about the model and systematically instructed in developing an MIP. They are required to develop an original MIP in any subject area reflective of their interests and appropriate for the children they will be teaching.

MIPs can be developed for every level—nursery school children to graduate students. Students have developed MIPs to teach topics ranging from the alphabet to instructing adults on completing job application forms. Students have shown creativity in developing fantastic MIPs, using teacher-made materials that are low in cost but are highly motivational. One student developed an MIP on Japan and included an actual Japanese kimono in one of the boxes, reminding the children that boys tie their obis in the front whereas girls tie theirs in the back, and invited the children to put on the kimono. That student even included a pair of zoris in the package. Another student boiled a chicken and cleaned off the bones to include in her MIP dealing with fossils and the methods used by archaeologists. These MIPS are only limited by the extent of their originators' creativity.

Early Childhood Education is another graduate-level course at Dowling College in which learning styles has been infused into the curriculum. Students learn about various paradigms of learning styles, including the models of the Dunns, Renzulli, Gregorc, and McCarthy. Aspects of brain research also are presented so that the students understand the concepts of hemisphericity and how the brain develops. Videos on brain research are shown to the students so they understand how persons learn from birth to adulthood. Students are asked to develop a paper on the brain using well-documented research to substantiate their presentations. Piaget's theory of cognitive development also is examined in this course on early childhood education and students are asked to conduct at least four of Piaget's experiments with a preschooler and an older child, to compare the differences in their cognitive development. Selected experiments included some of Piaget's classical observations of conservation of matter, liquids, and space. Once the two children's cognitive development has been classified according to Piaget's stages of cognitive development, students are asked to incorporate aspects of the Dunns' Learning-Style Model into the development of a curriculum for young children. *Teaching Young Children through Their Indi-*

vidual Learning Styles: Practical Approaches for Grades K to 2 (Dunn, Dunn, & Perrin, 1994) is used as the textbook.

The graduate students are particularly interested in the psychological strand of the Dunns' model and focus on the global and analytic elements of young children. *The Learning Style Inventory: Primary Version* (*LSI:P*) (Perrin, 1982) provides a tool for assessing young children's learning styles and differentiating between global and analytical thinkers. Then specific teaching strategies are recommended for an early childhood curriculum.

Graduate students in that Early Childhood Program have participated in research conducted by the Center for the Study of Learning and Teaching Styles at St. John's University. Dr. Angela Klavas came to Dowling College and explained several assessments to the students, including the *LSI:P* and the books *Elephant Style* (Perrin & Santore, 1982) and *Mission From No-Style* (Braio, 1988). Students volunteered to administer these instruments to young children and send the results to Dr. Klavas for inclusion in a large study of primary children and their learning styles. The data were processed at the St. John's University Center.

As previously stated, the Dunns' model of learning styles has direct practical applications in the classroom, which are clearly spelled out in detail in numerous books and publications. I personally believe no other model explicitly tells the classroom teacher what to do with the children. There is a marriage between theory and practice, which is what beginning teachers need to learn in their education classes. The graduate students at Dowling College have a year to learn everything—pedagogy, child development, methodology, and completion of student teaching. Most of these students have an eclectic background of trying other careers and now have decided to pursue a career in teaching. I have taught at least three lawyers, numerous former Wall Street persons, nurses, musicians, and business majors who have decided that they wanted to become teachers. Upon exposure to the Dunn and Dunn model, they all are impressed with the clarity of the model and the pragmatic applications for children in the classroom. In their student teaching experience, they are able to implement many of the concepts presented in the education methods courses described above. All agree that they love the direct applicability of the model in the actual classroom with children.

Education graduate students have conducted research projects for their master's degree theses at Dowling College. The names of the students and their competed projects on learning styles are listed below:

- Allers, Michael (1994). An analysis of the relationship between learning-style preferences of college graduate students and performance on the verbal section of the Scholastic Assessment Test.
- Alo, Michele (1995). Gender preferences toward perceptual learning styles.

- Batista, Secilia (1995). Sound as an element of learning style: Does sound have an effect on student test performance?
- Beckerman, Susan (1992). The facilitation of memory through direct instruction of learning strategies for disabled students.
- Brush, Nancy (1994). Effects of learning modalities on achievement.
- Pino, Louise (1996). Effects of tactual instructional techniques on elementary reading.
- Saul, Toni (1994). Learning-style preferences of high and low achievers in fourth grade.

Most of these research studies were mentored by Dowling College full-time professors. Dr. Beverly Joyce, who teaches the two-semester courses in which students are engaged in developing and presenting their research studies, has directed several of the projects on learning styles.

UNDERGRADUATE COURSES USING LEARNING STYLES

Besides incorporating learning styles into the specific graduate courses, various aspects of it have been included in the undergraduate teacher-education program. In the first education course in which undergraduates enroll, Education and Society, different models of learning styles are introduced. Students compare and contrast models and learn the positive and negative features of each. Dowling College has a unique undergraduate teacher-education program in which the students are involved during three full semesters of student teaching. Students are placed into three different classroom settings, and are supervised four times each semester; they thus are observed 12 times prior to graduation. Also, they meet at the college or in clusters in the schools where seminar leaders cover topics appropriate to the student-teaching experience. Learning styles is infused into the seminar classes. Topics such as inclusion and meeting the needs of Special Education students through learning-style strategies are focused on in depth during the seminars.

I recently had a cluster of student teachers in a New York State Blue Ribbon School of Excellence, Thomas Lahey Elementary School, Long Island, New York. The principal, Dr. Janet Perrin, conducted research and co-authored a book on learning-style applications at the primary level (Dunn, Dunn, & Perrin, 1994). Teachers and student teachers at Lahey have been taught how to use learning styles with children. Another school on Long Island that incorporates learning styles is the Setauket Elementary School. The principal, Dr. Thomas C. DeBello, also conducted research on learning styles and co-authored a number of articles and books with Dr. Rita Dunn (Dunn & DeBello, 1999). Dr. DeBello teaches education courses for Dowling College, as do Drs. Christina DeGregoris, Mary Cecelia Giannitti, Peggy Murrain, Thomas Shea, and Elizabeth Burton—all of whom have been involved in learning-styles research (Burton, 1980; De-Bello, 1985; DeGregoris, 1986; Giannitti, 1988; Murrain, 1983; Shea, 1983).

I have taught in higher education at various New York colleges for over 30 years. I find the Dunn and Dunn Learning-Style Model has a direct positive impact on learners. By applying this model, children learn, want to learn, and *do* learn! Students in teacher-education programs want strategies that they can apply practically in classrooms. We have seen an international movement to incorporate learning styles in schools, and teachers need to know how to implement them effectively.

LEARNING STYLES NETWORK AND CENTER

Dowling College is also part of the International Learning Styles Network (Dunn, Given, Thomson, & Brunner, 1997), which currently includes 21 centers across the United States and in Bermuda, Brunei, Finland, New Zealand, and the Philippines. The Center for Learning and Teaching Strategies at Dowling College is under the co-directorship of Dr. Bernadyn Kim Suh and Dr. Thomas C. DeBello. We attend Network board meetings and are involved in making decisions, conducting Network business, and exchanging ideas for cooperative research projects. Administrators at Dowling College, particularly President Meskill, Provost Al Donor, and Dean Kathryn Padovano, fully support our Center, as do our local districts, with which we have been using learning-style strategies on an ongoing basis.

In conclusion, the Dunn and Dunn Learning-Style Model has been a worthy paradigm for the Dowling College Teacher Education Program, both at the graduate and undergraduate levels. Prospective teachers are taught about elements of the model, and the specific applications for teaching are implemented directly with supervision from college personnel. Both the neophyte teachers and their own students enjoy the model's practical applications. As a result, teachers learn, children learn, and our ultimate educational goal is realized.

Chapter 9

A Paradigm Shift: Learning-Styles Implementation and Preservice Teachers

Karen Burke

In the best of all possible worlds, there is peace and prosperity. The sun always seems to shine and, even when it does not, there is a refreshing pleasantness to the rain. The natural order of things is seldom disturbed, and when the occasional unexpected event arises, it is viewed as a welcomed surprise. The car always starts, the checkbook always balances, and students have learned all that they have been taught.

However, this is not the nature of the world in which we live. Much of what we enjoy requires frequent attention. The car does not start unless we keep it serviced. The checkbook does not balance unless we keep accurate records. And many students do not remember much of what they have been taught, in spite of some of our best intentions and efforts.

We live in a real, rather than an ideal, world with an educational system that requires flexibility and ongoing change to achieve maximal success. Much of that necessary change is becoming an ongoing process in college classrooms.

PARADIGM SHIFTS IN COLLEGE CLASSROOMS

I was an undergraduate student in a small liberal arts college almost 20 years ago. Today, my experiences as an assistant professor at that same college and, for six preceding years as an adjunct instructor, have given me an interesting perspective on the changes that are occurring in higher education. At the very center of this change are today's students. Although neither they nor their instructors necessarily can predict where the changes will take us, together they appear to be providing the required cooperative leadership for improving education.

AN ENHANCED PROFESSORIAL ROLE

In September 1998, I began teaching an undergraduate education course by announcing, " Twenty years ago today, I sat in this same classroom as a college freshman!" One of my students boldly responded, "Twenty years ago today, I was born!" Another student proudly announced, "Twenty years ago today, I gave birth to my first child!"

It didn't take long for me to realize that people entering college today are radically different—in experience, expectations, and needs—from their counterparts of just two decades back. Examine our schools, examine the private sector and, for that matter, examine our personal lives and examples will abound. To respond to these changes, colleges have begun to make fundamental alterations in instructional methods, course content, and college living.

Students and faculty during the 1970s sensed a kind of holding pattern; the old order was over, but the new had not yet been defined. The relatively quiet, but intense, revolution taking place on college campuses since then has radically changed students' thinking, learning, and ways of relating to their professors, each other, and to social and political institutions.

A much clearer picture of the new type of student has emerged. It has been shaped, in part, by a global and universal perspective of human potential and has been enhanced by administrators and faculty with the courage to create new models of teaching, learning, and living. As a result, a paradigm shift is taking place in college teaching. The old paradigm of college education viewed teaching as the transfer of faculty knowledge to passive students with little acknowledgement of who they were as individuals involved in the learning process. The new paradigm of college education views teaching as one way to help students construct their own knowledge actively through their personal strengths and talents.

Quality is better assured by motivating students to exert extraordinary effort to learn, grow, and develop. This is largely accomplished through an awareness of individuals' learning styles and, through them, knowing students personally and becoming committed to their maximum intellectual growth, talent development, and ever increasing ability to take command of their own destiny.

> If you give a person a fish, you feed him for a day.
> If you teach a person to fish, you feed him for a lifetime.

This philosophical statement has long been applied to many areas of social responsibility. The message I hear in the new paradigm of education reiterates the same sentiment.

> When we give students knowledge, we educate them for now.
> When we teach students how to learn, we educate them for a lifetime.

LEARNING STYLES IN AN UNDERGRADUATE COLLEGE CLASSROOM

The goal of higher education is to educate people for a lifetime. It is a fascinating experience to be part of the process of dropping the old teaching paradigm and adopting a new one based on theory and research that has clear applications to instruction. By applying the theory of learning styles and paying particular attention to my students' strengths, the paradigm began to shift for my students and me. This shift continues in the courses I teach for preservice teachers at St. Joseph's College in Brooklyn, New York.

Identifying Students' Learning Styles

I administered the *Productivity Environmental Preference Survey* (PEPS) (Dunn, Dunn, & Price, 1982) to each student in my courses. The PEPS identifies the learning-style preferences of post–high school adults. The instrument consists of 100 dichotomous questions that elicit self-diagnostic responses relating to 18 discrete learning-style elements on a 5-point Likert scale. The Ohio State University's National Center for Research in Vocational Education reported that PEPS had "established impressive reliability and face and construct validity" (Kirby, 1979, p. 72). PEPS evidenced predictive validity in the investigations of Dunn, Bruno, Sklar, and Beaudry (1990); Dunn, Deckinger, Withers, and Katzenstein (1990); Lenehan, Dunn, Ingham, Murray, and Signer (1994); and Nelson, Dunn, Griggs, Primavera, Fitzpatrick, Bacilious, and Miller (1993).

This instrument identifies each person's preferred learning style. Components of style include:

- environmental (sound, light, temperature, and design);
- emotional (motivation, responsibility—conformity, persistence, and structure);
- sociological (learning alone, in pairs, with peers and/or authority figures, and with either variety or in patterns);
- physiological (perceptual, intake, time, and mobility); and
- cognitive (global/analytic) characteristics.

During initial class sessions, the PEPS was administered to students to identify how each preferred to learn and concentrate during challenging educational tasks. I explained students' respective profiles and how to use their learning-style strengths for studying during my classes.

Different Applications in Different Courses

The information from the learning-style profiles was applied differently in my methods course as opposed to in my research course. The various implementation procedures and students' reactions are explained in the next two sections.

An Undergraduate Math Methods Course. To link content, theory, and practice, every education major is required to register for methods courses while engaged in fieldwork in the local schools. The *ivory-tower* approach to learning is not part of these methods courses. Rather, students are expected to apply in their college field experiences with the public school classes they teach, what they learned during their college classes. Unfortunately, in this math methods course, many students often describe negative memories of their own experiences in math classes.

All my life I have hated math with an intense energy. I hope that I never have a student leave a math class I teach with the same feelings I had. If I can make my classroom into a place conducive to learning, then I will have done at least one positive thing to help other math students. (Nicky)

If future teachers like Nicky were ever to become successful math instructors, their attitude toward mathematics required radical change. It seemed to me that the only way I could make that change occur would be to model learning-style teaching strategies. Successful classrooms are those in which a variety of strategies are used so that each person's learning-style strengths can be addressed. Therefore, I try to design every lesson, whether it is focused on introducing a new topic or concept, practicing a skill, or reviewing prior knowledge, so that it contains some aspect of problem solving, decision making, exploration, manipulation, or discovery. I try to enhance my students' natural cognitive skills by incorporating tasks and resources that accommodate their diverse learning styles.

Lectures and lessons that focus solely on the textbook were inappropriate for many students in this math class. Based on their PEPS profiles, I knew that many were low auditory; although they could listen for 40 to 50 minutes, they then only remembered little of what had been said or discussed. The majority were tactual or kinesthetic; they needed to touch, manipulate, and be actively involved with the resources through which they were learning. They needed to learn through tactual materials, models, calculators, computers, simulations, and kinesthetic floor games (Dunn & Dunn, 1992, 1993). Knowing this, I introduced a variety of exploratory activities that went beyond arithmetic computation and required that students use instructional resources that actually taught or reinforced what either our readings or discussions focused on. Those materials helped my students expand their understanding of, and interest in, the processes of mathematics.

Rather than use large-group lectures or discussions with low auditory, high tactual, or high kinesthetic students, I incorporated other strategies such as small-group techniques like Circle of Knowledge for reinforcing knowledge and Team Learning for introducing it (Dunn & Dunn, 1992, 1993). They were permitted to work on assignments together so that students who needed to work with peers or in teams could do so; those who preferred to work independently could. These, and other alternative approaches to instruction, were mixed and matched to exemplify the varied nature of the learners, the learning process, and mathematics itself.

College Math Students' Reactions. Individual differences in learning styles dictate various teaching styles and approaches. A few weeks into the semester, students were asked to reflect on some of their reactions to my teaching strategies, course content, and the use of learning styles. Here is what they wrote.

When I was younger, math was mostly drill, repetitive numbers, and boring facts. Being in this class has made me realize that I am a global and need hands-on materials. I want the children I teach to enjoy learning. I will be certain to provide them tactual materials and help them to apply math to the real world. I don't want my students to feel overwhelmed by math or to dread it for the rest of their lives. (Rosann)

This class has taught us how to reach out to global, as well as analytic students. We created exciting new materials such as Flip Chutes, Learning Circles, Electroboards, and Task Cards. We also learned how to design activities such as Circle of Knowledge and Team Learning for peer-oriented children. Since every child has a unique learning style, it is important to provide many opportunities and experiences to help them learn. (Michelle and Mary Lou)

RESPONDING TO NCTM GOALS

Positive attitudes and beliefs, along with general student willingness to do mathematics, are referred to by the National Council of Teachers of Mathematics (NCTM) as a *student's disposition toward mathematics*. The adoption and implementation of learning-styles-based instruction has provided these preservice teachers with opportunities to learn mathematical skills and processes through their own styles, to observe their classmates learning with instructional resources responsive to *their* styles, and to develop and use tactual and kinesthetic materials with students effectively.

As the move to identify standards for improvement of mathematics instruction in the elementary school enters the new millennium, the importance of understanding mathematics content and methodology cannot be overemphasized. Combined coverage of both content and methods is creating future teachers who see the relationship between what they teach and how they teach.

Applications to an Undergraduate Educational Research Course

The participants in Thesis Seminar, an educational research course, are full-time college students in their senior year. They are enrolled in this course as a requirement for graduation with a degree in education. The course is viewed by students as a rite of passage to commencement and usually is accompanied by a great deal of anxiety. For example, one student wrote:

When I walked into my educational research class at St. Joe's in the spring of 1997, I remembered feeling as if I were walking the plank. Was I beginning a jail sentence? The thought of writing a thesis was enough to bring a strong woman to her knees. I was an *A* student, but wondered how anyone could ever complete such an incredible task. I learned a lot about myself in the months that followed that day. I learned about my emotional strengths and needs as a student. I learned about my level of motivation, my ability to be persistent, and my need for structure. I learned that I probably could do anything I wanted to do if I used my knowledge of how I learn and my strengths. For those lessons alone, CS401 is now, and will probably always be, one of my most valued courses and treasured memories. (Amy)

My students were taught educational research according to the department's established course outline and we covered all the course competencies. However, the instruction and class atmosphere were established through the use of learning-styles theory. The important strategies that I used included:

- identifying my students' styles with the PEPS;
- explaining their learning-style profiles to them so that they understood how they each learned;
- using their learning-style profiles to develop—and give to them—homework prescriptions that explained how they could study and do homework based on their learning-style strengths; and
- paying particular attention to their emotional learning styles.

Procedures

Student motivation appeared to increase immediately after being administered the PEPS and receiving personal feedback about their styles as I interpreted their profiles. I met with students individually to discuss their learning styles. We discussed how they could best complete their assignments through their strengths. Regardless of each student's motivation score on the PEPS, I saw an increase in their motivational levels as their learning styles began to be acknowledged, were given importance, and were responded to.

The objectives of this course require each student to complete a research study and a written thesis in a 15-week semester. This course historically has the highest percentage of students receiving an incomplete grade at the end of the semester. For this reason, I paid special attention to the students who scored low on persistence on the PEPS. These students were usually global and worked on several assignments simultaneously. They were able to complete their research within the time scheduled if I allowed them to work on several tasks and to sequence the work in their way. The finished product—a completed thesis—was due on the same day for all students.

These procedures also provided other opportunities for students who scored low on Responsibility. Such students are often non-conforming and respond well to a collegial relationship (Dunn & Dunn, 1992, 1993, 1999; Dunn, Dunn, & Perrin, 1994). Knowing this, I was willing to allow them some choices in the process. I often spoke with the students about my experiences and interest in doctoral research. I clearly wanted my personal experiences to help undergraduate students understand why the assignment I was asking them to do was *important to me.*

Certain students frequently asked many additional questions about the requirements. As indicated on their PEPS profiles, these were the students who needed a great deal of structure on the PEPS and very specific directions. I gave them additional time prior to or after class. I also offered all my students the option of telephoning or e-mailing me at home or school when they needed to discuss concerns or ask questions. Some of my more reflective students found this very helpful. They confided that it gave them time to process the information that I had presented in class and they felt confident when they could telephone to discuss questions or clarify information.

WHY USE LEARNING STYLES IN HIGHER EDUCATION?

The following specific questions were the basis for my initial desire to incorporate the learning-styles theory in my educational research course: (a) Does applying learning-styles theory to college instructional methods classroom make a difference in terms of how well information is learned and long-term assignments are completed?; (b) Does applying this same theory of learning styles make a difference with respect to college students' attitudes toward instruction and the course material?

To determine if there was a positive effect on academic achievement, data were collected regarding course completion and final course grades. To determine if there was a positive effect on attitudes toward instruction, data were collected from the final course evaluations.

My experience was consistent with the research of Buell and Buell (1987) and Mickler and Zippert (1987) at the post-secondary level regarding the application of the learning-styles theory. Specifically, the implementation of the learning-styles theory in my Thesis Seminar class had a significantly positive effect on the achievement, course completion, and attitudes of the students enrolled in that undergraduate educational research course.

Achievement

The typical sample population in Thesis Seminar is comprised, on average, of only eight students per semester. During each of the semesters in which I taught this class prior to using a learning-styles approach, achievement reflected the proverbial bell curve. For example, two or three students' final grades fell within the range of B, one or two received an A or A−, and a similar number reflected the lower end of the spectrum—C or C+. During the three semesters during which I used a learning-styles approach, no students received less than B+. Whereas other demographics may have contributed to the end effect, the groups were matched for grade-point average, gender, and reading ability and the same instructor taught the same content. The only thing that differed was the instructional delivery system.

Course Completion

When I first started teaching this course prior to the introduction of learning styles, at least half the students typically received grades of Incomplete at the end of the semester. After identifying the students' learning styles and sharing that information with them individually, I became aware of each of their idiosyncratic behaviors and, in turn, made them aware of their own strengths and behavioral patterns when studying or completing course assignments. Thus, students with low persistence scores on the PEPS frequently were reminded of the need to remain in focus and complete their assignment. Similarly, students who tended to be peer oriented were encouraged to check each other's end product; and those whose PEPS reflected an Authority Present orientation were provided lots of feedback from me on an ongoing basis. Gradually, students were heard reminding each other to remain in focus, stay on task, and work toward completion. Buddy helped buddy and individuals helped peers to "get the work done," "finish what you are doing," and "talk later; work now!" As a result, those friendly reminders served to help students complete their assignments and stay on task. What were the results? During the past three semesters, not a single student received an Incomplete and, simultaneously, all students' submitted papers reflected a level of sophistication unusual for undergraduates.

Evaluations of My College Classes

The *Students' Reaction to Effectiveness of Instruction, Form 4* (SREI-4) was administered each semester for evaluation purposes. A five-point Likert scale determined overall and specific reactions to the instructor, the class, and the course content. Although attitudes toward Thesis Seminar consistently appeared to be positive, past ratings tended to reflect the middle and upper part of the SREI scale. During the three semesters in which I initiated the learning-styles approach, every student reflected strong agreement with the most positive ratings on the continuum. It is virtually impossible to obtain significance with an n of 8; even without the application of statistical analyses, students' attitudes reflected the maximally possible positive end of the continuum.

Current concerns for quality in higher education often stress the importance of actively involving students in their own learning to obtain educational excellence. The identification of my students' learning styles, interpretation of their data into practical terms for studying and doing assignments, and suggestions for capitalizing on their strengths facilitated academic improvement with a minimum of effort on my part and increased involvement on theirs.

Synthesis

Through the use of learning-style practices, I got to know my students better. The process of discussing their learning styles, observing them with the knowledge that I had gained from their profiles, and then intervening seemed to create personal and informal interactions between the students and me. Apparently, addressing my students through their learning styles increased their overall satisfaction with the course and the instructor.

For me, formal lectures are a thing of the past. It is apparent that dialogues and discussions that actively involve teachers' and students' thinking are the hallmarks of stimulating and popular classes in colleges. Team Teaching and Team Learning reflect the growing awareness of world interdependence. In form, as well as in content, college professors are saying: "We all need to recognize individual strengths and depend on—rather than compete with—each other." Successful teaching currently is being done by instructors who are not afraid to go beyond disciplinary walls and who learn with, and about, their students as they model desired behaviors for their students to emulate.

Final Note

On July 15, 1982, Don Bennett, a Seattle businessman, was the first amputee ever to climb Mount Rainier. He climbed 14,410 feet on one leg and two crutches. When asked to state the most important lesson he learned from doing that, without hesitation he said, "You can't do it alone."

During one very difficult trek across an ice field in Bennett's hop to the summit of Mount Rainier, his daughter stayed by his side for four hours and, with each new hop, told him, "You can do it, Dad. You're the best in the world! You can do it, Dad." There was no way Bennett would stop climbing with his daughter yelling words of love and encouragement in his ear. Her encouragement strengthened his commitment to make it to the top and kept him moving forward.

Success in college occurs similarly. With instructors knowing their students' strengths, and encouraging their hops and strides, students amaze themselves and their instructors with what they achieve. Benjamin Franklin said it best. "Tell me and I forget; teach me and I remember; involve me and I learn." Higher education is really about this simple statement. I cannot help but wonder what a creative thinker like Franklin would make of this new paradigm of a learning-styles-based college classroom. My hunch is that he would be energizing others to assume the necessary leadership for bolting away from conventional teaching and electrifying young minds to take charge of their own learning with lightning precision!

Chapter 10

Learning Styles and College Teaching: My Experiences with Education Majors

Ann C. Braio

My husband is a philosophy professor. Need I say more? Our conversations, over dinner, travel along several well-worn routes. One is how to create a better world. Another is the meaning of our human existence. Still another is how to better reach the young people we teach.

The last question is always the one most talked about. We always have stressed that it is important not to lecture to students; the conventions of mere lecturing are alien to the conditions of human learning. Instead, we must find ways to foster our students' understanding of the meaning of what we are inviting them to learn. I often have thought to myself, *Easy to say; hard to deliver!* And then I realized that through research conducted with the Dunn and Dunn Learning-Style Model (1992), I not only could help school-aged children understand better, but also could help my own education major students at Manhattan College.

Although I had a full-time position in Special Education in a major public school system, I began as a part-time college instructor approximately 10 years ago. This decision easily was made as I always had enjoyed working with future teachers by advising and guiding them. These are *my* people! This work was also an outlet for all my creative impulses which my full-time work could not satisfy. Thus, I worked diligently in my classes to build a vital educational milieu. After several years of college teaching, I recognized that I had adopted the teaching style required by the lecture format of many of my former teachers. In addition, I had completely neglected the learning styles of my students with either a tactual or kinesthetic style. That realization made me willing to change how I taught.

Therefore, I immediately started revising the teacher-education courses I taught to make them more creative. First, I decided to administer the *Pro-*

ductivity Environmental Preference Survey (PEPS) (Dunn, Dunn, & Price, 1985) to all students in each of my college classes. By using this instrument, I was able to record and chart their learning-style preferences. After analyzing their individual and group profiles, I began to place them into specific sections of the college classroom without having explained the rationale to them. Thus, some were:

- seated near windows; others were seated far away from bright light;
- placed near where quiet music was being played on a recorder, whereas others were assigned to the opposite side of the room;
- advised to sit with one or two classmates whereas others were placed at nearby desks; the remaining individuals were assigned to a quiet corner to work independently; and
- offered diced vegetables or healthful snacks; others were offered none.

At first, these changes were not accepted. I am sure that there were many questions running through the students' minds. After all, doesn't a college professor only lecture and give out assignments? Why were they being treated differentially? Why weren't they permitted to sit with friends or by the closest exit? Why was this instructor creating such a divisive environment?

I then incorporated auditory, visual, tactual, and kinesthetic instructional resources for teaching the course content. A discussion style replaced the previous lecture format. I supplemented the discussions with group and individual activities, overheads, videos, compact discs, audio- and videocassettes, and students' short presentations and projects. This was quite a change! I also included anecdotes or short stories to introduce each new lesson globally for the global learners. Analytic learners were accommodated by a step-by-step handout. I continued teaching without telling my students the reason why I had so carefully planned my lessons and restructured the design of the room. They also were not told the reason for the different student groupings or why some were required to work alone. I neither revealed who (a) needed more or less structure; (b) was highly or less motivated; nor (c) were more or less persistent and responsible. I made certain to accommodate each student's preferences as had been revealed through the PEPS scores. Then, I waited patiently, or perhaps looking back, *not* so patiently, for the students to discover why I had made those unconventional changes.

Once the students recognized that these decisions had not been arbitrary and were facilitating their learning, they understood the value of implementing learning styles in the classroom. *An insight had occurred!* They understood the importance of knowing their own learning-style preferences and how accommodating them improved their ability to learn. Now in our classroom, we have multiple discussions relating to learning style—what it is, how it helps us, and how we can use it with any age of students we teach. All this was accomplished by simply administering the PEPS.

The PEPS had helped me focus on the specific needs of each of my students. It forced me to prepare for class differently, more thoroughly, and with a *styles* mentality. The upshot was that I began to create a new rapport with my students as we suddenly were speaking a common language. I believed in this method of teaching, and I knew it was an effective model. The challenge was to pass this message on to my students so that they could apply what they had learned about themselves in their future classrooms with their own students.

To continue this process, I had my students actually create and construct a classroom environment that accommodated their own learning styles. Some students built an imaginary classroom using boxes and paper cut-out furniture. Others drew pictures and pasted appropriate paper furniture onto cardboard. One group actually rearranged the furniture configuration in the room.

Again, some students worked on their projects alone while others labored in pairs or in a group. Each group chose one of its members to explain to the entire class why they had created their redesigned environment. Although each of the learning-style elements were used, all projects looked different from each another. Those students learned that there was no uniform way to design a classroom. What was necessary was to have a working knowledge of how different furniture and environmental configurations impacted on students' ability to concentrate and remember new and complex information.

Auditory-, visual-, tactual-, and kinesthetic-preferenced students all were more at ease in this environment than they previously had been. Each developed insight into what a transformed classroom environment could mean to someone trying to concentrate on difficult material. They realized that teachers could meet the varied preferences of their many students. It made them ask themselves searching questions such as:

- Why has it been the standard practice to configure desks and tables arbitrarily in classrooms?
- Why have rooms been organized in conventional ways even though their educational value has been questionable?
- Why have students' learning preferences not dictated classroom organization all along?

Focusing on these questions made them increasingly aware of the factors to consider when designing an instructional environment.

Another assignment that I required was for small groups of students to develop a learning-styles lesson, pretending that the rest of the students in the class were in a specific grade. Each group presented its lesson demonstrating to the entire class how to teach diverse topics in history, science, or literature while accommodating a variety of learning-style preferences. They sat some students near bright light and a window for coolness. Others were advised to work in teams, alone, or in pairs, to work on alternative activities that had been placed at designated stations.

For the global students, an overview of the presentation was given *first*. A floor game was provided for kinesthetic learners. Tactual resources were made for the hands-on learners. Each lesson was exciting to watch. Each was critiqued and suggestions were made for improvement. The understanding that learning occurs in different ways was illustrated concretely in these activities and made obvious to all.

The third teaching technique I introduced was a homework project. Students created a Programmed Learning Sequence (PLS) or a Contract Activity Package (CAP) (Dunn, 1992, 1993, 1999). Students understood that a PLS and a CAP had to accommodate a variety of different learning styles. On the final day, projects were presented to the class. Some students needed structure for this assignment, while others needed freedom and no limits. To motivate them, keep them responsible, and maintain their persistence levels, I elicited comments on the status of their work. Sometimes they shared their progress with each other and not with me. Students who did not prefer working with an authority figure functioned well with these options. On the other hand, those who needed an authority often sought my feedback. Weekly discussions of projects did not have to be lengthy.

All the PLSs and CAPs my students have created over the years make me proud and satisfied to be a professor of the future teachers of our nation! Because their projects were so unique, they were displayed in Manhattan College's Education Department Office. I always found this to be an effective way to end the semester. Students appreciated that their work was displayed, and welcomed the many comments I provided on the work they submitted.

Each semester terminates with student evaluations of the instructor and the course. I look forward to distributing the questionnaire each year, because the evaluations reflect the understanding that learning style reveals a completely new way of examining how my teacher education students learn and how they, in turn, can teach more effectively. Comments from selected evaluations included:

- Dr. Braio presented interesting ideas that I hadn't learned in any other education course;

- I feel confident that knowing about learning styles will make me a better teacher;

- Dr. Braio's course was the best I have taken. I learned so much in just one semester!;

- I really enjoyed our discussions. It was beneficial to learn about learning styles;
- This course made me enthusiastic about coming to school. For once, I really enjoyed it! What more can I say?

In conclusion, my love of teaching has been regenerated as a result of incorporating a learning-styles approach. Learning style has made me a more sensitive teacher and more discerning of the needs of my students. It has deepened my understanding of the meaning, value, and possibilities of education. May you have similar experiences and understandings!

Chapter 11

Tactual Learning at the Doctoral Level: A Risk Worth Taking

Barbara K. Given and Edward P. Tyler
with Nora Hall, William Johnson, and Margaret Wood

"I don't think undergraduate students will use tactual materials even if they have access to them," Bill offered in a class of doctoral students planning to teach at the community college level. "They might," countered Margaret, a computer-skills instructor. "It depends on what you're teaching."

"I teach Spanish," Emma spoke up, "and my students love the materials I make."

"Perhaps teaching a foreign language lends itself to manipulatives, since there is a discreet body of information to be learned," Freed offered. "Students would probably enjoy supplementing what they read and hear by interacting with the language."

Freed's comments revealed an intuitive grasp of matching content with student learning needs—a concept called learning-styles instruction. An individual's *learning style* pertains to the rather consistent "combination of many biologically- and experientially-imposed characteristics that contribute to learning, each in its own way and all together as a unit" (Dunn & Dunn, 1993, p. 2). Learning-styles instruction, therefore, accommodates an individual's visual, auditory, tactual, or kinesthetic modality preferences. As Freed implied, students who are tactual probably need a hands-on approach to foreign language vocabulary.

THE PROJECT

For the first time in her teaching career, the professor had the privilege of teaching a one-credit course on brain behavior for undergraduates and a doctoral class, "Community College Teaching through Learning Styles," during the same semester. Since both were highly experiential courses, she decided to design an embedded case study (Yin, 1984) to answer two questions: (a) will doctoral students make tactual resources for students in their community college classes? and (b) will undergraduates use and benefit from tactual resources to learn salient examination information? She kept the first question private, but entered the following discussion regarding the second.

"Later this semester," the professor announced during the first doctoral class session, "I will teach a one-credit, experiential course for undergraduates about the brain. There may be students in that class who are at-risk for college attrition, but most are expected to be strong academically. Would you, individually or as a class, be interested in conducting a mini-study to see for yourselves how undergraduates respond to hands-on materials like Electroboards and Flip Chutes when studying new and difficult information?"

"Do you mean actually make things for the undergraduates to use for learning about the brain?" Liz asked hesitantly.

Clearly, asking doctoral students to use rulers, colored markers, scissors, and glue as a way to investigate the teaching of undergraduates who are at-risk for dropping out of college seemed a bit bizarre in terms of traditional lecture and discussion classes. Quite frankly, it was doubtful that anyone would accept the challenge. Puzzled expressions seemed to say, "This is going to be a different type of doctoral class, but it sounds rather interesting." Enthusiasm began to build when Ed's soft but forceful voice caused every eye to turn in his direction.

"It seems to me that if education is to experience any lasting reform, two things are critical. First, teachers must fundamentally change their beliefs about how students learn. Second, educators across the board must seriously rethink how teachers teach." With his pronouncement, 10 of 11 students expressed enthusiasm for designing and executing a case study as a semester's class project. Basically, they wanted to learn how to implement learning-styles instruction in their classes. The eleventh person ultimately withdrew from the class.

In the set-aside time during the remaining classes, students explored specific research questions to ask, how to design the case study, and how to make tactual materials for undergraduate use. In the process of working out details, students were given a real-world experience in the frustrations of research design, scheduling, data collection, and data analysis while immersed in their own course content pertaining to learning-styles instruction.

This exploratory effort into learning-styles instruction at the doctoral level generated high student interaction, problem solving, and camaraderie while, simultaneously, providing an authentic laboratory for insights into the use of tactual materials by undergraduates. This cross-level, graduate/undergraduate opportunity was a mutually beneficial project due, at least in part, to the context or setting in which it occurred.

Setting

George Mason University's (GMU) student body of 24,000 is a rich mix of ethnic groups from 49 states and 108 countries learning together in a suburban area of Washington, DC. Because of the diversity of its student population, GMU provides alternative undergraduate and graduate programs in addition to strong traditional programs. For example, in 1996, 73 percent of the freshmen class enrolled in traditional programs whereas 27 percent selected one of three alternative programs; nine percent of them selected New Century College (NCC), the home of the one-credit brain course integral to this project.

Five qualities distinguish NCC from other program approaches at GMU. First, students progress through their freshman year in cohorts and complete much of their curriculum in study groups throughout their four-year program. Second, course content is integrated and taught by faculty teams from various content areas to avoid splintered course work. Third, courses are noted for their intense, short-term duration. Fourth, blocks of time are designed for service learning and one-credit experiential classes. Fifth, all NCC freshmen learn about their learning styles and are encouraged to capitalize on their learning-style preferences to attain academic success. The philosophy and design of NCC promote student understanding of self as learners, thinkers, and community advocates. Thus, learning-styles instruction is a core component of the teaching strategy at NCC.

The Doctor of Arts in Community College Education (DACCE) program is equally innovative, because it is one of only a few programs in the country designed for persons preparing to teach at the community college level. It is a discipline-focused collaborative effort with a variety of graduate programs. The 215 currently enrolled students study in 22 different academic disciplines.

Project Design

An embedded design was chosen, because use of tactual materials had no clear, single set of outcomes for either of the two groups: doctoral students (Case Study One) or undergraduates (Case Study Two). Further, boundaries between what we wished to study and the context were not clearly evident, because there was a strong reliance on students' reporting about behaviors rather than their actual observation of behaviors outside the class context. Additionally, student behaviors could not be manipulated for purposes of the project. Direct observation and review of class documents served as primary data sources. Project artifacts—tactual materials, response questionnaires, and reflective essays—were constructed as part of the project (Yin, 1984, pp. 23–25).

The major proposition for Case Study One was: If doctoral students construct tactual resources and observe undergraduates using them, they will be more likely to use manipulative materials in subsequent teaching at the community college level. For Case Study Two the proposition was: If provided tactual resources for learning information specific to a course examination, students will willingly use the resources for study purposes.

Instruments

Students in both case studies completed the PEPS (Dunn, Dunn, & Price, 1982)—a 100-item, self-diagnostic instrument designed to measure the learning-style preferences of adults. Upon receiving the results, undergraduates were asked to modify their study routines based on printed recommendations. Doctoral students used their feedback to develop a greater understanding of self and of learning-styles instruction. The PEPS 5-point Likert scale yields reliable and valid results as reported by Kirby (1979) and others (Buell & Buell, 1987; Clark-Thayer, 1987; Curry, 1987; Freeley, 1984; Lenehan, Dunn, Ingham, Murray, & Signer, 1994; Nelson, Dunn, Griggs, Primavera, Fitzpatrick, Bacilious, & Miller, 1993; Raupers, in press; Taylor, Dunn, Dunn, Klavas, & Montgomery, 1999/2000). Even though the PEPS provides learning preferences in 20 areas, for purposes of this study, I focused only on students' modality (visual, auditory, tactual, and kinesthetic) preferences.

Population

Doctoral Students. The five women and five men enrolled in the learning-styles course shared a common goal of developing skills and strategies for teaching students at high risk for college failure. They ranged in age from 32 to 54 years and their occupations included: vice president for an insurance training firm, systems analyst, intelligence analyst, data administrator, community college instructor, community college administrator, software systems engineer, family therapist, public school curriculum specialist, and accountant. The ethnic mix reflected the university as a whole with African American (n = 2), Asian-African American (n = 1), Asian American (n = 1), Latino American (Cuban) (n = 1), and European American (n = 5) representation. Their strong modality preferences were auditory (n = 2 prefer), visual (n = 2 reject), tactual (n = 5 prefer; one of these also rejected visual), and kinesthetic (n = 2 prefer). Their strong preference for tactual learning was in excess to that anticipated for a group of doctoral students with higher education teaching as a career goal.

NCC Students. The 16 undergraduate students (n = 12 women and n =

4 men) also represented ethnic diversity with African American (n = 1), Asian (n = 1), Greek (n = 1), Hispanic (n = 1), and European American (n = 12) representation. Their ages ranged from 18 to 45. Six were freshmen, four sophomores, three juniors, and three seniors. Three students had documented learning disabilities. Their intended majors ran the gambit from "I don't know" to pre-med, and their strong modality preferences included: auditory (n = 5 preferred); visual (n = 3 preferred, n = 2 rejected); tactual (n = 4 preferred, n = 1 rejected); and kinesthetic (n = 1 preferred and n = 1 rejected).

Procedures for Case Study One

Doctoral students generated several types of data, including: (a) individually constructed tactual resources; (b) approaches to group problem solving for data collection and analysis; (c) written observations of undergraduates as they used the tactual resources; (d) their own behaviors during those observations; and (e) their reflective essays regarding their use of tactual materials as community college professors and their involvement in this highly experiential learning course.

Doctoral students were given 16 question-and-answer pairs, directions for constructing Flip Chutes, Electroboards, and Task Cards, and freedom to design their own self-correcting tactual resources. Their products varied in size, color, design complexity, and aesthetic appeal. Prior to undergraduate use, each resource was critically reviewed by the professor and two members of the class. Suggestions for improvement were offered and the resources were refined, replaced, or modified as appropriate.

To ensure ownership of the tactual resource project, students debated how to phrase their specific research questions, how to develop survey questions to evoke meaningful feedback from undergraduates, and how to analyze the data. Various class members volunteered to: (a) tabulate undergraduate feedback; (b) enter all narrative responses on a spread sheet; (c) enter undergraduate PEPS scores and student examination scores in SPSS format; (d) construct graphs to identify meaningful relationships; and (e) analyze correlations between modality preferences and examination scores. Ed wrote a draft report, and the class reviewed it for content accuracy.

At the conclusion of the course, students submitted portfolios of their work with reflections on specific inquiries: Which work represents your most professional or personal growth? Describe your growth. Which is your best work and what *made* it best? Which was the most challenging and why? Which would you like to delete and why?

As the senior researcher, the professor analyzed their entries and wrote a draft of the embedded case study. During one of the last classes of the semester, she distributed the draft and for the first time, doctoral students realized they were subjects in an embedded case study design. The professor was apprehensive, because negative reactions to the course or the project could have resulted in anger and a sense of betrayal. Upon reading the draft, however, doctoral students demonstrated surprise, humor, and excitement at being both researchers and subjects. The entire class edited the draft. For several weeks after the semester's end, two students worked with the professor to further refine the manuscript and locate an appropriate journal for the manuscript's publication. It is now under review.

RESULTS OF THE UNDERGRADUATE CASE STUDY

In brief, undergraduate data revealed that students willingly used tactual resources when they were available, but only 40 percent said they would construct them—and then only if all the required materials were available and the resources were easy to make in a short amount of time. An *unwillingness* of undergraduates to construct self-correcting manipulatives was also illustrated in a study by Dunn, Deckinger, Withers, and Katzenstein (1990) who found that, of 47 students, only ten (21%) agreed to implement the researchers' homework suggestions. Those ten achieved significantly higher scores than did either of two control groups that did not modify their homework approaches.

Undergraduates in our study expressed enjoyment when working with resources that had bright colors, those that needed little time or effort to figure out, ones that were portable, and those that were neither simple nor complex. Sixty percent of the resources were rated as more helpful than other techniques previously used.

The final quiz revealed a high 81 percent average correct score for questions studied with the tactual resources. Three circumstances prevented the average from reaching a higher level: (a) limited time with the materials, (b) the need to explore several different resources to overcome the novelty effect of learning with tactual resources in college, and (c) the scientific difficulty of the information to be learned. Overwhelmingly, students expressed the need for more in-class time to work with the resources and a desire to do so.

A tactual student with a learning disability made the second highest score (98% accuracy score) in the class on questions presented with tactual resources and those provided for home study. She wrote:

I really enjoyed the hands-on tactual materials. These materials really gave me the opportunity to throw myself right into learning the functions and terms needed. I also liked the idea that they were colorful and game-like experiences. This made the materials easier for me to remember.

No comparison could be made between student results on 19 e-mail questions and the tactual questions, because several students failed to read their e-mail in time to study for the test. Nonetheless, the research question, *will undergraduates use and benefit from tactual resources to learn salient examination information?*, can definitely be answered in the affirmative. Not only did they use the resources, they expressed interest in having much more time to practice with them.

RESULTS OF THE DOCTORAL CASE STUDY

The major purpose of this study was to explore the incorporation of authentic learning-styles instruction in a doctoral class of mature adults preparing to teach students at risk for community college failure. First, students explored their own learning styles and experimented with them throughout the semester. One woman wrote:

I did not consider myself a tactile learner, and could not see students using the tactual resources as well. However, . . . I created several resources for myself as study tools during previous classes, but didn't identify them as tactual resources. The discussions that followed via e-mail and in class helped me realize the significance and value of tactual resources in a teaching environment. I don't think I would have had the same response had we not gone through the steps to develop, discuss, and see tactual resources in use in another class.

One man, who scored as a strong tactual learner, created attractive and clever resources that were engaging and easy to use. He wrote:

I believe that learning is enjoyable and perhaps an intoxicating experience when it provides an opportunity for one to indulge in his or her dreams or passions. The opportunity to design and build tactual resources was one such experience because it permitted me to indulge in my artistic desires. For the past four years, as a result of professional and doctoral program demands on my time, I have had to restrict my indulgence in the arts. Thus, I welcomed the tactual resource activity with glee.

According to the PEPS, not one of the ten students demonstrated a strong visual preference, but one woman, who scored at the moderate level for "does not prefer" tactual learning, wrote:

The new design of learning/teaching devices, which were introduced in EDCC 802, has opened new avenues of approach to certain areas of learning in my Spanish language classes. The tactual resources required an inordinate amount of design and construction time, but the final effort was rewarding because I used several of them in successfully teaching [an] aspect of grammar which is often repetitious and tiring. The students, who range in age from 20 to 70, were amused at first. But each one commented favorably about the interesting aspects of the tactual devices. "It puts a new slant on the verb 'to be,' " they said, jokingly.

By contrast, a student with a strong preference for auditory learning and a strong preference against visual learning offered the following response when asked if she would make tactual materials for her students:

No, I would not create these resources; however, I will take a more hands-on approach to teaching in my subject area. I would not use these tools because of the extra time it takes to create them. However, it is definitely a good suggestion to offer to students.

Throughout the semester, interest in the undergraduate case study remained highly enthusiastic in spite of the lack of clear structure that accompanies exploratory research design. As procedural concerns surfaced, first one and then another volunteered out-of-class time to organize responses, run statistical analyses, coordinate their analyses of student responses, and write drafts. While the extent and type of participation varied considerably, each student tapped into his or her areas of expertise, creativity, and collaborative spirit to conduct a creditable class-directed mini-study. The answer to the research question, *will doctoral students make tactual resources for students in their community college classes?* seems to depend upon the learning style preference of the doctoral student or potential community college professor. However, even those with a strong dislike for tactual learning plan to offer hands-on learning options for students in their courses.

CLOSING COMMENTS

During the semester, doctoral students were encouraged to use the course as a catalyst for developing specific techniques they could use in their teaching. They willingly constructed materials for a course project, and many constructed additional materials for classes they teach or plan to teach. These efforts—in spite of heavy course load demands, full-time employment, family responsibilities, and no extra credit in terms of course grades—clearly convinced me that construction and implementation of authentic tactual resources offer viable instructional approaches for mature adults in a doctoral program. Whether this would be true for a class where half the students are strongly auditory or visual rather than tactual remains to be explored. That exploration, however, can be risky for professors in traditional programs where (a) students are conditioned to expect lectures, term papers, and examinations, and (b) annual evaluations, tenure decisions, and salary increases depend upon high student ratings. Professors willing to explore learning-styles instruction at the doctoral level, however, will find that taking the risk is well worth the effort. As Ed so poignantly stated in his reflective portfolio:

Whenever we commit ourselves to learn, I believe that we indulge in an opportunity for risk-taking. Depending on one's outlook, it is the risk of success or the risk of failure. Specifically, we may succeed in understanding a new concept; in gaining proficiency in a new knowledge domain; or in acquiring a new skill. On the other hand, we may fail. No matter the result, we are certain of one outcome—we would have learned from the experience. Thus, if we embark on a life-long commitment to learning, then we commit ourselves to make risk our business. As a class we made risk our business, and we succeeded!

Chapter 12

Divergent Styles, Common Goals: Implications for Counselors

Shirley A. Griggs

The counselor education faculty of St. John's University meets regularly to review the progress and status of matriculated students in the program. Most faculty members had worked with Joya and Mary, fraternal twins who were in their second year of the school counseling program. Dr. Sims opened the discussion of the twins by observing, "It's difficult to believe that these two young women are twins; they are radically different in their perceptions, skills, and general approach to counseling their clients." Professor Harmon followed-up with:

They are both excellent students and will develop into highly effective counselors. In my theories course, Joya embraced cognitive-behavioral approaches to counseling and was a soul-mate of Albert Ellis', whereas Mary was most effective in using creative counseling approaches with clients and demonstrated skill in using art, music, and play therapy with youth.

The discussion concluded when I reported that I would have the twins in my Case Studies in Counseling course that semester and planned to assess my students' learning and cognitive styles to contribute to their self-knowledge and understanding and how their styles impacted the counseling process. My hunch was that their cognitive styles were divergent, with Joya being an analytic processor and Mary being a global processor.

The phenomenon of fraternal twins possessing different learning styles was clarified by Dunn and Dunn, who stated:

Everyone has strengths, although parents' strengths tend to differ from each other's, from their off-springs', and from their own parents'. Thus, mothers and fathers often learn differently from each other and from their children. In the same family, members usually learn in diametrically opposite ways. (1992, p. 1)

It is always interesting to graduate students in the Counselor Education Program when they recognize the diversity of learning styles within a classroom of approximately 25 to 30 students.

ASSESSMENT OF LEARNING AND COGNITIVE STYLES

Two instruments are used to assess learning style and cognitive style, including the *Productivity Environmental Preference Survey* (PEPS) (Dunn, Dunn, & Price, 1990) and the *Hemispheric Preference Scale* (HPS) (Zenhausern, 1988; see Appendix B). The PEPS provides a detailed printout on each student's learning-style characteristics in the five stimuli—environmental, emotional, sociological, physiological, and psychological domains. The HPS is self-scoring; class results can be scored and plotted on a continuum from extreme left to integrated to extreme right (Appendix C). Research indicates that an analytic cognitive style positively correlates with (a) left hemispheric specialization, (b) inductive thinking involving moving from parts of a concept and building toward the whole concept, and (c) field independence. Conversely, a global cognitive style positively correlates with (a) right hemispheric specialization, (b) deductive thinking involving grasping the whole concept and subsequently addressing the parts, and (c) field dependence (Dunn & Griggs, 1995). An interpretation of the cognitive-style characteristics of analytic versus global processors is found in Figure 12.1, with analytic processors characterized as logical, highly verbal, objective, and sequentially oriented when problem solving. Global processors are emotional, highly visual, subjective, and simultaneously cope with several problems.

Group discussion of cognitive processing modes reveals that most students have some awareness of their preferences prior to the formal assessment, but are not cognizant of how these preferences impact the counseling process.

LEARNING-STYLES COUNSELING

Conflict in relationships and among groups is widespread in our society and many youth do not have effective role models for resolving problems. Their parents and other significant adults often use physical and verbal violence and/or emotional abuse in attempting to resolve tensions. Counselors need to work with children, adolescents, and adults both individually and in groups to help them explore conflict and find effective ways to resolve it.

Table 12.1
Cognitive Styles

Analytic Processors	Global Processors
• recognize/remember names	• recognize/remember faces
• respond to verbal instructions	• respond to visual and kinesthetic instructions
• are systematic and controlled when experimenting or learning	• are playful and relaxed when experimenting or learning
• are inhibited emotionally	• are responsive emotionally
• are dependent on words for meaning	• interpret body language easily
• produce logical ideas	• produce unusual ideas
• process verbal stimuli	• process kinesthetic stimuli
• process information objectively	• process information subjectively
• are serious and systematic when solving problems	• are playful and non-conforming when solving problems
• are task oriented	• are people oriented
• dislike improvising	• like improvising
• are not psychic	• are highly psychic
• rarely use metaphors and analogies	• frequently use metaphors and analogies
• are responsive to logical appeals	• are responsive to emotional appeals
• cope with one problem at a time	• cope with several problems simultaneously
• think sequentially	• think holistically
• use language when thinking	• use images when thinking
• tend to be time conscious	• tend to be time indifferent

In my Case Studies in Counseling course, graduate students engage in experiential activities designed for use with either global or analytic processors. To demonstrate a global approach to dealing with conflict, students are instructed to form dyads. Each pair is given an 8½- × 11-inch paper with the following instructions: "This paper represents something very important and valuable to each of you. Only one person may have the paper ultimately. If the paper is torn or mutilated, both parties lose. Begin this exercise with each person grasping the paper between his or her thumb and index finger."

After each dyad has completed the exercise, the methods by which the conflict was resolved are identified and discussed. Students are encouraged to classify their responses to resolving conflict as *ineffective* (denial or withdrawal, suppression or smoothing over, power or dominance) or *effective* (compromise, negotiation, or collaboration). The emotional reactions that this conflict elicits also are identified and include frustration, incompetence, indignation, anger, and irritation.

Another global technique for helping individuals experience conflict is a visualization exercise, which is described as follows:

Get into a comfortable position and close your eyes. In your mind, picture a person with whom you presently are experiencing conflict. Get in touch with the thoughts and feelings that you encounter as you focus on this person.

When you are ready to discuss your reactions, open your eyes. Similarly to processing the paper conflict, students are encouraged to express the thoughts and feelings that interpersonal conflict generates.

Analytic processors find Table 12.2's *Basic Conflict Resolution Procedure* compatible with their approach to resolving conflict.

After these seven steps have been reviewed and discussed, students form dyads and role play conflicting situations, using the procedures outlined. For example, students are given some of the following scenarios to role play:

• You learn that your best friend has just told a number of her friends and acquaintances something that you revealed in confidence.

• You have just been denied a promotion at work and learn that a colleague has erroneously told your boss that you engage in recreational reading during working hours.

• You and your spouse have agreed that you will divide household responsibilities because you both have demanding jobs. However, all week he has arrived home too late to prepare dinner and you have had to assume that task.

• Your daughter has agreed to spend less time on the telephone and more time doing homework, but she continues to spend hours on the phone with her friends.

At the conclusion of the role-playing exercises, the activity is processed and students evaluate the extent to which they successfully engaged in the conflict resolution procedure.

After involving students in these experiential activities designed for differing cognitive styles, a lecture and discussion period follows. These activities address: (a) the basic assumptions of learning-styles counseling, (b) classic counseling theories that are suggested for persons with global versus analytic cognitive styles, and (c) counseling techniques and compatible learning-style preference patterns.

The basic assumptions of learning-styles counseling are as follows:

1. Individuals are unique and they are central to the counseling process. Counseling theories and techniques must be tailored to accommodate individual differences.

Table 12.2
Basic Conflict Resolution Procedure

Step 1: Use Active Listening to Determine How the Other Person Perceives the Conflict

Draw out the person. Attempt to understand his/her point of view. Do not yet express your own views. Instead, encourage the other person to explain his/her position. When he/she has finished, summarize what you have heard and ask whether your summary is accurate. Remember: accurately understanding another's point of view does not mean that you are agreeing with it or giving in.

Step 2: Describe How YOU Perceive the Conflict

Now it's your turn. Tell the other person how you see the situation. Explain your point of view. Don't rush to seek a solution yet—just tell how it looks to you. Point out how your position is similar to and different from the other person. If the other person interrupts you, politely ask him/her to wait until you've finished, then ask him/her to summarize what you've said in order to check whether you've communicated your position clearly.

Step 3: Ask the Other Person to Explain What He/She Wants

Encourage the other person to describe what the ideal state would be. In short, "What do you want if you could have your way?" Urge him/her to talk about specific behavior rather than vague generalities. Resist the impulse to tell the other person why it's impossible for you to do these things. Summarize the things the person wants, to make sure you've understood them.

Step 4: Tell the Other Person What YOU Want

State as specifically as you can what you want. Try to describe specific behavior rather than vague generalities. If the other person starts to tell you that it's impossible, politely ask him/her to wait until you've finished, then ask him/her to summarize what you've requested.

Step 5: Seek a Solution

Attempt to find a solution that gives both of you as much of what you want as possible. This may require some "horse-trading" and you should look for new, creative alternatives as well as more obvious ideas. Try brainstorming all the possible ways both of you could get what you want. Invite the other person to suggest alternatives.

Step 6: Agree on a Solution

Choose the best solution from those suggested. Do not agree to a solution that you really cannot support. That only postpones the conflict. Make sure the other person genuinely supports the solution.

Step 7: Develop an Agenda

Establish explicitly what each of you is going to do to implement the solution. Set a time for checking back to make sure the solution is working. If it is not, agree on a new solution.

2. Learning styles are not related to intelligence, mental ability, nor actual perform-ance. No learning style is better—or worse—than any other style.

3. Counseling is fundamentally a learning process that, if successful, involves positive changes in the attitudes and behavior of the counselee.

4. Individuals have learning-style preferences, which, if attended to, will facilitate the learning process.

5. The client is knowledgeable in terms of identifying his/her learning-style prefer-ences and can report accurately these preferences on a self-report inventory.

6. Counselors can plan interventions that are compatible with the learning-style pref-erences of each client.

A fundamental tenet of counseling for individual learning style is as fol-lows: *If the counseling approaches are compatible with the individual learning-style preferences of the client, the goals of counseling will be achieved.*

STUDENTS' APPLICATION OF LEARNING STYLES

Graduate students recognize that, just as knowledge of their learning-style preferences is empowering, the same applies to their clients.

The twins, who were discussed initially in this chapter, came to recognize that their cognitive-style differences resulted in favoring some counseling interventions over others. As an analytic processor, Joya embraces Ellis's (1994) Rational Emotive Behavior Therapy, which views the counseling process in a logical sequential manner, using the A, B, C, D, E, F symbols:

• A is the *activating* event in the life of the client.

• B is the client's *belief system* and the major focus of counseling.

• C represents the client's *emotional and behavioral consequences* to the event or crisis.

• D is the application of the scientific method by the counselor to help the client *dispute* his/her irrational beliefs.

• E is the development of an *effective philosophy* by the client.

• F represents a newly developed *feeling response-set* by the client.

Conversely, Mary is a global processor and is attracted to Carl Rogers's (1986) *Person-Centered Therapy* that focuses on the whole person rather than the problem. The counselor's role is to project attitudes of genuine caring, respect, acceptance, and understanding of the client, which results in the client experiencing self on a deeper level and moving toward increased independence and integration.

There are counseling techniques that are appropriate for students with certain learning-style strengths (Griggs, 1992). Several of these techniques are identified, described, and linked with compatible learning style charac-teristics as follows:

1. *Art therapy* utilizes activities, such as drawing, painting, clay modeling, and collage construction to provide emotional release and stimulate thinking. This technique is appropriate for individuals with tactual perceptual preference, low need for structure, and varied sociological preferences.

2. *Bibliotherapy* involves the counselor in carefully selecting reading material for the client based on that individual's age, emotional issues, and personality needs. Follow-up discussion is designed to increase the client's insight and self-understanding. This intervention is appropriate for persons with a visual perceptual preference, high need for structure, high degree of motivation and responsibility, and preference for learning alone or with an adult present.

3. *Puppetry* is the technique of manipulating small-scale figures to create or re-enact situations or events for therapeutic purposes. This strategy is compatible with youth who report kinesthetic and visual perceptual preferences, a low need for structure, and a global cognitive style.

4. *Autobiographical writing* involves the client in writing about self, including values, interests, goals, family constellation, and significant past events. The paper is shared in a counseling session. This approach is congruent with the person's exhibiting strong tactual and auditory preferences, high need for structure, high responsibility, and being a self-learner.

5. *Charade games* are used in a group counseling setting in which students act out their feelings in relation to specific theme areas (anger, failure, jealousy, guilt), while other group members try to guess the message. This strategy is used with individuals who are peer-oriented, global processors, with kinesthetic and visual perceptual preferences.

OUTCOMES AND EVALUATION

Knowledge about our styles, preferences, strengths, and assets is empowering and enables us to capitalize on the processes through which we learn. Counselor education students experience personal insight into their learning and cognitive styles and recognize that their clients can benefit from this self-knowledge with similar outcomes. Additionally, graduate students recognize and understand why some counseling theories and techniques are more attractive to some than to others, because of their congruence with personal preferences. However, these same counseling students realize that their clients' styles may be diametrically opposed to their own, and the burden of accommodation rests with the counselor. Thus, these students understand the need to:

- increase their repertoire of counseling interventions;
- move beyond the traditional *talking* approaches in counseling; and include action-oriented and experiential techniques congruent with a wide variety of learning-style characteristics.

As part of their final examination in the Case Studies in Counseling course, students develop an essay-type response to the following question:

Describe a way to apply learning and cognitive styles in your work with children, adolescents, college students, or rehabilitation clients when engaged in individual or group counseling in academic or career planning. Explain how that application would vary if your clients were regular or Special Education students.

Chapter 13

Teacher Training in Progress: Giving It Our Best Shot

Katy Lux

THE HOPES AND ASPIRATIONS

Alan was going to set the world on fire! He knew what he wanted to do, was relatively certain he could do it, and understood his processing style well. The world was his playing field and he was ready to play.

Shannon's enthusiasm for learning could almost engulf you and sweep you away totally. She was relentless in her mission to become an outstanding teacher, sought out each and every extra opportunity for professional growth and involved herself in every aspect of educational development.

REALITY: THE NEXT PHASE

After working with Alan over a period of two years, I lost track of him in the shuffle of life in general for the undergraduate student. Some years later I saw him in a classroom opposite mine and excitedly ran to speak with him. As it turned out, he was working with his father in media productions, was only on campus for that effort, and had dropped out of school.

Shannon met me in a reading class and never let go. She embraced the concepts of learning styles totally and began to blossom in her understanding of herself and the field of education. She eventually graduated with a master's degree.

What is it that haunts me about examples like this? Is it the difference in maturity that caused one to drop out and the other to graduate? Is it the region, the town, the family, the grocery store, or the water? What is it?

The quest for that answer led me into another life-long venture to revisit the way we teach and the way we address student learning in higher education.

THE INSTITUTION OF HIGHER EDUCATION

Aquinas College is a small, private liberal arts college situated among hundreds of wonderful old trees in the heart of a small community in Grand Rapids, Michigan. For the most part, our students come from this and surrounding communities in Michigan, as well as from other parts of the state, nation, and foreign fields. From its inception, Aquinas has focused on the individual student, and still prides itself on the small, personal contact possible with a smaller population. Teaching is the core of emphasis, with a secondary thrust toward the academic field of publishing and professional recognition.

In 1991, the Aquinas College Midwest Regional Teaching and Learning Center was established to assist in the process of working with faculty, community educational structures, classrooms, teachers, students, parents, and interested populations in developing research and disseminating information on the process of learning and teaching. We joined a cadre of national/international groups to explore these issues and strengthen the forces of investigating the process of how people actually learn and how that translates into the classroom at any level. We took a hard look at the issues of learning and teaching and began working with our own student population with a new zest and perspective.

THE TEACHER-EDUCATION PROGRAM

Our process began on a small scale in the Education Department. In the first required course of all students aspiring to go into the field of teaching, we provided a formal introduction to the concepts of learning—how we learn, what factors influence the process, which things serve as distracters, what we know and don't know about analyzing learning processes, brain functions, and preferences of style. We assessed our students and provided the interpretations and information they needed to understand themselves, and, hopefully, to understand the classrooms of students they would eventually work with.

More than half our student population is in the category of nontraditional age. They come to us from other fields, varied professions, to finish something begun years ago, or simply to change their lives and pursue that which always has been attractive to them. Our education program graduate students outnumber our undergraduate population, and the initial certification program has become very attractive to those wishing to change careers, or realizing that teaching still can become a reality, even at different stages of life, or with different undergraduate degrees.

Over and over again, we hear how delighted our students are to discover what they instinctively have known about themselves in the learning process. Many find great comfort in the fact that we can confirm what they know, and provide assurance that they need to honor what they know and find strength in that confirmation. Many, for example, who entered other fields when receiving their undergraduate degrees, find out that they can, and do, fit into the education system. By assessing their styles of learning and the approaches they use, we begin to help them understand that there is no one absolute way to learn, and that there is no right or wrong of the learning process. This, by far, has been a powerful discovery for many of our students. We have also discovered that our education system, as a whole, has a long way to go to provide for this new knowledge we now have, and to make allowances for the actual techniques and processes needed to enhance the occurrence of learning.

It was our goal to have the first formal exposure to these learning theories and processes enable our students to develop a foundation for the additional issues in learning and teaching they would encounter in the subsequent education classes. This did, indeed, happen. However, even more powerful were the unanticipated results of our efforts. Each semester, students come forward to share their own revelations and relief in discovering that their particular learning processes and preferences were worthy of acknowledgment and even use! Never before had they been told that their own individual styles are perfectly acceptable and should be honored. They are in awe that they have spent an entire lifetime (or close to it) in academic settings and have never been assisted in determining how they go about processing information, or recognizing which things influence their academic concentration.

A CASE STUDY EVALUATION

Of particular impact have been the scenarios of students whose various labels attest to their learning differences. There's Kerry Ethridge, for example. She is a traditional, older learning-disabled student, in her fifth year of college and planning to enter the teaching profession. Kerry struggled through her entire school career believing that she had far fewer capabilities than her valedictorian brother. The messages she invariably received were always that she needed to apply herself more, focus harder, be more like her brother, and so on. She was eventually put on Ritalin at the suggestion of some of her teachers who saw her as having Attention Hyperactive Deficit Disorder (AHDD), but she became jittery, upset, and developed severe insomnia. On her own, she wisely decided to throw the bottle of Ritalin away. It wasn't until her senior year in high school that she was diagnosed as borderline dyslexic. Her own private school couldn't help her, so arrangements were made to have her spend a portion of every day at the public school nearby and participate in their Individualized Learning Center. It was a great relief for Kerry to discover that she was not a *dummy* and that she did not need to cheat in her classes in order to succeed.

Her struggles to get into college are another whole story, but Aquinas accepted her with the foresight of our Academic Achievement Center Director, who works with all our special-needs students. It was her own instincts that told Kerry to pursue this avenue and allow us to work with her.

Her freshman year was not without struggle. Kerry worked weekly with individuals who assisted her in setting up study schedules, learning to take notes, strengthening her study skills, providing test-taking strategies, and teaching her to use color-coding for chapters—among many other finely detailed instructions and directions. Working with the information provided through the assessment of her learning styles, we also were able to determine that Kerry needed to be involved personally in every plan we proposed. When that occurred, she readily took responsibility for her own learning.

One of Kerry's strongest preferences attested to her need to concentrate on challenging material in the late afternoon. This was perfect for some of her required difficult classes that were offered at optional times of the day. Kerry's strength in the tactual area also was capitalized on by having her rewrite her notes immediately after every class and highlighting each main point on the left side of the page. Not only was this necessary for working around her disabilities, but it enabled her to use her tactual strength to absorb the material.

We taught her to use various colors to: underline required information, transfer required facts onto flash cards or Task Cards, use different-colored cards to represent varied subjects or concepts, use hands-on learning resources, and capitalize on those processes that enabled her to function as independently as possible.

Kerry speaks proudly of only failing one class during her program here at Aquinas. She describes that first math class with triumph as well as pain. It happened to be a night class with no late afternoon option available. The subject was difficult enough for Kerry, who had failed every math class during her previous school experiences—with the exception of Geometry. The time of the class wasn't the point of contention for Kerry, since she had successfully negotiated her other evening classes. What did make the difference was the *instructor*. This particular professor did not appear to be approachable to Kerry and was not willing to allow her to take the course tests in a different setting (as had been advised). Time constraints and pressure always have been Kerry's enemies, but under reduced tensions in less formal settings, such as an easy chair or soft music in the room, Kerry manages quite well. The request to make such an allowance for Kerry proved to be very uncomfortable for the instructor and, unfortunately, led to an unfriendly relationship between the two of them.

There was no apparent respect for Kerry's needs, and the harsh tones in the instructor's voice suggested that no option or compromise was available. Kerry tells us that this was the only instructor at Aquinas who could not, or would not, be flexible in requirements or, as Kerry perceived it, *helpful*. It is not, however, assumed that this is the only such instructor on campus.

Kerry finds that her experiences have made her all the more sensitive to those learners who need different approaches to learning, and whose style isn't always met or recognized. She has a passion for working with the *bad* children—those she describes as *throwing fits, moving around*, and causing disruption and chaos. She says that she often *felt like doing those things*. During her years at Aquinas, Kerry has taken every opportunity to learn everything she could about special-needs students, investigate their options, and tell others about their needs. She is comfortable in understanding her own strengths and is relentless in her message to others that they not view themselves as failures in school merely because they cannot learn conventionally. Her mission seems to be clear, and she delivers her message with great conviction.

IMPACTING OTHER DEPARTMENTS AND STUDENT SERVICES

The faculty's collaborative efforts to work with our students expanded as well into the counseling department of the college. The director of that department calls upon our expertise to assist whenever questions arise concerning the academic connections that might help in completing the puzzle for any student—whom they describe as our *clients*. Many of our non-traditional and/or older students often begin the college venture with fear and trepidation because they have been away from such a setting for a significant number of years—or have never been in such a setting at all. These are often learners who did not understand their instructional needs at a younger age and, at times, still didn't understand them. Repeatedly, through our learning-styles approach, we have been able to add another dimension to helping individuals understand themselves and acknowledge their own processing styles.

At its earliest inception stages, staff at the Midwest Regional Teaching and Learning Center were asked to work with the Aquinas faculty, staff, and adjuncts. It began on a small scale with the request for a workshop primarily for our adjuncts. The emphasis was on providing information on how students actually learn and what that meant as we translated this information into how we teach. More than 90 participants spent the day immersed in discovering what research is telling us about the learning process and what we, as professors and instructors, can do to meet the needs of our students.

From that initial workshop, we presented information in a variety of formats over the next several years, always trying to respond to the needs and requests of faculty by providing practical suggestions. One workshop, Alternatives to Lecture, was particularly well received, and provided us with critical insight into what our faculty actually wanted in their search to hone their teaching skills. Not only was it important to look at the learning processes and analyze the styles involved, but we also needed to address specifically the delivery systems of instruction. A more amazing revelation, however, was made in discovering that our faculty members, in general, were receptive to, and really interested in, examining the learning and the teaching process. Lest we make this sound too good to be true, there were, and still are, the collective groups who represent the *been there, done that* edict, or those who simply have no interest in these areas.

Within the last six or seven years, we have been able to work with the majority of faculty either in an introductory or in a more in-depth format. Frequently, we are asked to analyze the learning styles of a particular class and provide an in-depth session to assist in the interpretation and application of that information. Among the departments that are particularly aware of providing this service and information are Sociology, Graduate Management, International Studies, and Business Administration. More specifically, the Education Department in particular continues to provide these services as part of its core efforts in preparing future teachers. This department has adopted formal procedures for including learning-style analyses for every education student. In addition, the development of a graduate class to specifically address issues of brain research, learning styles, and teaching styles has proven to be immensely popular, and provides numerous opportunities for analyzing these issues in greater depth.

In our continued quest to improve the academic delivery systems at Aquinas, we encourage innovation and the re-thinking of traditional formats. As such, we have seen beginning attempts to change things as simple as a syllabus, starting with our own efforts in the Education Department. We took the basic information from the traditional, analytic format used on most syllabi (see Appendix D), and provided an overview format often needed by holistic, global students (see Appendix E). The feedback was instantaneous. We saw students selecting the format that made the most sense to them and telling us how much they appreciated being able to understand where we were going in the course and how all the pieces fit together. Many asked why hadn't we thought about this sooner!

A FINAL NOTE

We now continue to develop these concepts slowly and gradually. We have come to the revelation that we cannot do it alone, and that we need each other to not only preach to change, but actually to be a part of demonstrating change. We have also come to realize that our students can provide us with new perspectives and can teach us how to become *better at allowing them to learn.*

The future is filled with plans, aspirations, and hopes. We have been invited to become a viable force in the development of a formal mentoring program at the college. Not only would we work with new faculty, but we would help interested tenured faculty to develop the expertise needed to be more successful teachers, as well as continuing learners. What a challenge, and how wonderfully appropriate for a teaching institution!

Chapter 14

Project Learn: A University-Initiated Consortium of Science Educators and Practitioners

Barbara S. Thomson

RATIONALE

During the past 40 years, numerous books and articles have been written criticizing teachers and teacher educators for the low academic achievement of students in reading, mathematics, social studies, English, and the sciences. In order to be accountable, standardized tests and proficiency examinations designed to meet national and state standards were administered to obtain student achievement data. Based on the data obtained from those assessments, attempts to reverse declining achievement scores among the diverse U.S. student population have spawned numerous intervention strategies. Although teams of educators and academicians repeatedly have massaged and reworked the curriculum with content innovations and provided continual professional training for teachers to implement these new programs, we still are not meeting appropriate expectations or academic goals for our children (NCTAF, 1996). Everyone realizes that the continued success of our country depends on the academic excellence of *all* students and a commitment to that goal is more important now than at any time in the history of this nation. However, until we focus on how students internalize and retrieve new and difficult material so that we can ensure quality learning for all students, we shall continue to grasp for that elusive variable—academic excellence. How *do* our children learn new and difficult information?

LEARNING STYLES AS A BASIS FOR ACADEMIC IMPROVEMENT

For more than 30 years, researchers working with learning and teaching styles have accumulated substantial documentation to support the belief that most students *can* learn (Dunn & Dunn, 1978, 1992, 1993, 1999; Dunn, Griggs, Olson, Gorman, & Beasley, 1995). The *process* through which students learn is called their *learning style*.

It is critical that teachers: (a) accommodate individual learning-style strengths; (b) remediate learners using their strengths; and (c) abandon the practice of introducing new bandwagon cure-all curricular programs. All educators from many different teaching communities must collaborate to provide appropriate learning strategies that produce academic excellence for all students. It is no longer appropriate to continue focusing only on content revisions and strategies for teaching new content. We must consider and act on the research that indicates that teaching students through their learning-style strengths, instead of remediating learners emphasizing their weaknesses, not only enhances test scores but also impacts positively students' attitudes and behaviors (Brunner & Majewski, 1990).

Teacher-education partnerships designed around student learning styles can catalyze quality learning for both students and professional partners. A community of learners, reaching for this vision of excellence and improved academic capabilities, can create a difference for students, preservice interns, and inservice teachers as we make student learning power our primary focus. We cannot continue to teach students in exactly the same way and watch them struggle when we know they can achieve when they are taught through their learning-style strengths (Andrews, 1990; Klavas, 1993; *The Buffalo Experience*, 1993).

PROJECT LEARN

To close the achievement gap, we have established a Professional Development School (PDS) partnership called *Project Learn*. It is comprised of classroom practitioners, clinical and teacher educators, administrators, parents, and students from 12 schools representing diverse populations and socioeconomic groups. This consortium seeks to provide excellence in education by using learning styles. Ohio State University's College of Education, in collaboration with individual building teams from local school districts, initiated this partnership in 1991. Participants in Project Learn are trying to close the achievement gap by sharing strategies for learning with all partners. Students and practitioners are identifying their learning strengths to increase their competence. As a result of our outcomes, we believe that everyone interested in promoting quality education should become a participant in a collaborative partnership. It no longer is appropriate to continue to work on new content for a revised curriculum and neglect individual learning styles. Successful collaborative change, designed around teacher education and learning styles, requires a consortium.

Historically, teacher educators from colleges and universities used a top-down management model to insure quality control similar to business and industry. However, contemporary management learners have evolved toward a horizontal partnership that creates the framework for this Project Learn PDS partnership. Senge (1990) argued that we can build learning organizations in which: (a) people continually expand their capacity to create the results they truly desire; (b) new and expansive patterns of thinking are nurtured; (c) collective aspiration is set free; and (d) people continually are learning *how* to learn together. Further, Senge indicated that organizations that excel in the future are those that discover how to tap people's commitment and capacity to learn at all levels. The capacity of organizations to optimize learning and realize human potential depends on commitment to cope with institutional interconnectedness (Senge, 1990). Teacher educators must function by using a similar model in our organizational framework as integrated partners reaching for a vision of learning that benefits every student.

Project Learn is building a teacher-education PDS learning organization that can be distinguished from the traditional vertical decision-making structures found in many universities. The Holmes Partnership goals (1995) helped Project Learn partners to expand their learning-styles vision across many arenas, including:

- high-quality professional preparation for educators;
- simultaneously interlocking renewal;
- equity, diversity, and cultural competence;
- scholarly inquiry and programs of research;
- faculty development; and
- policy initiation.

The Holmes goals and the Senge horizontal model provided Project Learn partners with a working model for change and opportunities for learner success.

A horizontal model using learning styles as a focus across key teacher-education goals is not always a match for the traditional vertical model used by many higher education colleges and universities. Being mismatched with the current framework can unravel some of the strengths of a horizontal framework. Using the Holmes goals (1995), a Senge (1990) model, and focusing on learning style strengths as our priorities provided some challenges. Conventional teacher educators who are comfortable with their current ways of working often found this partnership to be disconcerting. Conversely, many of the early adopters on the faculty embraced the opportunity to pilot new strategies in an attempt to improve teacher education at all levels. Others found this model to be personally inappropriate and did not participate. However, Project Learn partners had made a major commitment of time, energy, and expertise to integrate teacher education into a comprehensive educational, horizontal-growth model using learning-styles and brain research to reach that vision of learning and achievement for all students.

TEACHER-EDUCATION PARTNERSHIP FOCUS

A diversity of partnership is crucial for a teacher-education organization to function properly since education is interconnected with so many different components. Our learning-styles partnership, Project Learn, includes 10 key groups:

1. Students in classrooms are our most important element in this partnership. Schools exist to help students learn. Everyone in this partnership has the responsibility to use expertise to help all students reach their potential by using their personal learning-style strengths.

2. Family members can support or unravel a viable partnership. Communication and contributions within the family framework are critical. Commercial free educational videotaping is done by some families using Cable in the Classroom programs to expand classroom learning resources. Educational web sites such as Eisenhower National Clearinghouse (ENC) and Web Teacher provide links to quality resources that some families access and share.

3. Classroom teachers are with students on a daily basis and have a major impact on learners. Teachers help to weave a fabric for learning and establish an environment for success. Teachers use the *Learning Style Inventory* (LSI) (Dunn, Dunn, & Price, 1991) to identify student processing strengths and use this information to enhance students' learning power. Teachers also work collaboratively with OSU graduate students and preservice interns to integrate learning styles into the district courses of study. The mentoring of these groups by classroom teachers blends these partners into the total learning framework. Interns are our future teachers and graduate teaching associates are the teacher educators of tomorrow.

4. Teacher educators weave the theory piece into practice as they work collaboratively with classroom teachers. Assisting teachers in the workplace, contributing resources, examining our own practice, and creating a collaborative change environment are a few of the important roles of university educators. Developing an instructional supervision network for preservice interns using a horizontal model is another component essential for this learning-styles partnership.

5. Preservice interns are our future colleagues in classrooms. Interns have a unique opportunity to learn, through partnership collaboration, how students can increase achievement using their personal learning-style strengths. State and national standards, benchmarks, and district courses of study all have statements suggesting that educators should accommodate student

learning styles. The Project Learn partnership helps everyone explore implementation strategies to make this happen.

6. Clinical Educator (CE) positions were initiated by Dean Nancy Zimpher at Ohio State University (OSU). She negotiated with schools in the PDS partnership to use funds from OSU to hire a PDS classroom teacher to work in a university PDS partnership 50 percent of the time. Thus, one of our PDS teachers could become a Clinical Educator (CE) and spend 50 percent of the time in the PDS partnership with the university. This released time is critical. A dual-role classroom practitioner in the morning and a teacher educator in the afternoon/evening has great credibility with all partners. Districts continued to pay the fringe benefits for each CE. The CE also had access to extensive professional development in learning and teaching styles.

7. A Field Professor (FP) is a key teacher in each building site. This educator has been an early adopter of learning styles and is using this model effectively in the classroom. The FP has no monetary compensation, but does have opportunities for intensive professional development in teacher education and learning styles.

8. Administrators are the curricular and instructional leaders for the school district. They are also the liaison to the community, board of education, and the business sector.

9. Community leaders in business and industry subscribe to the Secretary's Commission on Achieving Necessary Skills (SCANS). The SCANS competencies (U.S. Department of Labor, 1991) define the skills needed for employment. Learning style creates a dissemination strategy for SCANS competencies. This is an important segment of the partnership.

10. Teacher-Education graduate students who work in the area of learning styles become equal partners with all of the participants. This partnership empowers graduate students and provides many avenues of professional development for them. Attending and/or presenting at conferences, writing articles with Project Learn partners, and team teaching are just a few of the professional development experiences our students have had as important members within this partnership. These students are our future university colleagues who are helping to build a learning framework for teacher education. Many of these partners' dissertation research explores learning-styles questions.

LEARNING AND LEARNING STYLES IN TEACHER EDUCATION

All certified teachers have had numerous university courses that review the historical and contemporary work of learning theorists. Skinner, Piaget, Bruner, Gagne, Ausubel, Vygotsky, Posner, and others provide glimpses into ways people learn. However, these theoreticians each pose only a single process for all—and each propose a different *process*. Educators must have data on how *individual* students learn to maximize learning for each student. Another key is implementation. Once we have the individual profiles of students, what can do we do to help learners capitalize on their strengths? Project Learn uses the LSI profile and its homework computer disc prescriptions to increase learners' strengths (Dunn & Klavas, 1990). Strategies for each student based on his/her strengths are provided by this computer program based on LSI scores.

Currently, there are many learning-style instruments available. Thirty years ago, instruments were just evolving. As we move into the twenty-first century, it is critical to use instruments that have established manuals that provide reliability and validity data and a strong research base developed over time by numerous researchers.

After piloting many instruments, Project Learn PDS selected the Dunn and Dunn Learning-Style Model. This model includes different instruments for assessing the learning styles of young children (Dunn, Dunn, & Perrin, 1994), elementary students (Dunn & Dunn, 1992), adolescents (Dunn & Dunn, 1993), and adults (Dunn & Dunn, 1999). Thus, we profiled our entire team along with their students to determine everyone's learning style. Implementation keyed to stimuli and elements is an integral part of the framework for using the Dunn model. Thies (1979, 1999/2000), a child psychologist at Yale University's School of Medicine involved with investigating brain processing, indicated that the variables in this model match recent and emerging brain research findings.

Many educators erroneously believe that perceptual modalities (auditory, visual, tactual, and kinesthetic) are the only learning-style components. Many other variables are critical components for learning, including environmental, emotional, sociological, and psychological aspects. The Dunns' model has evolved to incorporate learning-style elements with extensive research to support their inclusion in the model (*Research on the Dunn and Dunn Model*, 1999). Project Learn works with all these learning-style elements.

Implementation is the key to success in learning achievement. Knowing each person's learning strengths and knowing how to study new and difficult information is part of the Dunns' model. Partners receive their own personal learning-style profile. A computerized study-skill printout is also part of the individualized learning package. All interns, classroom teachers, students in the schools, and teacher educators make learning packages to use in their classrooms. Kindegarten to grade 12 students create materials that accommodate their own personal learning power. Workshops are provided for parents to learn about implementation. Parents also can have their own learning-style profiles by request.

Our partners use *Everything You Need to Successfully Implement a Learning-Styles Instructional Program: Materials and Methods* (Dunn,

1996). This publication is an inexpensive but comprehensive strategy to jump-start the implementation in a learning-styles partnership in which each partner must develop ways to enhance his/her personal learning strengths. Knowing your own learning strengths is important for success.

ACTION RESEARCH

Current educational literature is filled with articles encouraging teachers to examine their own practices. Action research is a wonderful way to evaluate classroom practice and its impact on student learners. Because teachers are overloaded with so many extra tasks each year, Project Learn created a classroom partnership consisting of an intern, classroom teacher, and supervisor who collaboratively conduct action research partnership projects. This action research can be replicated by another intern later in the year if desired.

Interns are in classrooms for a half day each Monday through Thursday. This provides interns and teachers with time to explore an instructional problem or question that is important for that particular classroom. Intervention strategies are often part of the action research plan. This project becomes a team effort among the teacher, intern, and supervisor. Sometimes the research involves working with a small group of students and, at other times, the entire class. The partners make collaborative decisions about their own classroom action research project and each team may have a different focus.

Using learning styles to conduct action research illuminates the importance of using learners' strengths and not remediating with students' weaknesses. If a student is having difficulty reading in a district that uses only phonics, identifying the learner's strengths is very important. Also, showing students ways to do their assignments by using their own personal learning style often makes a substantial difference. For example:

Jeff and his teacher were interested in strategies to improve mathematics achievement. The teacher had taught the students for the first six weeks of the semester. Jeff taught the students for the next three weeks using the same strategies, profiled a group of six students who could not pass the math quiz each Friday, and identified the personal learning strengths of each student. For the following two weeks each student studied mathematics using homework prescriptions based on personal learning-style computer analysis.

Two of the students improved their grades from E to A. The other four students raised their grades to above a C. During the next two weeks, Jeff requested that they return to the original study plan that they had been using all semester and that they not use their newly identified learning-style strengths. The six students found that, once they had been empowered to understand their own strengths, they could not revert easily to the way they had been learning when they were failing math.

Patty was fascinated with the informal seating and global processing research. Can a global student, who needs an informal area in which to study and take a test, demonstrate grade improvement? As an intern, Patty took over one section of a mathematics middle school class. She used strategies, assignments, and tests similar to those of the regular teacher. After three weeks, she introduced learning styles and shared the profile information with the students. For the next three weeks, only those students who needed informal seating studied and took their tests in a comfortable chair or seated on the carpeted floor. Those eight students were global, informal processors and had been underachievers in the class. After three weeks of changing only the students' seating preferences, six of the eight had raised their math grades to satisfactory or above. Patty had planned to reverse the process, but the classroom teacher, students, and parents did not want this to occur.

Music research and learning styles fascinated Peter. Many adolescents as well as adults have a preference for sound when they are studying or taking a test. Peter, as an intern, acquired equipment and appropriate 60-beats-per-minute tapes without vocalizations for his high school unified science class in an urban setting. The profile of the students indicated that a high percentage of these adolescents needed a sound-present environment while learning. Peter provided the sound tapes during labs and examinations. Seventy percent of the students who needed sound increased their scores on weekly tests. Peter and his teacher were surprised that the manipulation of one critical variable in the environmental category could make a difference.

Combining teacher, intern, OSU supervisor, Clinical Educator, and Field Professor to support a mini-action research project is a great way for partners to examine their own practices. Classroom teachers have many questions about the way their students learn. The LSI profile and homework prescription used to explore a question the team finds relevant is productive for the classroom students and provides professional development for the entire team.

CHALLENGES

In every institution there are early adopters, skeptics who observe and wait to see what will happen with an innovation, and those who are comfortable with the status quo and refuse to change. Project Learn found that the early adopters wanted to join as partners immediately. Eventually, others joined also. Although we are working to enhance the learning of all students and provide professional development for all educators, some teachers and professors are unwilling to break with tradition. Therefore, students are taught by teachers and interns to study using their learning-style strengths. If teachers in other classes are not willing to accommodate students' learning preferences, then students need to study according to their learning-style strengths *after* class to achieve their maximum potential.

Challenges occur within all the partnership categories. Most, but not all, educators are eager to experiment to determine if learning styles might help their students. Some family members only want the basics taught in our classrooms. Certain administrators want a top-down approach and are uncomfortable with any partnership that empowers others. Certain university professors want to maintain the tradition of the university with the expert at the top making decisions. Community learners seem to be most flexible. They want young people to be capable of meeting the demands of the workplace. Because learning styles is a perfect match for the SCANS competencies (1991), community leaders usually are supportive of learning-styles implementation. They are appreciative that we are using a well-researched instrument.

Every change has detractors and resisters (Kolb, 1979), but the talent of our educators and students is too precious to waste. It is important to remember that the early adopters will help initiate the change process. Once families and children begin to work with their learning styles, they will promote quality changes in other classes. Hilliard High School students wrote an article for their school paper that stated: "Teachers need to appeal to students if they ever want to teach them. If this learning-styles test reached further than just the science department, then maybe teachers could create an atmosphere in which all students can learn" (McElheny, 1995).

IMPLEMENTATION WORKSHOPS AND SEMINARS

Professional development for all partners is needed. Identifying what is important is a decision made by the partners. In Project Learn, we created university credit and non-credit partnership programs determined by the team. Some examples are:

1. You've Got to Know Your Learning Power: A PDS Learning-Styles Orientation Workshop

2. Learning Styles I : A Graduate Credit Course

3. Learning Styles II: A Graduate Credit Course

4. Instructional Supervision and the Learning-Style Connection: A Graduate Credit Course for University Supervisors

5. Learning Is for Kids: A Workshop for Students Grades 5–12

6. Electronic Portfolios for Teachers: A Graduate Credit Workshop for Teachers and Graduate Students

7. Learning Styles: The SCANS Connection—A Community Presentation for Business and Industry Partners

8. Learning Style for Administrators Seeking Solutions: A Credit or Non-credit Course

9. Learning Styles and the Proficiency Exam Partnership: Students, Teachers, Graduate Students, Professors, Clinical Educators, Parents, and Administrators

10. Underachieving Students and Learning Styles: A Seminar for Kids and Teachers as Partners

SUMMARY OF THE TEACHER-EDUCATION LEARNING-STYLES PARTNERSHIP

Teaching suggests that when teachers teach, students learn. Teaching and learning are interwoven, but we need to have appropriate information to determine how each student can use his/her learning potential. The LSI (Dunn, Dunn, & Price, 1991) and the PEPS for adults (Dunn, Dunn, & Price, 1994) provide the data to determine learners' strengths. When evaluating the progress of students with learning difficulties, it becomes apparent that we are not teaching to their learning strengths. For example:

Paul was disruptive in school. He was argumentative at home when parents insisted that he sit at the kitchen table and do his homework each evening after school. He never finished his work without inappropriate interactions between himself and his family members. His LSI revealed that Paul is a global processor who has a strong energy peak in the evening. He works in short bursts, needs an informal place to study, and brief personal breaks every 20–30 minutes. Paul is not an auditory learner but most of his work in school is provided through lectures and discussions. Paul is tactual and kinesthetic, which suggests that he needs to move while learning.

After seeing Paul's profile, his parents set up a study time after dinner in his room and scheduled several short breaks. Paul works on each subject for approximately 10 minutes and then moves to another subject until he has rotated through all of his homework areas for the evening. He then takes a 10-minute break, which usually means it is also snack time. Paul returns to this pattern and does another rotation until all assignments are done. Parents review his work and help with corrections.

The very first evening the family initiated the new procedures, Paul completed his homework without any arguments or tantrums. He has improved his grades and now understands his personal learning strengths and weaknesses. The PDS partners were surprised at Paul's change in school. He has better attendance and is no longer a major discipline problem, although he still has his moments. When Paul experiences stress, he needs a mentor to assist him to refocus on his strengths—but he has made significant progress.

If we want to be outstanding teachers, we must teach students about their own personal learning strengths. If students have teachers in other classes who are not willing to accommodate diverse strengths, then students must learn the material outside that classroom. Students who are mismatched with certain teachers can teach themselves during homework time. PDS partners can help them. Mismatched students may need mentors.

CONCLUSION

Project Learn participants realize that it is time to stop jumping on each curricular bandwagon and begin to examine and capitalize on students' learning strengths. The Dunn and Dunn model has given Project Learn a focus and strategies for success and excellence in education. It is time to identify how students learn using a PDS partnership model. Students are our future. The interns and graduate students are our teachers and teacher educators of tomorrow. The Project Learn partnership creates a community of learners. We verbalize that everyone can learn, but we need to become aware of the variety of ways in which individual learners process new and difficult information and what is appropriate for each. Creating a partnership around the strengths of learning styles will make the twenty-first century the place to be for life-long learners.

Chapter 15

Teaching Graduate Students with a Learning-Styles Approach: Adding Zest to the Course Ingredients

Laura Shea Doolan

Rushed and harried after a busy day, I answered the phone on its second ring. It was a call from the university. "Are you available to teach Education 7232? It starts on Tuesday of next week."

I was excited. This was the area in which I was most interested—a graduate course on learning styles! But I had so many things to do this semester, and I was preparing to leave for Bermuda as a Teaching Assistant for another course on learning styles.

"May I call you back on Monday? I have to see if I can adjust my schedule," I asked. And so, I had a few days to ponder what and how I would teach a course on learning styles while using a learning-styles approach.

TEACHER EDUCATION

I realized that graduate students with varied backgrounds register for this master's-level course. According to Dunn and Dunn (1999), at least part of the continuing need for teacher education is based on one or more of the following widely recognized problems in school districts throughout the nation. There is a widely acknowledged:

- lack of research-based instruction that evidences increased student achievement and improved attitudes toward schooling across the board;
- use of *new* instructional approaches for which advocates claim remarkable gains—without research documentation;
- failure among educators to insist on published experimental studies to demonstrate the accuracy of the elaborate media claims of either traditional or innovative programs' successes;

- failure of many programs or innovations because they have been implemented for entire classes or schools without thought about for which students they were likely to be effective; and

- lack of time and classroom assistance provided for teachers required to implement new approaches.

With these above factors to consider, why would using a learning-styles approach be important to teach a graduate course? Would such a course on still another approach impact on experienced—or new—teachers? Could it make a difference? According to Dunn and Dunn (1999):

The requirement for ongoing inservice also may be an outcome of the general inadequacy of Teacher Education Programs and the institutions that permit them to continue offering the same courses in the same program by the same faculty who teach "their" courses in the same way—and sometimes with the same notes and lectures. (p. 4)

The Dunns insist that it is not possible to be an outstanding college teacher without conducting ongoing research with your own classes and the methods you use and teach your students to use. Therefore, it is imperative that all teaching instructors become aware of (a) the differences among how individuals learn and (b) how to teach new and difficult information through strategies that match students' individual learning-style preferences.

WHAT IS LEARNING STYLE?

Learning style addresses the biological uniqueness and developmental changes that make one person learn differently from another. Individuals *do* change in the way they learn. Evolving maturation impacts one's biologically determined learning-style preferences (Restak, 1979; Thies, 1979, 1999/2000). Similarly, developmental aspects relate to how we learn but, more predictably, follow a recognizable pattern (Dunn & Griggs, 1995).

RATIONALE FOR USING A LEARNING-STYLES APPROACH WITH GRADUATE STUDENTS

Since 1970, St. John's University's faculty have conducted research, published extensively, and prepared educators in teaching students through their individual learning styles. The doctoral program, Instructional Leadership, emerged from that background of professional commitment. Courses specifically devoted to identifying individuals' styles provide the core of the program. Advanced courses on how to conduct staff development through the participants' learning styles and develop consultant skills provide the basis for effective supervisory education. These courses were an outgrowth of the successes realized when teaching students in all subject areas through their learning-style strengths. This approach is the vehicle for increasing students' standardized achievement test scores while simultaneously increasing their positive attitudes toward school (Dunn & DeBello, 1999).

The underlying mandate of the past three decades has been that teachers, as educational leaders and change agents, need to teach all students through instructional strategies responsive to their unique strengths. Consequently, this commitment promotes students' competence, interest in, and enthusiasm for all subject areas. According to GOALS 2000 (1996), "every school in America will ensure that all students learn to use their minds well, so they may be prepared for responsible citizenship, further learning, and productive employment . . . The nation's teaching force will have . . . the opportunity to acquire the knowledge and skills needed to instruct and prepare all American students for the next century" (p. 1).

Thus, the enactors of GOALS 2000 state that students must use *their* minds and teachers need the skills to prepare *all* students. Therefore, we must concentrate on teaching students about their learning-style strengths if we are going to teach diverse learners (Dunn, 1995). Classroom strategies used for all students in the same class damage many learners. If we take responsibility for teaching all learners, we must break with tradition. Dunn (1995) states that "When children do not learn the way we teach them, then we must teach them the way they learn" (p. 30).

Learning-styles-based instruction has been effective with students at all academic levels, and with teachers involved in professional development (Buell & Buell, 1987; Dunn, Dunn, & Freeley, 1985; Raupers, in press; Taylor, 1999/2000). In addition, those teachers who were exposed to a learning-styles instructional approach during inservice were more likely to use a learning-styles approach with their students, in comparison to teachers who were not exposed to a learning-styles approach. Why would it not be beneficial for all teachers?

THE MODEL FOR TEACHING TEACHERS

It seems logical that those involved in teaching teachers need to use each teacher's learning preferences as the basis for the instruction they provide. Thus, to help educators teach through their students' learning-style preferences, it makes sense that one should provide a model for teaching them through a learning-styles approach.

The teachers enrolled in this course taught students on the primary, middle school, and secondary levels. I began the first class with a global introduction that was as humorous as I could be when relating the overall course content to teachers' usual classroom experiences. For example, I explained learning styles in terms of what teachers at different grade levels normally see in class—despite their well-prepared lessons. I described the learning-style traits of youngsters who:

- fall asleep;
- talk to each other when they should be listening to the teacher;
- surreptitiously munch on snacks while listening;
- cover their ears when thinking;
- hum to themselves while taking a test;
- fall off their seats while listening;
- move their bodies continually while doing assignments;
- can't keep their hands to themselves;
- need peer-group approval more than they do adult approval;
- say "No!" just for effect;
- rarely do as they are told;
- repeat the words we say verbatim;
- can't/won't take notes while listening;
- ask us to repeat words we have just said;
- ask us to check their work long before they have finished it;
- require constant feedback; or
- frequently ask for interpretations of what they are reading, and so forth.

I encouraged my students to examine several Multisensory Instructional Packages (MIPs) that I had brought to class (Dunn & Dunn, 1992, 1993, 1999; Dunn, Dunn, & Perrin, 1994). MIPs include analytic and global titles, a Contract Activity Package (CAP) (see Chapter 20), a Programmed Learning Sequence (PLS) (see Chapter 16), several hands-on tactual instructional resources, and a kinesthetic Floor Game—all with identical, clearly stated objectives and tests.

After examining and handling these materials, students asked whether they were going to make them in the course, and I assured them that they would, but that I would help. I also told them that they were to develop a complete MIP based on *difficult* content that they often found youth struggling with in their classes. End of class one.

When we met for the next session, I administered the PEPS (Dunn, Dunn, & Price, 1987), a measurement of the learning-style preferences of adults. Waiting for the return of their personal profiles, we spent the next sessions further discussing learning-style strategies and talking about ways teachers might use these different approaches in their classes. I emphasized that these approaches were all effective—but not for all students. I assured them that they quickly would become aware of which of their students responded best to each strategy; the youngsters *tell you and everybody else voluntarily and enthusiastically!*

The students enrolled in my course were a mixture of veteran and new teachers. They were used to teaching students traditionally, but were willing to try using learning styles in their classrooms. Indeed, they verbalized that *this* course (as opposed to some) had *practical applications* for their daily problems!

I implored them to let me know of both their problems and successes when using learning-style strategies. One of the teachers reported that some of his students' parents had wondered why he was changing the way he had been teaching. At the next session, I gave him an article on parents' perceptions of their children's learning styles to share with those parents. During each class session, we worked on different learning-style strategies—CAPS, PLSs, small-group techniques for peer-oriented students, tactual materials for the hands-on children, and Floor Games for the kinesthetic youngsters. While working with the latter resources, one of my students groaned and acknowledged that she had absolutely no kinesthetic ability and felt handicapped. Others agreed, but added, "See what we do to our students who have to sit and just listen and look? Now we understand how they feel when learning something that is hard for them! For the first time, I realize that those must be the tactual/kinesthetic students!"

Throughout the semester, I used visual aids—Power Point transparencies, the chalkboard and overhead, films, charts, and graphs. I also taught them how to develop each set of materials through the materials themselves; for example, I gave them a CAP on how to write a CAP, a PLS for learning what PLSs included, and so forth. When I taught globally, I included anecdotes, samples, and humor. When I taught sequentially, I provided printed lists, outlines, and directions. Thus, I used approaches that were congruent to the processing styles of both global and analytic students who, based on the PEPS, were in my class.

Before receiving the PEPS information, some of my adult students were unaware of their need for an informal environment, intake, and comfortable seating and they remained in conventional seating throughout the semester. They may have been conditioned to learning in a traditional environment for too long a time to change. Nevertheless, they really were interested in the dichotomy between how they positioned themselves in graduate classes and how they studied at home. They *always* studied informally at home! That knowledge of their personal styles was fascinating to them and several suggested that they had succumbed to either their parents' or teachers' admonitions years before when they were young students. A few remembered resisting, but reported that they eventually had *given in*!

My students were required to administer the *Learning Style Inventory* (LSI) (Dunn, Dunn, & Price, 1990) to at least three of their students and provide a homework prescription (Dunn & Klavas, 1990) for each because several studies verified increased student achievement when using them (Doolan, 1999). As an added component (optional), teachers wrote about the learning-style strategies they had used with their students during that week. These are some of their comments.

- I adjusted the lights and allowed the kids to put their desks wherever they chose as long as they did not interfere with anyone else's style. I allowed intake and soft music during math. I asked the kids to bring pillows, cushions, or small rugs to sit on. To my amazement, they have been well behaved and *happy*.

- I allowed a few students to get out of their seats and quickly stretch during a lesson. I permitted others, who needed an informal design, to lie on the carpet in the back of the room and read—as long as they were quiet. During one social studies lesson, I allowed some tactual students to actually touch the globe during a map lesson.

- I tried approaching my global-processing students by turning off one bank of lights and reviewed what I was teaching on an overhead. To my surprise, the next day several asked if I would work with the overhead again. They had found it helpful!

- I've already enlisted the help of my school custodian and my husband to help re-design my classroom during the February break. I also moved some children's seats based on their requests. I had one student who asked to sit by himself at the back table, and I found that he now stays in his seat and talks less.

- This week, we discussed learning styles and changing the classroom. We also discussed how they "like" to do their homework. I tried using a global opening today and it seemed to work well. I told students to have their parents phone me if there were any problems—either from their point of view or the children's.

- This week we turned bookcases on their sides to create partitions and began constructing Flip Chutes. Tomorrow we will complete those and begin making small Flip Cards. Students are studying with those manipulatives more than they ever studied before.

- Yesterday, I decided to bring in a box of donuts for the first period class in which most are global learners. The majority had a donut but, to my surprise, none were distracted during the lesson. They seemed to pay more attention than usually. Had they skipped breakfast and merely needed nourishment? Were they just appreciative of the donuts? Was it the great lesson I had prepared? Or is there just something magical about responding to students' learning styles?

Throughout the semester the teachers would comment on how some students were performing better in class and on tests than before. These educators were now using the learning-style strategies and resources that I demonstrated in class. They freely discussed the problems of turning the lesson *control* over to the students but each week they continued to use new approaches.

This course was targeted to future educators who wanted to use research-based methods with their students. They designed and developed innovative instructional materials for individualizing instruction. After each session during the semester, they took the new strategies and materials that had been introduced and transferred the techniques and resources to their own classrooms at their own discretion.

Dunn and Dunn (1999) state that we need to improve the quality of teaching and help teachers become successful learners so that they, in turn, can model strategies for their students successfully. Perhaps now that these teachers are equipped with effective, researched strategies and resources, *all* students in their classrooms will use *their* minds and GOALS 2000 will become a reality.

Part III

Applications in Health-Related Professions

Chapter 16

Incorporating Learning Styles into the Curricula of Two Programs in a College of Health-Related Professions

Joyce A. Miller and Rose F. Lefkowitz

INTRODUCTION

College professors! Hear the clarion call! Imagine, for a moment, that you are a student in your own classroom. The professor is lecturing for about two hours and you are bonded to your seat required to listen. By nature, you are a visual and tactual learner and prefer to have some hands-on experience when learning new and difficult information. You want to see some videotapes, slides, and/or transparencies and the professor provides none. Maybe you would like to get a feel for the new material by manipulating models or touching the keyboard of a microcomputer. In this scenario, the professor is teaching, but is the student learning?

Are you aware that learning-styles-based teaching significantly improved the academic achievement and attitudes of college students (see Appendix I)? Despite a plethora of supportive research, on the college scene, acceptance of diversity among learners and the need to accommodate various styles has *not* been the rule. In fact, after identifying the learning styles of 109 undergraduate college students Miller, Alway, and McKinley (1987) recommended that faculty teach the students skills so that they could *adopt* a better learning style! That style may be *choice* has been negated by Restak (1991), Thies (1979), and Milgram, Dunn, and Price (1993), who argued that almost four-fifths of learning style is *biological* and further embedded in cultural norms. Learning-styles interventions also have been found to be effective in maintaining college enrollment (Nelson, et al., 1993) and for showing students how to study and do their homework through their style strengths (Lenehan et al., 1994).

However, in our College of Health-Related Professions, two programs,

Diagnostic Medical Imaging and Health Information Management, have implemented learning-style techniques with successful outcomes. This chapter describes how we incorporated learning styles into our curricula.

PART 1: DIAGNOSTIC MEDICAL IMAGING AS REPORTED BY JOYCE MILLER

In the Very Beginning

The students in this program were introduced to the concept of learning styles in an informal class discussion. I defined the construct of learning styles to them as Dunn and Dunn do—"the way in which individuals begin to concentrate on, process, internalize, and retain new and difficult information" (Dunn & Dunn, 1993, p. 2). After informally eliciting comments from students as to how they like to study, I presented the learning-style variables that comprise the Dunn and Dunn model. They found the illustrated description of the model very intriguing and volunteered to take a learning-styles assessment to identify their styles.

Identifying College Students' Learning Styles and How They Each Should Study

I tested each of my classes with the PEPS (Dunn, Dunn, & Price, 1991) and, when the students' individual printouts were returned, offered each an individual counseling session so that I could explain the results. I entered each student's standardized PEPS scores into the Dunn and Klavas (1990) Homework Disc—a computer software package that interprets individuals' PEPS profiles and prescribes printed guidelines for studying based on each person's learning-style strengths. Students were receptive to, and grateful for, these analyses. Some stated that they were aware of their learning style before the counseling session, but learned much more about how to capitalize on them. From the analysis of their strengths, I was able to offer them concrete and effective study options.

Interpretation of my students' PEPS printouts alerted me to the fact that many young adults in the program had styles very different from those ordinarily met by traditional college lectures. Some students had strong tactual, kinesthetic, and mobility preferences that certainly could not be addressed by my lectures—which are essentially effective only for auditory and visual learners. It immediately became clear that I had to incorporate at least some learning-styles theory into my teaching style!

Practical Applications of the Findings

I began to modify my lectures by beginning lessons tactually—with physical examination of anatomic models prior to discussion. I encouraged students to handle the equipment probes and to perform ultrasound scanning with the help of volunteer students in the laboratory. I then reinforced that introduction with a lecture and slide presentation on the topic by presenting the information to which my students previously had been exposed tactually and experientially. I permitted students to work on lab assignments according to their sociological preferences—either alone, in pairs, or groups of three. It immediately became apparent that the students were more attentive and more actively involved in the learning process.

I developed several Programmed Learning Sequences (PLSs), an instructional resource that is designed to present new and difficult information in small discrete steps to promote learning without direct supervision by an instructor. They are appropriate for students who prefer structure, a quiet environment, have visual strengths, prefer to learn individually or in a pair, and are motivated and persistent (Dunn & Dunn, 1993, 1999). I developed two PLSs for my ultrasound class—one in book format and the other in multimedia computerized format. The book PLS covered the topic of normal renal ultrasound and was entitled *Joe Montana Learns All About Passing—a Kidney Stone That Is!* In a humorous vein, the text described the anatomy of Montana's kidneys and the protocol for performing a sonogram. I included diagrams, sonograms, and many jokes (to which global learners respond). After each frame (page) of the material, the student was questioned about information that appeared on it, and then received immediate feedback from answers provided on the following frame.

The multimedia interactive PLS, entitled *A Saga of Footballs and Kidneys*, was a sequel that delved into the complex topic of renal pathology. It involved critical thinking skills that synthesized the anatomy and pathophysiology of renal diseases processes. This PLS began with Joe Montana being *pink-footballed* from his team, falling into a dream state, and being scanned for renal pathology by Sophie the Sonographer. I developed this resource using *Multimedia Toolbook* 3.0 by Assymetrix, a Windows-authoring package that creates multiple screen applications with pages in a book. More than 20 sonograms delineating various pathologies were scanned into the program, which also included graphics, diagrams, free-hand cartoons, puns, and rhymes.

For my cross-sectional anatomy course, I developed a book-format PLS entitled *Axial Anatomy of the Brain: Sam the Sonographer Sneaks a Snack at a Smorgasbord*. Beginning with a humorous introduction, the text content included a detailed anatomy of the brain using computerized tomography scans, diagrams, charts, cartoons, and jokes. Information was mastered by reading the text and accompanying illustrations, answering questions at the bottom of each frame, and seeing the immediate feedback . My students enjoyed the PLSs, especially the jokes! But even more important, they obtained excellent test scores that were significantly better than those recorded when they had studied traditionally (Miller, 1998).

We then assigned the task of constructing PLSs on various ultrasound topics to the students, who were permitted to work independently, in pairs, or groups of three. The results were astonishing! PLSs on heart disease, placentation, congenital birth defects, gallbladder pathology, maternal diabetes, and so forth, were designed that covered the topics thoroughly and in a most captivating manner. Two students, who previously were very quiet and laid back, spent over 100 hours developing a sophisticated computer PLS on the anatomy of the brain! We have incorporated student construction of learning-style resources into the course curriculum of our program. We obtained permission from the student developers to duplicate their materials for the benefit of future classes!

Learning-styles theory also has made our faculty aware of how important the physical environment is for optimal learning. To accommodate various styles in our scanning laboratory, we re-organized the equipment and resources to provide separate sections. In one corner, students can sit at formal library-type tables and chairs, whereas in another, students are able to lounge on a donated couch. We also permit snacking, as long as the students clean up and maintain a neat environment. One corner of the lab is dedicated as a media center that contains a slide projector, television, and videocassette recorder. Another corner of the lab was established for ultrasound scanning—to allow students to actually scan each other, or to work on assignments using the ultrasound simulator equipment. The lighting in the lab can be adjusted and adapted to different tasks.

For almost three decades, our program has graduated diagnostic medical sonographers who excel in both didactic and clinical experience. The learning-styles approaches we adopted resulted in even higher achievement outcomes and more positive students' attitudes (Miller, 1998).

PART 2: HEALTH INFORMATION MANAGEMENT AS REPORTED BY ROSE LEFKOWITZ

As a college professor, I have been teaching courses in health information management for over 17 years. Prior to 1990, I always lectured to my college students who, thus, were compelled to listen to everything I said in a traditional classroom setting. One very fortunate day, my colleague, Dr. Joyce Miller, asked if she could speak to my students on the topic of learning styles. At that time, Joyce was involved in a project on learning styles and sought my students' participation. Listening attentively to her presentation on the Dunn and Dunn Learning-Style Model, I decided to explore various methods of teaching to present my course content based on learning-style strategies. Further, I asked Joyce for some research studies on learning styles so that I could understand the concept in greater depth. The more I read, the more my interest and curiosity intensified. Then, after trying some of the learning-style-responsive strategies with my students and observing the positive effects on their classroom participation and grades, I enrolled in St. John's University's doctoral program to learn directly from the expert on styles—Professor Rita Dunn.

As Chapters 1 and 2 describe, the Dunn and Dunn Learning-Style Model impacts on multiple dimensions of both learning and teaching. It emphasizes that the classroom itself either stimulates or inhibits people's initial concentration and that whether people are analytic or global determines the way in which they take in (*process*) information, for example, from the facts to the concept or from a holistic understanding of the content to the facts. In addition, individuals' need for mobility, as opposed to being able to sit passively, and *with whom* they learn contribute to their ability to concentrate. The modality through which content is first introduced makes a difference as to how well the student grasps it and, even more important, retains the information for future application.

I realized that, as a typical college professor, I had expected my students to sit for three to four hours of didactic instruction and to master the content merely by listening and taking notes. And I had assumed that all students learned that way. However, their PEPS printouts evidenced how misinformed I had been! I have learned that, to help each student perform well, it is my responsibility as their professor to adjust my teaching style to respond to their learning styles. This is my story.

In the Beginning

My junior class in health information management received a short presentation on the background and supporting research on learning styles. Students voluntarily participated in completing the PEPS (Dunn, Dunn, & Price, 1991) to find exactly what their learning styles were. Each student was given a computer-generated printout that interpreted his/her particular style. The style profile was translated into an individual prescription generated by the Homework Disc (Dunn & Klavas, 1990) to enable the student to reinforce how to study and do homework outside the classroom setting. Each student was counseled to interpret the results—how to study and do homework, thereby maximizing learning potential in and outside of the classroom.

Next Steps

I kept a copy of each student's learning-style assessment and the group summary so that I could adjust my teaching methods to accommodate my students' learning styles. I rearranged the classroom to provide (a) a media center on one side so that individuals could use resources most responsive to their modality strengths, (b) round tables so that groups could interact at the other end of the room, (c) chairs and desks for students who wanted to work independently in formal seating, and (d) informal seating on a couch and lounge chairs that had been brought indoors for storage) for those students with this preference. My students' subsequent test scores demonstrated that they did not have to sit in neat rows to learn!

My teaching style varied according to the styles most present in each class. Using information in the individual printouts, I became aware of who was global and who was analytic. And, with the knowledge of each student's primary perceptual strength, I varied my teaching presentations accordingly. I used visuals, auditory material, tactual simulations in the microcomputer laboratory, and kinesthetic resources or actual experiences out in the field. Within just a week or two, it was evident that effective teaching is not necessarily lecturing to students but, rather, is introducing content in ways that help each student learn well and enjoy doing it!

Consider the Textbooks We Require

I then realized that the textbooks I had been requiring for my health information courses must have been written *by analytics* for *analytics*. Each chapter basically provided sequentially presented facts with none of the characteristics valued by global learners who comprised the majority in some of my classes; no anecdotes, no humor, no short summaries, and no connections with *their* lives! And these textbooks contained a significant portion of the material tested on national certifying examinations!

My students' PEPS group summaries indicated that many had visual and tactual strengths, were motivated, and needed structure. The best way to reach these students was an instructional resource known as PLSs, which is ideal for teaching those who need structure and have visual and tactual preferences (see Appendix H). It can be used to either introduce or reinforce knowledge or skills in a classroom, library, corridor, or in resource centers as well as at home, because it allows for each student's environmental and physical preferences (Dunn & Dunn, 1993, p. 203). But I had developed only one PLS on what I teach and had no free time to develop more. But there *was* a solution!

Overcoming Problems of Limited Resources and Time

I required that each student, individually or in a pair, by choice, select one chapter in the textbook and design an original PLS based on its content. I distributed instructions on the correct format for a PLS (Dunn & Dunn, 1993) and encouraged them to be as creative as possible. Their PLSs had to include:

• both an analytic and global title, to appeal to both types of learners;
• a humorous beginning story related to the content, to appeal to global learners;

- frame-by-frame structured presentation of information followed by questions and illustrated answers;
- visual/tactual periodic reinforcements, such as a word search, crossword puzzle, and tactual manipulatives.

Students developed excellent PLSs on the following topics.

- Content of the Mental Health Patient's Record: Use Your Head!
- Managing Health Information Management Department Personnel: Don't Get Personal with Personnel.
- Nomenclatures and Classification Systems: What's in a Name?
- Development and Content of the Hospital Medical Record: There Are None So Blind as Those Who Will Not Document.
- Legal Aspects of Medical Record Information: Unspeakable Acts.

Students' creativity amazed me. One student presented the PLS in the form of a diary and lock; its title was *The Legal Aspects of Medical Records Information: Record Dismissed.* The introductory story was in a *Dear Diary* format chronologically sequenced. The content of the chapter was well presented and well organized in a unique, entertaining style. Students created their PLSs directly from the textbook and, despite the complexity of the material, they really enjoyed doing this assignment. They mastered the chapter's content as they created the PLS and reinforced it with the hands-on resources that were required. Learning became an active process that continued from the classroom to the home—and back.

CONCLUSIONS

As a result of incorporating PLSs and learning-styles theory into the course, students increased their scores on examinations based upon the material learned in class and the development of their PLSs. They exchanged their creative projects and learned from each other. Furthermore, most projected more positive attitudes toward learning difficult material on health information. Learning styles proved to be the key to unlocking students' minds and enabled me, the professor, to reach each and cultivate his/her learning potential.

Part IV

Applications in Schools of Law, Engineering, and Liberal Arts

Chapter 17

Bringing Learning-Style Instructional Strategies to Law Schools: You Be the Judge!

Robin A. Boyle

"Here's a dime. Call your mother. Tell her there's serious doubt about your becoming a lawyer."

In the 1970s movie *The Paper Chase*, these words were proclaimed by an intimidating contracts professor to a weary law student surrounded by his classmates in a large lecture hall, insinuating that he should quit law school. Although exaggerated, the movie nonetheless reflected some truths about how law teaching has been conducted. It is true that many law students feel alienated by traditional law school teaching methods because of their impersonal nature, as the movie scene depicted (Guinier, Fine, Balin, Bartow, & Stachel, 1994; Teich, 1986). Law professors who teach to diverse learning styles among their student population will likely diminish negative student reactions to classroom learning.

TRADITIONAL TEACHING METHODS

It is also true that like the movie *The Paper Chase*, law professors at American law schools traditionally have used two teaching approaches—the case method and the Socratic method (Friedman, 1985, p. 610). In using the case method, the professor asks students to study individual court cases on a particular legal topic. Students are expected to construct from cases an understanding of the overarching legal principles and laws. Thus, in order to know the forest, students initially learn about each tree.

To arouse students' interest and to spark intellectual and analytical thinking about assigned cases, professors have used the Socratic method, which attempts to simulate the ancient Greek philosopher Socrates in a dialogue. In the law school context, as with Socrates, the dialogue occurs between the teacher and one student at a time. When the student has answered the teacher's questions to his or her satisfaction, then the teacher moves on to another student. The emphasis with Socratic method is to extract the substance of the lesson from the student, rather than to have the professor "feed" the information too easily.

Professors who use these instructional methods, to the exclusion of other methods, are neglecting the needs of many, if not most, of their students. For example, the case method is based upon the premise that all student audiences learn by piecing small concepts together into a bigger picture. Analytic learners prefer such a step-by-step approach (Dunn & Dunn, 1993, pp. 4–5, 47–48), and, therefore, the case method may be ideal for them. However, global learners do not share this preference, and instead excel when they understand the concept first and then concentrate on the details later (Dunn & Dunn, 1993, pp. 4–5, 47–48). The case method would not be the most effective teaching strategy for both types of students because it caters to analytics more than globals.

The Socratic method also is based on the premise that all students have high auditory strengths. However, few students possess high auditory strengths; many possess visual, tactual, or kinesthetic strengths (Dunn & Dunn, 1993, p. 143).

Reportedly, some law professors gradually have been employing non-traditional law teaching methods in their repertoires, such as group learning. For the most part, these professors have not been assessing their classes for their learning-style preferences. This author suggests that law professors continue to experiment with a variety of teaching methods that reach the majority of the learning-style preferences within their classes, and where possible, that law professors assess their students to become aware of their learning-style preferences. A learning-styles assessment reveals how one learns new and difficult material. The one used in this study is only one of many learning-styles assessment methods available.

OUR FINDINGS FROM LEARNING-STYLES ASSESSMENTS

In challenging these fundamental presumptions of both the case and Socratic methods, Dr. Rita Dunn and this author tested first-year law students in Legal Research and Writing classes in 1996 (see Tables 17.1 and 17.2), and in 1997 (see Tables 17.3 and 17.4) at St. John's University School of Law. We used the PEPS (Dunn, Dunn & Price, 1997) as the assessment instrument.

PEPS consists of 100 statements that elicit self-diagnostic responses on a five-point Likert scale, and can be taken in approximately 25 minutes. For

Table 17.1
Productivity Environmental Preference Survey: Group Results of 1996 Class, Standard Score of 40 or Below

PEPS Area	Subscale	Responses	Percentage
Noise Level	1	16	21.05
Light	2	12	15.79
Temperature	3	9	11.84
Design	4	14	18.42
Motivation	5	10	13.16
Persistent	6	4	5.26
Responsible	7	19	25.00
Structure	8	1	1.32
Learning Alone/Peer Oriented	9	23	30.26
Authority Figures Present	10	4	5.26
Learn in Several Ways	11	3	3.95
Auditory	12	4	5.26
Visual	13	9	11.84
Tactile	14	4	5.26
Kinesthetic	15	5	6.58
Requires Intake	16	8	10.53
Evening-Morning	17	28	36.84
Late Morning	18	21	27.63
Afternoon	19	1	1.32
Needs Mobility	20	5	6.58

Number of Students 76
Total Responses 200

instance, one statement reads, "I prefer working in bright light." The student would then fill in one of the following circles: strongly disagree, disagree, uncertain, agree, or strongly agree. The data collected from that assessment yields a computerized profile of each individual's preferred learning style. A software package (Dunn & Klavas, 1990) then analyzes each individual's preferred learning style based on the PEPS computerized profiles.

Tables 17.1 and 17.3 indicate students' responses on the PEPS revealing low preferences for the specified categories. For example, these tables show the percentage of students who strongly prefer no background noise—or quiet—while learning new and difficult material. On the PEPS scale used to measure this population, students who scored a 40 or below indicated that they strongly did not prefer each of the elements assessed (such as structure or mobility). Learning alone, temperature, and time-of-day are the exceptions to the rule.

Tables 17.2 and 17.4 indicate students' responses on the PEPS that have a high preference for the specified categories. For example, they show the percentage of students who strongly preferred background sound while

Table 17.2
Productivity Environmental Preference Survey: Group Results of 1996 Class,
Standard Score of 60 or Above

PEPS Area	Subscale	Responses	Percentage
Noise Level	1	14	18.42
Light	2	18	23.68
Temperature	3	15	19.74
Design	4	14	18.42
Motivation	5	8	10.53
Persistent	6	7	9.21
Responsible	7	12	15.79
Structure	8	51	67.11
Learning Alone/Peer Oriented	9	8	10.53
Authority Figures Present	10	18	23.68
Learn in Several Ways	11	4	5.26
Auditory	12	20	26.32
Visual	13	6	7.89
Tactile	14	16	21.05
Kinesthetic	15	12	15.79
Requires Intake	16	20	26.32
Evening-Morning	17	2	2.63
Late Morning	18	6	7.89
Afternoon	19	43	56.58
Needs Mobility	20	19	25.00

Number of Students 76
Total Responses 313

learning new and difficult material. On the PEPS scale used to measure this population, students who scored a 60 or above indicated that they strongly preferred each of the elements assessed (such as light or temperature).

The remainder of the students, who expressed no strong preferences for particular elements, received scores ranging between 41 and 59 for those elements; these scores were not presented in the tables because they are less significant for purposes of this study. Twenty elements were assessed, and they are listed in each table.

The 76 students from the class of 1996 were divided into three class sections, two of which were taught by this author (Boyle & Dunn, 1998). The 42 students from the class of 1997 were divided into two class sections, both of which were taught by this author. Each class section met once a week for 21 weeks, spanning two semesters. Class sections generally ranged in size from 25 to 35 students for the Legal Research and Writing course.

Our findings showed that the law school populations, for both 1996 and 1997, were diverse in their learning-style characteristics. Therefore, using the same teaching method for all students would be ineffective—whether the Socratic method, case method, or straight lecture were used.

Table 17.3
Productivity Environmental Preference Survey: Group Results of 1997 Class,
Standard Score of 40 or Below

PEPS Area	Subscale	Responses	Percentage
Noise Level	1	1	2.38
Light	2	5	11.90
Temperature	3	5	11.90
Design	4	5	11.90
Motivation	5	5	11.90
Persistent	6	4	9.52
Responsible	7	10	23.81
Structure	8	1	2.38
Learning Alone/Peer Oriented	9	9	21.43
Authority Figures Present	10	1	2.38
Learn in Several Ways	11	2	4.76
Auditory	12	1	2.38
Visual	13	5	11.90
Tactile	14	2	4.76
Kinesthetic	15	0	0.00
Requires Intake	16	1	2.38
Evening-Morning	17	17	40.48
Late Morning	18	7	16.67
Afternoon	19	1	2.38
Needs Mobility	20	2	4.76

Number of Students 42
Total Responses 84

For instance, in the 1996 and the 1997 classes, students with high auditory preference ranged between 26.32 percent (Table 17.2) and 28.57 percent (Table 17.4). Only 25 percent of high auditory students will remember 75 percent of what they hear in a normal 40- or 50-minute lecture (Dunn & Dunn, 1993, p. 402). Additionally, the Socratic method would be even less effective for the remaining 75 percent of the students who are not high auditory. The Socratic method's premise, which is that *all* students learn by listening to answers given by other students, conflicts with the PEPS results indicating that approximately 8 students out of our total population of 118 would internalize and retain the oral exchange between teacher and classmates. For the same reasons, straight lecture would be less effective for a majority of the students as well.

Traditional law school instructional methods do not aim to reach high tactual nor kinesthetic students. These students would be disadvantaged in a traditional law school classroom where high visual and auditory strengths would be advantageous. In our population, there was a sizable percentage of both high tactual and kinesthetic students (Tables 17.2 and 17.4). Students who were high tactual ranged from 21.05 percent (Table 17.2) to

Table 17.4
Productivity Environmental Preference Survey: Group Results of 1997 Class,
Standard Score of 60 or Above

PEPS Area	Subscale	Responses	Percentage
Noise Level	1	5	11.90
Light	2	10	23.81
Temperature	3	12	28.57
Design	4	9	21.43
Motivation	5	4	9.52
Persistent	6	4	9.52
Responsible	7	3	7.14
Structure	8	20	47.62
Learning Alone/Peer Oriented	9	5	11.90
Authority Figures Present	10	14	33.33
Learn in Several Ways	11	2	4.76
Auditory	12	12	28.57
Visual	13	3	7.14
Tactile	14	10	23.81
Kinesthetic	15	5	11.90
Requires Intake	16	16	38.10
Evening-Morning	17	5	11.90
Late Morning	18	6	14.29
Afternoon	19	23	54.76
Needs Mobility	20	14	33.33

Number of Students 42
Total Responses 182

23.81 percent (Table 17.4). Students who were high kinesthetic ranged from 11.90 percent (Table 17.4) to 15.79 percent (Table 17.2).

In our population, we found that at least 20 percent were global processors and 20 percent were analytic. The case method approach is not particularly effective for the globals because it focuses predominantly on minute details of cases with less emphasis on the synthesis of legal principles. Therefore, the case method would not be an effective instructional approach for the majority of students.

TEACHING TO DIVERSE LEARNING STYLES

Due to the diversity of learning-style preferences in our law school population, I gradually began to incorporate new instructional methods for my classes. These new methods were more tactual, visual, and kinesthetic, and less auditory. I also added methods that aid students with high preferences for structure, mobility, small-group learning, and the presence of an authority figure.

There are two reasons why I began to move away from straight lecture, and from the case and Socratic method approaches. First, the meta-analytic research on teaching to diverse learning styles in undergraduate schools revealed impressive academic-achievement gains (Dunn, Griggs, Olson, Gorman, & Beasley, 1995). Second, I realized that my own students were disengaged from the traditional law school teaching methods that I was employing.

I discovered that my students would do the graded written and research assignments, but they either were not doing their weekly reading assignments in preparation for class, or were doing the readings but had not sufficiently absorbed the key concepts. This led to increasing tension between them and me during classes. When I attempted to engage them in the Socratic-method format of asking questions, very few hands were raised to offer answers. When I called upon students, their answers were either non-responsive or ranged from poor to average. I tried various carrot-and-stick tactics to encourage my students to be prepared for class, such as extra credit for participation, but none of these tactics worked.

The PEPS data supported my growing personal observation that my students were non-responsive. In both the 1996 and the 1997 populations, the percentage of students with high visual strengths was less than 8 percent (Tables 17.2 & 17.4). This indicated that even if all my students did their homework readings, a significant percentage would not readily absorb and remember the material (Dunn & Dunn, 1993, p. 407). Even visual learners remember only 75 percent of what they read or see (Dunn & Dunn, 1993, p. 402), and therefore, only a tiny percentage of our law school populations would remember 75 percent of what they read for homework.

I also observed that my students needed me constantly. They asked me questions frequently in my office and in class. I rarely ended a class without several students approaching me for clarification of the lecture. For a while, it felt good to be needed by my students, but after teaching the course for four years, their demands became exhausting. I also wondered why students were not grasping the fundamental concepts from their readings or class experiences.

Again, the PEPS data supported my observations. Large percentages of my students preferred structure, ranging from 47.62 percent (Table 17.4) to 67.11 percent (Table 17.2), in contrast with a small percentage of students who preferred low structure (choices), ranging from 1.32 percent (Table 17.1) and 2.38 percent (Table 17.3). Significant percentages in both populations, ranging between 23.68 percent (Table 17.2) and 33.33 percent (Table 17.4), also preferred working with an authority figure. The data demonstrated that my guidance would benefit a large percentage of my students.

THE *QUIZ* STRATEGY

To relieve classroom tension and to ensure that students were absorbing the materials, I changed my instructional strategies. One new instructional strategy that I developed was the *Quiz*. Rather than asking my students questions in class and expecting them to engage in Socratic dialogue, I prepared written questions, from their homework readings, that covered the same material. An example of such a *Quiz* is in Appendix F.

The *Quiz* theoretically could cover any range of questions. For example, on the topic of writing an argument for a legal brief, one *Quiz* question asked where in the argument the student/lawyer should address a case whose outcome is adverse to the position of his or her client. The proper answer, as gleaned from the assigned legal writing text, was that the adverse case should be addressed after the author has sufficiently presented favorable cases for his or her client.

The *Quiz* was the first in-class exercise I would use in a two-hour class session. I announced it as an Open-Book *Quiz*. I relieved any anxiety the students had upon hearing *Quiz* by telling them it would not be graded and that I would not ask to see their answers; however, *Quiz* impressed upon them its importance. For those who had done the reading and could potentially feel frustrated by the repetition of information, I explained that this *Quiz* should *reinforce* concepts from their reading.

Thus, I gave them both structure for the exercise and an enticement to do it by forewarning them that they would be called upon to provide their answers after a set period of time (usually 20 minutes). To accommodate those with small-group preferences as well as those who preferred to work alone, I gave them the option of working in groups or independently.

While the students were working with their books and writing their answers, I walked around the classroom to see if any needed help. Those who preferred to work with an authority figure, took advantage of my approach to their desks.

The students appeared to have fun with the quizzes. Quizzes provided those with high tactual strengths, of which I had significant percentages, an opportunity to use their hands while flipping through their books and writing answers. For those with moderate to low auditory strengths, of which I also had significant percentages, this exercise provided them with written answers that they could retain and refer to when necessary.

When their time expired, I asked for volunteers to provide answers. More students volunteered their written answers from the *Quiz* than had responded to my oral questions in prior classes. In fact, students seemed to feel more confident having researched the questions and having the written answers in front of them. They also joked with each other, and in proper balance with the seriousness of the subject matter, the humor confirmed that the *Quiz* was a successful learning tool.

I reinforced the material by going over the *Quiz* answers orally. I gave them oral feedback on their *Quiz* answers; this helped to provide structure and was appreciated by those with auditory strengths. In addition, at the conclusion of the exercise, I gave the students written answers to take home and use when preparing their longer research and writing assignments. An example of answers to a *Quiz* is found in Appendix G. From start to finish, the *Quiz* and its oral reinforcement took approximately 45 minutes.

THE *PRACTICAL APPLICATION* STRATEGY

For the remainder of class, I gave the students a Practical Application of the legal writing principles that were covered by the *Quiz* by assigning the Practical Application, in-class exercises from their required legal writing text-book. Generally, the assignment provided a fact pattern of a legal case, which the students would read silently (if it was long) or aloud (if it was short). Questions about the assigned legal writing principles for that class followed the fact pattern. These questions involved using more critical thinking skills than the *Quiz*; students had to apply the legal writing principles they learned from the *Quiz* to a hypothetical client problem.

For example, I directed the students to read excerpts from trial court documents regarding a hypothetical lawsuit brought by parents of a child who played with a chemistry set that exploded. Students also read excerpts from related case decisions. Then they were asked to construct elements of an appellate brief for the injured child's parents who were seeking a remedy in torts, and for the manufacturer in its defense. Students were asked questions such as "What is your client's strongest issue?" They also were asked about topics they could include in an argument for the manufacturer on appeal (Dernbach et al., p. 249).

As with the *Quiz*, the students were given a time frame, told that they could work with others or independently, and were asked to write their answers to the assigned questions. I sometimes left the room for a few minutes to allow students to collaborate with each other comfortably. If time allowed, I copied their answers onto a transparency and projected it on an overhead for the class to critique. If we had a lot of time, I had them write their answers on the blackboard. Alternately, if short on time, I had them give their answers orally.

The Practical Application usually brought some excitement to the class. There often was more debating and joking among students with this exercise than the *Quiz* because there was more room for opinion and for them to demonstrate their knowledge. If it did not take too much class time—nor detract from the seriousness of the material—humor made the learning process enjoyable. It also made the students feel more comfortable with me as a collegial authority figure. Students often said that this exercise gave them a break from the traditional teaching methods that occurred in their other doctrinal courses, which I perceived as a compliment.

From a learning-styles perspective, the application exercise was visual (reading the fact pattern/questions and viewing work of others), tactual (writing), auditory (listening to the answers provided by others), and kin-esthetic (moving around the classroom to write on the blackboards and to engage in peer-group discussions). I always provided feedback when reviewing their written or oral answers, and this accommodated those with a need for structure. Students also asked me questions as the exercise progressed, providing an opportunity to supply further structure.

ADDITIONAL INSTRUCTIONAL STRATEGIES

There were a few other techniques that I incorporated to make the classroom experience one that reached as many students as possible. For the global learners, I tried to smile, be pleasant, and provide some humor when I began my class. Admittedly, I am not a stand-up comic. At the least, I tried to engage the full class so that its members could respond as a group. For instance, I would ask loudly and with enthusiasm, "How is your research assignment progressing?" Often, I heard groans; sometimes I heard positive remarks. I would take this a step further and lightly comment. From there, I would launch into a few serious sentences about the topic for the day.

For global students, I overviewed what I had planned for the class, although I assumed that this would make the analytics secure in the knowledge that I have a lesson plan (law school evaluations rate whether students believe their teacher is organized). For those who needed mobility, I provided a 10-minute break in the middle of my two-hour session. But for those who needed extensive mobility, I told students that they could take a break as soon as we got to the application exercise, usually 45 minutes into class. When they voluntarily divided into groups, I let them move around and congregate.

These new approaches appeared to be successful. In the students' recently graded assignments, I saw a significant improvement in that they all grasped the legal writing principles that we covered in class, as opposed to the prior papers in which significant numbers of students missed key concepts. In addition, students stopped crowding my desk after class with questions about what I had just covered. In the past, many had sought my advice in conferences about getting started because they felt lost before beginning to write. Now when students visit me in conference, they arrive with prepared written materials and are seeking my critique. Dramatically, the classroom tension has dissipated. Hopefully, students will feel more enthusiastic about learning legal research and writing because class time is more comfortable, productive, and nurturing.

The high percentage of tactual students in the 1996 and 1997 populations has inspired me to collaborate with a graduate student, Lynne Dolle, who is earning a doctoral degree in Instructional Leadership from St. John's University. Together, we are exploring ways to teach legal research effectively, using structured PLSs for visual and tactual learners (Dunn & Dunn,

1992, 1993, 1999). The results of our study will be reflected in Ms. Dolle's forthcoming dissertation.

CONCLUSION

My observations, supported by the PEPS results, have led me to conclude that straight lecture, the case method, and the Socratic method are not effective instructional strategies for significant percentages of the legal writing classes that I teach in a law school. When I used in-class exercises that were tactual, visual, auditory, and kinesthetic, my students responded positively. These in-class experiences have proven to be both enjoyable and effective for *all* students.

Chapter 18

Meeting the Academic Challenges of an Undergraduate Engineering Curriculum

Joanne Ingham

INTRODUCTION

Chris was accepted into the Electrical Engineering program at a competitive engineering university with a scholarship. He was ranked in the top 10 percent of his high school class, had earned a 90 average and was considered smart in science and math. However, despite his track record, Chris ended up on academic probation after his first semester at college. Chris had never learned to study new and difficult information; he had never been challenged academically. The academic work in high school was so easy for him that his study skills never were developed. He would boast about how little time he spent studying or writing papers. After completing the Academic Skills Seminar that helped Chris learn about his individual learning-style strengths, his second semester grades were significantly better because his approach to learning new and difficult information was dramatically changed.

Approximately 25 percent of the freshman class at an engineering university were placed on academic probation each year. Students remaining on probation for more than one semester often were disqualified or withdrawn. Tinto (1993) reported that many students leave college as a result of unclear individual goals or intentions, a lack of connectedness with the institution, or academic underachievement. Tinto (1993) further suggested that by identifying the problems students encounter and offering appropriate interventions, an increase in persistence might result.

Several interventions with students on probation have been described with varied course content including study skills, time management, goal setting, and career orientation (Carver & Smart, 1985; Lipsky & Ender, 1990; Newton, 1990). Programs were based upon differing theoretical frameworks (Coleman & Freedman, 1996; Simmons, Wallins, & George, 1995). Studies also have been conducted exploring self-efficacy and academic success (Astin, 1993; Hackett, Casas, Betz, & Rocha-Singh, 1992; House, 1993; Quilter, 1995; Wilhite, 1990). Brown, Lent, and Larkin (1989) documented the interactions between aptitude and self-efficacy. Results indicated that strong academic self-concept was particularly important to the success of moderate-ability students and also were predictive of persistence and good grades in the sciences and engineering.

Researchers have examined meta-cognitive approaches using awareness of individual students' learning styles as the focus (Clay, 1984; Lenehan, Dunn, Ingham, Murray, & Signer, 1994; Nelson, Dunn, Griggs, Primavera, Fitzpatrick, Bacilious, & Miller, 1993). Previous experimental research with learning styles was conducted in the undergraduate content areas of math (Dunn, Bruno, Sklar, & Beaudry, 1990), marketing (Dunn, Deckinger, Withers, & Katzenstein, 1990), education and nursing (Buell & Buell, 1987), study skills (Napolitano, 1986), anatomy (Cook, 1989), and biology (Miller, 1998). In addition, Marsh and Craven (1997) suggested providing learning opportunities *within programs* to complement the individuals' preferred learning styles.

This engineering university provides freshmen with information on learning styles and maintains a supportive educational climate. Freshmen are introduced to learning-styles concepts in Freshman Orientation Seminar. These new students complete the PEPS (Dunn, Dunn, & Price, 1993) and are provided with an explanation of their individual learning-style profiles. Older students in difficulty, who want to learn more about their strengths, also are assessed. From the first moment students enter the classroom they are provided with information about how to learn.

Students can request tutoring through the Learning Center on an individual basis, small- group review sessions, and large-group exam reviews. Students are encouraged to explore the library and find a place where they can study productively. The library provides varied settings for studying. There are beanbag chairs in one corner where classical music softly plays. There is always an art exhibit on display, plants for ambiance, and a fish tank for relaxation. Some may select the solitary study carrels on the opposite side of the room where it is quiet. There are soft couches in the center area for small-group discussions, as well as tables and chairs for those requiring a more formal setting. Students also are permitted to talk softly and to bring in snacks to munch on while concentrating on their work.

The campus provides varied settings and support services enabling students to work in ways that complement their learning-style preferences. The *challenge* is to open students' eyes to the choices they make and to encourage them to develop the study skills and habits required for success at a university with a very demanding curriculum. Unfortunately, some students fail first, before their eyes, ears, and minds are open to exploring who they are as learners. The Academic Skills Seminar is one program that appears to provide the vehicle for academic self-awareness and an opportunity to explore individual learning-style differences.

THE ACADEMIC SKILLS SEMINAR HISTORY

In December 1993, the University Retention Team proposed the creation of an Academic Skills Seminar designed to help students in danger of being retained. Statistics collected over a five-year period indicated that students who had achieved less than a 2.0 cumulative grade-point average for more than one semester were at risk for withdrawing or disqualification. The persistence rates of 82 first-year students, placed on academic probation in spring 1993, were tracked for a two-year period. After two years, four students (5%) remained in good standing, 16 (19%) continued on probation, 12 (15%) were disqualified, and 50 (61%) withdrew from school. To address this concern, the Academic Skills Seminar was proposed.

The faculty approved the Seminar in October 1994 as a non-credit, eight-week, one-hour-per-week course open to all first-time probationary students and *required* of all first-year, first-time probationary students. The Academic Skills Seminar was taught as a formal course for the first time during the spring 1995 semester. All sections of the Seminar were taught by this author; students were evaluated on a pass/fail basis.

The curriculum is shaped by individual self-examination of learning-style preferences and strengths. Weekly meetings consist of group discussions on topics including identifying what went wrong, setting short- and long-term goals, study skills, time management techniques, and stress management. Activities also were included to increase students' knowledge of careers in engineering and motivational strategies to shape short-term and long-term goals.

In addition to assigned readings and small-group experiences, weekly journal entries were required to enhance and develop their self-awareness as learners. Invited guest speakers included former probation students who had succeeded in graduating and in securing work as engineers. The lively discussions covered a host of survival strategies proven successful to the guests. These discussions often were reported by students as very helpful and highly motivating. A final paper was required that asked students to synthesize the insights they gained about themselves as learners and what steps they had taken to be more academically successful.

SUBJECTS

A total of 261 undergraduate freshman students were included in this evaluation report. Students attending this engineering institution were

Table 18.1
Registration Status of Students Registered for the Academic Skills Seminar, Spring 1995 through Spring 1997

	Passed Seminar		Failed Seminar		Total	
Students Registered as of 6/97	113	(43%)	28	(11%)	141	(54%)
Students Disqualified	27	(10%)	33	(13%)	60	(23%)
Students Withdrawn or Not Registered	46	(18%)	14	(5%)	60	(23%)
Total	186	(71%)	75	(29%)	261	(100%)

drawn from high schools in the New York metropolitan area. They tended to be first in their families to attend college, were from middle- to low-income families, and were ethnically diverse. They typically had been within the top 10 percent of their high school graduating classes and had obtained average combined SAT scores over 1100.

A TWO-YEAR ANALYSIS OF THE ACADEMIC SKILLS SEMINAR, SPRING 1995 THROUGH SPRING 1997

This evaluation is based on data for 261 undergraduate students registered for the Academic Skills Seminar during the spring and fall semesters since spring 1995. To determine the relative success of this seminar, the following basic questions were posed:

- Do students who complete the Seminar persist?
- Do students who complete the Seminar return to and remain in good academic standing?
- Do students who complete the Seminar demonstrate higher grade-point averages?
- Has the Academic Skills Seminar impacted retention rates among first-year probation students?

Please note that students completing the seminar during the spring 1995 semester would be entering their fourth year at the university so, consequently, no graduation data are available at the time of this submission.

1. Do students who complete the Seminar persist at the university? Table 18.1 reports the registration status of all students who enrolled in the Academic Skills Seminar during the two-year period beginning in Spring 1995 as reported by the Registrar's Office, June 1997.

A number of observations about student persistence can be made. Students who passed the Seminar persisted at a greater percentage rate (43% vs. 11%) than those who failed the seminar. Of those freshmen placed on

Table 18.2
Academic Standing of Students Registered in Academic Skills Seminar, Spring
1995 through Spring 1997

Academic Standing	Total
Academic Warning	2 (1%) *2 Pass**
Initial Probation	23 (9%) *18 Pass/ 5 Fail***
Continued Probation	77 (30%) *55 Pass/ 22 Fail*
Final Probation	40 (15%) *31 Pass/ 9 Fail*
Disqualified	60 (23%) *27 Pass/ 33 Fail*
Dean's List (GPA > 3.4)	3 (1%) *3 Pass*
Returned to Good Academic Standing	33 (13%) *28 Pass/ 5 Fail*
Maintained Good Standing	23 (8%) 22 Pass/ 1 Fail
Total	261 (100%) *186 Pass/ 75 Fail*

*Passed Seminar; **Failed Seminar.

probation during this period, 54 percent persisted overall. Students who passed the Seminar were disqualified less frequently (10% vs. 13%) than those who failed the Seminar.

Students who passed the seminar left or withdrew at a slightly higher percentage than those who failed. Perhaps the experiences and insights gained in the Seminar triggered these students to transfer to a less academically rigorous college or transfer to a different academic major and return to being a *big fish in a little pond*. Some chose to go to work full-time.

2. Do students who complete the Seminar return to and remain in good standing? Table 18.2 provides the academic standing of the Seminar students as of June 1997. The academic standing descriptors indicate relative length of time on probation. Students in difficulty typically pass through a series of levels of probation. Academic standing is evaluated at the end of each academic semester. Maintaining good standing indicates that students have achieved a cumulative grade-point average of at least 2.0 for a year or more.

Of those registered for the Seminar, 22 percent were in good academic standing, while 78 percent continued on probation. Those remaining on probation might require more than one semester to sufficiently raise their grade-point average above the 2.0 level. The disqualified students (23%)

Table 18.3
Mean Cumulative Grade Point Average (GPA) of Students Who Passed or
Failed Academic Skills Seminar, Spring 1995 through Spring 1997

	Passed Seminar	Failed Seminar
Mean Cumulative Grade Point Average (GPA)	1.87	1.33
Median GPA	1.93	1.41
Minimum GPA	.16	0.00
Maximum GPA	3.43	2.36
Count	186	75

earned grade-point averages substantially below minimal levels required by the university.

In all academic-standing categories, the number of students passing the Seminar was higher than the number failing, except in the category of disqualification. Those whose performance was very poor also tended to be those who did not complete the basic requirements of the Seminar to earn a passing grade.

3. Do students who complete the Seminar demonstrate higher grade-point averages than students who do not complete the Seminar? Table 18.3 reports the mean cumulative grade-point averages of students who either passed or failed the Seminar.

Table 18.4 indicates the results of a t-test to determine if the difference between the mean GPA of students who passed the Seminar was significantly different from the mean GPA of students who failed the Seminar.

Students who passed the Academic Skills Seminar achieved a significantly higher cumulative grade-point average (.54 on 4.0 scale) than students who failed the Seminar.

4. Has the Academic Skills Seminar impacted retention rates among first-time probation freshmen when comparing pre-seminar probation freshmen retention rates and post-seminar probation freshmen? Table 18.5 reports the comparative academic status of pre-seminar and post-seminar freshmen who were on probation.

The persistence rate among freshmen on probation increased by 7.6 percent after the introduction of the Academic Skills Seminar. Further, the persistence rate for freshmen on probation who passed the Seminar increased by 11.5 percent as compared to the two years prior to its inception.

DISCUSSION

Students are required to write a final paper reflecting on their learning strengths and defining what they need to do to be academically successful

Table 18.4
t-Test: Two Samples Assuming Unequal Variances*

	Passed Seminar	Failed Seminar
Mean	1.87	1.33
Variance	0.26	0.47
Observations	186	75
df	111	
t Stat	6.10**	

*Results of the F-test revealed a significant difference between the reported variance of the groups. Therefore, the t-test for unequal variance was employed.
**$p < .05$.

Table 18.5
Comparative Persistence Rates of Freshmen on Probation Before and After the Seminar Intervention Was Institutionalized

	Spring 1993 Freshmen on Probation, 1992-1994 Persistence Rate Pre-Seminar	Spring 1995 Freshmen on Probation, 1995-1997 Persistence Rate Post-Seminar	Spring 1995 Freshmen on Probation Who Passed Seminar 1995-1997 Persistence Rate
First-Year Probation Students Who Persisted	20 (23.7%)	26 (31.3%)	25 (35.2%)
Disqualified	12 (14.6%)	23 (27.7%)	15 (21.1%)
Withdrew	50 (60.9%)	34 (40.9%)	31 (43.6%)
Total	82 (100%)	83 (100%)	71 (100%)

at the university. These final papers were placed on file and provided insights into the qualitative and human side of academic life at the university. Students described their overwhelming sense of feeling "stupid" after finding out that they had been placed on probation. Many had never failed a course before, let alone failed a semester at college. They believed that their peers were brilliant and that they were the only freshman failing. Upon walking into the Seminar the first day of classes and finding they were among a classroom full of freshmen who had failed, they reported feeling much better about themselves as students. Hearing other students who failed speak about their eventual success was reported as giving them hope and providing motivation to tackle a new semester. They reported that the weekly discussions helped them achieve their short-term goals for the semester. Some found the weekly meetings helpful reminders that they were on probation and provided the impetus to keep them on track academically.

Students also reported that becoming more aware of their learning-style strengths and reconsidering how, where, and with whom they studied were valuable strategies. Many attributed their eventual success to this information.

In summary, data suggest that the Academic Skills Seminar should be continued as a supportive freshman program. Students who complete the seminar earn grade-point averages significantly higher than those students who fail the course. Further, probation students were retained at a higher percentage rate after the Academic Skills Seminar was introduced, as compared with a control group. Clearly, these significant results speak to the rewards reaped by the university when these at-risk students are provided a supportive program in which they are taught how to learn and how to navigate a rigorous engineering curriculum. The students report their feelings of being empowered to learn and their increased sense of self-esteem. Their patterns of persisting in the engineering program hopefully will enhance their behaviors as life-long learners.

Chapter 19

The Writing Portfolio as a Learning-Styles Tool in a College English-as-a-Second-Language Course

Herbert D. Pierson

INTRODUCTION

Early in the fall semester, one of my students, an immigrant from the former Soviet Union, unexpectedly brought her 10-year-old son to the university because she had to take him to the doctor immediately after class. The youngster sat next to his mother seemingly absorbed in drawing, writing, and reading—unaware of the class dynamics. However, a few days later I discovered he hadn't been so oblivious to what was going on in the class. He astutely observed that, while I was conducting the lecture and discussion, neither his mother nor her classmates had raised their hands; he scolded her for "not knowing the answers!" I felt that, in a very poignant way, I had witnessed a modern version of the learning-styles generation gap.

Why I thought this way went back to graduate school during the early 1970s when one of my professors first introduced the concept of learning styles and I had found it interesting. However, once I returned to the daily demands of teaching large English-as-a-Second-Language (ESL) classes, with piles of papers to edit and grade, I had fewer moments to reflect on the earlier enthusiasms and idealism of graduate days. Learning styles were lost from memory or simply eclipsed by the daily routine of teaching. Although the tenets of learning styles were far from my consciousness, the instinctive way I taught my classes and questioned fixed ideas about instructional practices were evidence to me that those rich concepts from graduate school were deeply rooted, only waiting to be actualized at the proper time.

After years of teaching, I now realize that I have been on a joyous intellectual journey that has led me back to the great ideas of graduate school.

I now have a more mature understanding of what I was once taught and believed and have become a practitioner of learning styles.

I owe much to the work of Joy Reid (1995) and Lynn O'Brien (1989) for this understanding. I am deeply indebted to the work of Rita Dunn and Ken Dunn who, through their learning-style model and workshops, have not only led me to a deeper appreciation of the potential of learning styles for my students, but also to its potential for my academic discipline ((Dunn & Dunn, 1993). This, in turn, has produced a new confidence and enthusiasm for my work as a college ESL teacher.

As I continue to deepen my understanding of learning-styles theory and practice, I am resolved to engage in action research guided by the learning-style model. However, in this chapter I describe, in practical terms, how a learning-styles philosophy has been impacting on my present teaching. I demonstrate how, through a learning-styles approach, I have converted an innovative instructional and assessment tool—process-writing portfolios, into a learning-styles tool. I do this with reference to my own academic department and show how a learning-styles approach can significantly enhance instruction and make it more productive and rewarding.

Based on my own experiences during the past few years, I show how an understanding and acceptance of key elements in the learning-styles philosophy have helped my college-level ESL students use learning styles in compiling their individual process-writing portfolios and, ultimately, become better writers.

THE CONTEXT

To put this chapter in context, I briefly say something about the teaching department and university where I teach. Since my university is located in New York City, one of the largest urban immigrant centers in the nation, it naturally attracts a culturally diverse student body, as well as a number of international students. The university has a tradition, dating back 100 years, of having educated waves of immigrant children who settled in the New York's metropolitan area. In the early years, this implied a focus on students from Roman Catholic families. However, with the huge demographic changes that metropolitan New York has experienced during the past 30 years, this mission has been extended significantly to embrace immigrant and foreign students of every conceivable ethnic and religious background. A typical cohort is comprised of foreign and international students who emigrated from China, Taiwan, Hong Kong, Macao, Russia, Columbia, Poland, India, Indonesia, Iran, Iraq, Africa, Vietnam, Ecuador, the Ukraine, Israel, Chile, Korea, Japan, Brazil, and the Philippines, and is now in the ESL Program.

The academic English-language needs of these matriculated international students, who usually are limited speakers of English, are met by my department in a credit-bearing program that offers advanced and intermediate courses in writing and speaking. The aim of these courses is to prepare students to meet the academic demands of regular university study. Thus students are assigned to courses on the basis of their performance in the department's placement test. In addition, international students are permitted to enroll concurrently in content courses in their major field of study while taking the credit-bearing ESL courses.

WRITING PORTFOLIOS AS LEARNING-STYLES TOOLS

Although I have been inspired by my deeper understanding of learning styles, I deliberately decided not to engage in that area of research for the time being. Rather, I decided to observe, listen, and learn. Nevertheless, I was motivated to integrate a learning-styles approach and philosophy into the process-writing portfolio activities of my students. The portfolios would be the means by which I integrated learning styles into my writing classes at the intermediate and advanced levels.

To encourage a learning-styles approach among my student writers, I introduced the process-writing portfolios to them. Originally, I required my students to maintain writing portfolios as a convenient filing system. Later, I used it as an auxiliary assessment tool to showcase or store exemplary work, just in case a good student did not pass the exit test at the end of each semester.

The process-writing portfolios differ from storage portfolios in that they help student writers become more aware of themselves as writers. Process portfolios encourage student writers to recognize their strengths and identify areas of needed improvement because, as we will see further on, they encourage student reflection about the whole—or part of the—writing process.

Process-writing portfolios also differ from the fine arts, exemplary, or résumé portfolios in that they consist of only products of outstanding achievement, whereas the process-writing portfolios consist of everything students write as they move toward becoming better writers. The process-writing portfolio is an instructional tool that manifests the stages and efforts in the writing process. It also contains completed, unfinished, abandoned, or successful work. Process-writing portfolios typically contain brainstorming activities, clustering, diagramming, outlining, free writing, drafting, redrafting in response to teacher/peer review, and so forth. Thus, a picture of the current state of an individual's composing process is revealed. The two essential pedagogical elements in the process-writing portfolio are student reflection and teacher inquiry.

The writing portfolio is the means by which students can speak honestly, authoritatively, and with documentation about their writing. It enables them to distance themselves from the tediousness of revising and editing. By compiling a process-writing portfolio, students learn to discern and talk about their writing improvement with pride. In short, the process-writing portfolio is a useful means to disclose the story of a writer in-the-making.

LEARNING-STYLES APPLICATIONS

I am of the opinion that process-writing portfolios are entirely compatible with explicit elements of the learning-style model as proposed by Dunn and Dunn (1993). Of the 21 elements delineated in this model, all are relevant in some way to process-writing portfolio tasks. They provide insight for students and teachers.

Although I have not formally assessed the learning styles of individual students, my current observations and interactions with students have given me the sense that my students represent the entire spread on the Dunn and Dunn Learning-Style Model (1992, 1993). For example, I have students who (a) simultaneously complain about the heat or cold in the classroom, (b) seldom partake in group work even when encouraged to do so, (c) come to class with the cafeteria's plat du jour; and (d) find it difficult to concentrate on class activities with the hum of air conditioners.

With learning styles in mind, I observed that undergraduates approach the task of developing process-writing portfolios in different ways. Disciplined, self-starting students compile their portfolios with few explicit directions, and usually ask few question about how to proceed. The majority of students constantly ask questions or show their work to me to be certain that they are doing it the *right* way. To cater to all the learning styles represented in the class, I have devised two short handouts that give explicit instructions on how to compile this portfolio. I generally distribute the first handout at the second class meeting, while another handout is distributed approximately one month before the end of the term. I have discovered that I cannot assume that all undergraduates have strong visual perceptual strengths. Therefore, I have found that I must read the entire handout in class, line by line, in order to minister to those undergraduates whose auditory and kinesthetic perceptual strengths far outweigh their visual strengths.

Originally, my portfolio handouts were lengthy, repetitious, and verbose, but over the years I have tried to simplify the language. Now the language is much more precise and elegant, benefiting students who thrive on explicit directions. Nevertheless, the handouts are deficient, as they lack concrete examples and illustrations that some students seem to crave. To mitigate this problem somewhat, I have made the uncollected portfolios from the previous year available to students. A quick handling and perusal of these portfolios by tactually or visually oriented undergraduates is worth a thousand elegantly written words.

My work on the process-writing portfolio has demonstrated that I have to be sensitive to the diverse learning-style elements among my students. The Dunn and Dunn (1993) model has identified five stimuli. *Environmentally*, students contend with sound, light, temperature, and the furniture in the college classroom. *Emotionally*, I become increasingly aware of students' motivation, persistence, and responsibility levels as I work with and observe them. As the semester comes to a close, I provide more or less structure for each student. *Sociologically*, I am sensitive to their individual preferences for working alone, in pairs, or in groups. *Physiologically*, perceptual strengths (visual, auditory, tactual, or kinesthetic), time-of-day energy levels, and the need for intake and mobility require more of my consideration. *Psychologically*, the information-processing styles of learners—global or analytic—and impulsive or reflective reactions still need to be examined and considered when explaining and elaborating on the process-writing portfolio tasks.

INTEGRATING PORTFOLIO METHODOLOGY WITH LEARNING STYLES

What follows is a practical account of how I attempted to integrate learning styles and process-writing portfolios during the past year. With a learning-styles mind-set, I tell my students on the first day of class that they are required to compile a writing portfolio. I describe this as a folder with two pockets, in which they are to keep *all* written work they do for this course, including notes, outlines, exercises, revisions, homework, in-class assignments, reactions to reading, essays, first or second drafts, and so forth. In addition, I require them to keep a separate journal book to comment on what they have read, how they feel about it, and what they think. Students are urged not to throw away anything they write during the course; not even the roughest notes. I tell them to add the date to everything they insert in the portfolio.

The primary purpose for keeping a writing portfolio is to give both students and me an opportunity to share and measure their progress as writers. This is helpful information for global processors, but often is ignored by the analytics. Since the portfolio is a collection of everything students write from the first day of the course to the last, it ideally should give them—and me—a meaningful chance to compare earlier and later work to see how well they are developing as writers.

The portfolio is a concrete, collective record of the efforts students are making in the course. As a result, the more students refine their written work, the better I can assess their efforts and progress as writers.

The portfolio is an ongoing, continuing body of their work in progress. I reiterate at the end of the course that the writing portfolio is the means by which they present themselves as writers.

SUBMITTING PORTFOLIOS AT THE END OF THE SEMESTER

Before the end of the semester, I invite students to look through their portfolios and reflect on them carefully. As they review their portfolios, I ask them to select three samples of work that best illustrate their effort and development as writers. These samples should be work that the individual student writer believes best demonstrates his/her effort to become a better writer.

Subsequently, I ask the students to write a letter to me in which they introduce the three samples. Examples of what would be considered samples are any compositions written out of class, revised and re-written compositions, any in-class compositions, journal entries, reactions to in-class or out-of-class readings, and so forth. The letter should explain what it is about each sample that caused the student to select it. Here students are urged to be as specific as possible. For instance, if a student has selected a sample because he/she attempted something not previously accomplished, the process in the development of the work should be described.

Finally, the portfolio provides each student with a valuable opportunity to review his/her effort and growth during the course. Hopefully, they feel a sense of accomplishment about, and pride in, their portfolios.

CONCLUSION

In the beginning, students, especially those needing structure and constant support of the teacher, were very puzzled about my purpose in asking them to compile a portfolio. They were even more puzzled when I asked them to make the selection of three samples and write a letter of introduction to me. I believe, judging from the writing products and personal insight that have been achieved, that this strategy has worked well. I have, in the past three semesters, received some exceptionally perceptive letters from my students. There is a consensus among the students who do the work and take pride in developing their portfolios, that they have learned from the experience and have acquired personal insight about how they write and under what conditions they do their best work. By integrating process-writing portfolios with an awareness of learning-style preferences, I believe we are on the way to good results.

Part V

Applications in Colleges of Business

Chapter 20

Contract Activity Packages in Higher Education: The Flexible Flyer of Pedagogy

Heather Pfleger Dunham and Barbara-Jayne Lewthwaite

It is the first day of a new semester, and Professor Roundemup has just overviewed the entire semester's schedule with his students, assigned them to working groups, and noted the dates for their presentations. As those undergraduates filed out at the end of the class, he mentally congratulated himself on his organizational skills. However, as he turned to pick up his brief case, his desk was surrounded by three concerned young people.

- The first was a professionally dressed young man who told the professor that he had just received a promotion that required travel. Unfortunately, he would have to miss several classes and wondered whether the professor could make some schedule adjustments for him.

- The second was a charming, obviously expectant young mother who explained that her physician had prohibited her from driving and that she would have to forgo the pleasure of working with classmates on assignments. Would the professor permit her to complete the assignments and the presentation independently?

- The third had family that had fled from the Serbians in Yugoslavia. She had to fly there to try to locate parents and two siblings, but promised to have all assignments done and submitted as soon as she and her husband returned. Would he allow her to do that?

Today's college and university populations are different and more diverse than previously. The student body represents a broad spectrum in terms of age, experience, culture, ethnicity, levels of preparedness, and scheduling challenges. As a result, it has become a real chore for instructors and support staff to meet the needs of all students.

We have found that Contract Activity Packages (CAPs) are an innovative instructional strategy that addresses the different needs of today's students. A CAP provides incredible flexibility in that it allows students and faculty to explore further their own interests while capitalizing on their learning-style strengths. The CAP also demands that students actively participate in the learning process.

CAPs are effective for the following reasons: they are self-pacing; they respond to varied learning styles and academic levels; they allow for independence as well as student collaboration; they reduce frustration and anxiety; they capitalize on individual student interest (Dunn & Dunn, 1993, 1996). The well-integrated design of the CAP accounts for its effectiveness as a learning strategy. Critical to the design are the elements contained in the CAP, including: Behavioral Objectives; Activity and Reporting Alternatives; Resource Alternatives; small-group techniques; pre- and post-tests. Let's examine how each of these components contributes to the CAP's unique success.

Behavioral Objectives identify the course content that the student is expected to master. They are expressed in a way that requires that the student take the initiative to identify how the objectives can be attained. For example, in a college-level economics unit on foreign trade, a Behavioral Objective might be: *Demonstrate knowledge of the difference between absolute and comparative advantage in foreign trade with 90 percent accuracy on a written examination.*

Each Behavioral Objective is followed by Activity Alternatives, which provide choices for accomplishing the objectives. They accommodate multiple perceptual strengths and therefore individualize the students' experiences. Examples might include: *Create an overhead presentation that identifies the differences between absolute and comparative advantage in foreign trade,* or *Develop a list of at least five (5) countries, select a product from each, and decide whether the country has an absolute or comparative advantage in that product and why.*

Consider how this active approach to learning differs from Professor Lecturelots's methodology of preference.

Professor Lecturelots was annoyed. She had just finished the usual 75-minute lecture on monetary theory. She loved this particular topic, and always found herself caught up in the equations and graphs. Typical of many of her peers, she used a podium and microphone to address the students gathered for class in the lecture hall. This was a style she had perfected over the years and with which she was extremely comfortable. In fact, the tenure committee had praised her style of delivery. The professor's only problem was the students who persisted in asking questions about the material discussed after the lecture. There never was enough time to address their individual concerns. "How does administration expect me to get my research done when I have to re-teach this material for students after class?" she wondered. "Why doesn't the registrar do a better job of screening students so that I don't have to be all things to all people?"

A CAP could go a long way toward helping Professor Lecturelots successfully deal with students who require extensive structure.

WHAT IS A CAP?

A CAP is one easy-to-use instructional method for individualizing course content and responding to how different students in the same class learn and demonstrate the knowledge they gain. CAPs include:

Behavioral Objectives that clearly spell out (a) exactly what has to be learned and (b) how students demonstrate that they *have* learned what was required.

Resource Alternatives that permit students to learn the content through a choice of multisensory resources and small-group strategies that respond to their individual perceptual modalities. Included might be relevant library reserve readings, available research material, multisensory instructional materials, internet resources, textbook peripherals such as study guides and tutorials, tactual and kinesthetic manipulatives that the students create in response to homework assignments, or any other materials that are pertinent to the subject.

Activity Alternatives and matching *Reporting Alternatives*. The Activity Alternatives require that students *apply* the new information they are learning in a creative way by making instructional resources to teach that same information. Reporting Alternatives address how students share the Activity Alternative they created with each other. Examples of Reporting Alternatives that show how Activity Alternatives can be shared might include: "Demonstrate the overhead presentation in class" or "Display the countries' products on original posters. Arrange the posters around the classroom as an exhibit to be used to generate discussion."

The alternatives should respond to varied students' learning styles and should capitalize on students' perceptual strengths. In this example, the first alternative will be attractive to the student who is a visual learner, and the second to one who prefers a tactual, visual, and/or kinesthetic perceptual modality. Motivated students appreciate the challenge and diversity built into the Activity and Reporting Alternatives (Dunn, 1996); poorly achieving students cannot retain difficult information without them (Dunn & Dunn, 1993, 1999).

Consider how appealing these components can be to both Suzanne SuperStudent and Colin I'mConfused.

Suzanne SuperStudent was perturbed. She enjoyed the subject material in her class, but was dismayed by what she perceived as a low motivation level among her classmates. She was frustrated because the instructor spent what she regarded as too much time explaining things over and over again. Suzanne was concerned that the course content would be reduced in both substance and quality.

Colin I'mConfused has no problem with interrupting his professors' lectures with an exasperated "Maybe I'm the *only* one who doesn't understand what you are saying, but I'm Confused!" He then listens to the repetition of what was said and continues to shake his head as if the explanation was of no assistance.

Resource Alternatives can be used to provide more challenges and avenues for enrichment for students like Suzanne, and reinforcement for those who require more time with the basics, like Colin.

Small-group techniques are a key component of any CAP. They can be used to introduce or reinforce new and difficult information. They are effective because they enable students to learn the content through either collaboration, if they are peer oriented, or constructive competition, if they enjoy vying for grades (Dunn, 1989).

One useful small-group technique is Team Learning that provides peer interaction and support when new and difficult material is being introduced. In Team Learning, difficult content, such as a research or technical article, is distributed or assigned. The instructor develops questions pertaining to the reading, which incorporate a variety of intellectual levels, ranging from knowledge acquisition to application and evaluation. Students work on the questions in small groups, and report to the larger group at the conclusion of the allotted time (Dunn & Dunn, 1992, 1993, 1999).

The Circle of Knowledge, which is a review technique, is also effective (Dunn & Dunn, 1992, 1993, 1999). Here student groups would be given a short time frame, such as three or four minutes at most, and would be asked to identify as many terms as they can that pertain to the unit being studied. Groups compete against each other to compile the most comprehensive list of correct answers. Other small group techniques, such as Brainstorming, Case Studies, or Simulations, also provide an effective addition to a CAP.

The CAP is a winner once again in the evaluation category. Students demonstrate theoretical knowledge and competence via the difference between their pre- and post-test scores. This is perfect for assessment purposes. Students also demonstrate performance-based attainment of skills and information via their completed Reporting Alternatives.

Let's review the parts of a CAP (see Tables 20.1 and 20.2).

Now that you have an idea of how they work and what they contain, let's consider some additional, creative problem-solving uses of CAPs together.

Case Study Applications of CAPs

The effective coordination of internships is always a challenge. Dean Mywayhyway, who is in charge of many important things, supervises the student internship program. The participating students have been complaining that their experiences are not meaningful because they don't seem to fit their

Table 20.1
Summarization of the Parts of a CAP

Element	Purpose
Behavioral Objectives	Identify the course content that students are required to master.
Activity Alternatives	Provide student choices for showing they mastered each objective.
Reporting Alternatives	Identify how the activity alternative is demonstrated or shared with the class.
Resource Alternatives	Provide different ways of learning the information cited in the objectives.
Small-Group Techniques	Are used to introduce or reinforce new and difficult information and allow for higher-level cognitive skill development.
Pre-/post-test Assessments	Allow students to demonstrate mastery and to verify what has been learned.

individual needs to be very organized. She is perplexed as to what to do because she can't possibly become personally involved in designing and supervising each individual situation. A CAP would allow for some aspects of a consistent experience in terms of Behavioral Objectives, while still providing individual options through the Activity and Reporting Alternatives.

Providing alternatives to distance learning is another way to capitalize on CAPs. Vice President Microslick wants to offer distance learning to students, but the institution just does not have the resources to do it. In addition, some students like the independence involved in that concept, but would like to touch base with faculty and colleagues on a human-to-human basis on occasion.

CAPs represent an ideal compromise solution for students who prefer a distance learning environment because of the independence it affords, but find distance learning itself too isolating. Here, a CAP provides the best of both worlds. The student who prefers to learn in a non-traditional setting uses the CAP to frame a flexible program of study. The isolation is removed because the CAP incorporates at least three small-group activities that allow for interaction between and among students. Furthermore, although the CAP individualizes how information is learned, demonstrated, and evaluated, it can be used easily in a traditional classroom setting. Thus, students can complete the Activity and Reporting Alternatives independently, but are able to benefit from the socialization provided by classmates.

Inflexible semester beginnings and endings can be a real deterrent to *just-in-time education*, a concept that is becoming a market force in our world.

Administrator Newblood has been urging the Curriculum Committee to devise ways in which accomplished adult learners might obtain development and assistance when they need it. It has been his all-too-frequent experience that the non-traditional adult learners he meets often need to begin a course

Table 20.2
Sample CAP

Objective 1: List at least three (3) learning-style elements accommodated by CAPS and at least six (6) components of a CAP.

ACTIVITY ALTERNATIVES:
1. Write an essay that discusses at least three (3) learning-style elements accommodated by CAPS, and explains at least six (6) components of a CAP.
   -or-
2. Create a rap that includes at least six (6) components and at least three (3) learning-style elements contained in a CAP.
   -or-
3. Document three (3) research articles that discuss the components of a CAP and the learning styles accommodated by CAPS.
   -or-
4. Create a PowerPoint overhead that cites at least six (6) learning-style elements accommodated by CAPS and also shows the parts of a CAP that respond to them.

REPORTING ALTERNATIVES:
1. Read the essay to three (3) colleagues of your choice. Have each explain the extent to which a CAP would respond to his/her style.
   -or-
2. Perform the reap for a small group of your peers. Ask for feedback.

   -or-
3. Submit the documentation to your teacher/session leader for analysis.

   -or-
4. Display the overhead to at least five (5) of your colleagues and ask for feedback.

Objective 2: Explain the purpose and benefits of using small-group techniques in CAPS, and identify at least two (2) types of small-group techniques that frequently are used.

ACTIVITY ALTERNATIVES:
1. Make a chart that outlines at least two (2) of the purposes and benefits of small-group techniques.
   -or-
2. Write a poem that portrays the purposes and benefits of small-group activities in CAPS.
   -or-
3. Create at least two (2) small-group original techniques.

   -or-
4. Develop a PowerPoint demonstration on the purposes and benefits of small-group techniques.

REPORTING ALTERNATIVES:
1. Display the chart to three (3) colleagues. Answer any questions they may have.
   -or-
2. Recite the poem to at least two (2) colleagues and have them react to it.

   -or-
3. Try your new strategies with eight (8) to ten (10) colleagues. Obtain their feedback.
   -or-
4. Show the demonstration to at least three (3) peers and have them critique it.

Table 20.2 (continued)

Objective 3: List at least four (4) specific uses of CAPS with adult learners.

ACTIVITY ALTERNATIVES:

REPORTING ALTERNATIVES

1. Create a short video on the uses of CAPS with adult learners.

   -or-

2. Write an analysis of how CAPS can be used with adult learners.

   -or-

3. Prepare a chart that portrays uses of CAPS with adult learners.

   -or-

4. Develop a Floor Game on how to use CAPS with adult learners.

   -or-

5. Create a Team Learning on the uses of CAPS with adult learners.

1. Show the video to at least five (5) colleagues and have them critique it.

   -or-

2. Submit the analysis to the instructor or session leader for review.

   -or-

3. Display the chart during the session. Ask for feedback.

   -or-

4. Play the Floor Game with one (1) or two (2) colleagues. Ask for their reactions.

   -or-

5. Have at least three (3) colleagues use the Team Learning and evaluate it.

Objective 4: Develop strategies for negotiating the CAP with adult learners.

ACTIVITY ALTERNATIVES:

REPORTING ALTERNATIVES

1. Prepare a written analysis on strategies for negotiating the CAP with adult learners.

   -or-

2. Create a model of strategies for negotiating the CAP with adult learners.

   -or-

3. Develop a Role Play Activity in which strategies for negotiating the CAP with adult learners are reviewed.

   -or-

4. Construct a Floor Game that uses strategies for negotiating CAPS with adult learners.

1. Submit the analysis to the instructor or session leader for a grade.

   -or-

2. Display the model for the group, explain how it will be used, and ask for feedback.

   -or-

3. Act out the Role Play Activity with a couple of colleagues. Have them evaluate it.

   -or

4. Demonstrate the Floor Game to at least three (3) peers. Have them critique it.

OBJECTIVE 5: Explain why CAPS are beneficial for staff development purposes.

ACTIVITY ALTERNATIVES:

REPORTING ALTERNATIVES:

1. Construct a chart that identifies staff development activities that are enhanced by CAPS.

   -or-

1. Show the chart to at least four (4) colleagues. Explain how it could be used, and ask for their reactions.

   -or-

Table 20.2 (continued)

2. Create Task Cards on the benefits of using CAPS for staff development purposes.

-or-

3. Develop a paper that explains the benefits of CAPS for staff development purposes.

-or-

4. Prepare a presentation that markets the benefits of CAPS in staff development.

-or-

5. Write a song or a rap that lists the benefits of CAPS for staff development purposes.

-or-

6. Create a videotape on the benefits of CAPS for staff development.

2. Use the Task Cards with at least three (3) colleagues and ask for their feedback.

-or-

3. Submit the paper for publication to a staff development journal.

-or-

4. Make the presentation to a group of staff development leaders. Request their reactions.

-or-

5. Sing or read the song or rap to at least three (3) peers. Have them discuss the accuracy of the material.

-or-

6. Show the videotape to at least five (5) colleagues, and have them evaluate it.

Creative Uses of CAPS for Adult Learners: Doing It Their Way!
Activity Log

Name _____

Objective:	Activity Alternative:	Reporting Alternative:
1.	_____	_____
2.	_____	_____
3.	_____	_____
4.	_____	_____
5.	_____	_____

Date Completed: _____

Resource Alternatives

Books

Dunn, R. (1996). *How to implement and supervise a learning style program.* Alexandria, VA: Association for Supervision and Curriculum Development.

Dunn, R., & Dunn, K. (1993). *Teaching secondary students through their individual learning styles: Practical approaches for grades 7–12.* Boston: Allyn and Bacon.

Dunn, R., & Dunn, K. (1999). *The complete guide to the learning styles system.* Boston: Allyn & Bacon.

Recommended Journals

Educational Leadership
Innovative Higher Education

Table 20.2 (continued)

Journal of Counseling & Development
Journal of Staff Development
Journal of Staff, Program, & Organization Development
Research in Higher Education

Instructor-Made Materials (These should be used first)
Computer Presentation
Kinesthetic Floor Game
PowerPoint Slides
Task Cards

Pre-/Post-test

Answer each of the following questions as completely as possible:
1. List at least six (6) components of a CAP and identify at least three (3) learning-style elements accommodated by CAPS.
2. Explain the purpose and benefits of using small-group techniques in CAPS and identify at least two (2) types of small-group techniques that frequently are used.
3. List at least four (4) specific uses of CAPS with adult learners.
4. Develop strategies for negotiating a CAP with adult learners.
5. Explain why CAPS are beneficial for staff development purposes.

References

Acheson, K. (1992). *Techniques in the clinical supervision of teachers: Preservice and inservice applications.* White Plains, NY: Longman.

Berliner, D., & Calfee, R. (Eds.) (1996). *Handbook of educational psychology.* New York: Macmillan.

Braskamp, L., & Ory, J. (1994). *Assessing faculty work: Enhancing individual and institutional performance.* San Francisco, CA: Jossey-Bass.

Dunn, R., & Dunn, K. (Eds.) (1998). *Practical approaches to individualizing staff development for adults.* Westport, CT: Greenwood.

Dunn, R., & Dunn, K. (1999). *The complete guide to the learning-styles inservice system.* Needham Heights, MA: Allyn & Bacon.

Hoy, W., & Forsyth, P. (1986). *Effective supervision: Theory into practice.* New York: Random House.

Kauchek, D., & Eggen, P. (1989). *Learning and teaching: Research-based methods.* Needham Heights, MA: Allyn & Bacon.

Kristensen, E., & Moulton, D. (1993). Challenges for faculty developers and department chairs: When faculty arrive from professional settings. *To Improve the Academy: Resources for Faculty, Instructional, & Organizational Development, 12,* 39–52.

Luna, G., & Cullen, D. (1996). *Empowering the faculty: Mentoring redirected and renewed.* Washington, DC: ASHE-ERIC Higher Education Reports.

Mintzberg, H. (1981). Organization design: Fashion or fit? *Harvard Business Review,* 81106, 103–116.

spontaneously—when they suddenly become motivated or find that they have the scheduling freedom. However, highly structured college schedules do not permit flexibility. This is where a CAP can be extremely beneficial. Well-written CAPs can be used for independent studies that begin when the student needs or can take advantage of them. CAP Activity Alternatives can be negotiated between the instructor and the student and included in the Contract itself. In addition, the project orientation of the Activity Alternatives provides great networking opportunities for the self-starter.

Consider the plight of Nancy Non-conformist who does not require or appreciate a structured learning environment. For this type of adult learner, a CAP can provide an alternative learning environment where the methods used in accomplishing the course objectives, the pacing of the learning, and the projects completed by the student are all able to be negotiated. The independent adult learner has a great deal of control over the learning process, and has the ability to choose among options. There is variety in the choice of the Activity and Reporting Alternatives, which allows the non-conformist to find his or her own best method for acquiring knowledge.

Department chair Dr. Sos is completely overwhelmed. His staff is constantly complaining about the standardized, one-size-fits-all faculty-development efforts put forth by the institution. Faculty regard it as meaningless and perfunctory, as well as ill-suited to individual needs and a formative process.

Just think about how the CAP would allow for individual efforts that could be self-generated by the individual faculty member—think of the faculty roundtables that could be generated via Reporting Activities. Faculty can improve in ways that are important to them and to the institution, and can share information gained with other interested colleagues. Now there is a win/win situation!

The traditional college classroom is an environment where learning is transmitted from the instructor to the learner. "In the beginning was the word—and the word was pedagogy. Derived from the Greek roots *pais* (boy), and *agogos* (leader), the term literally means one who leads, or teaches, children" (Somers, 1988, p. 1). In a traditional model of learning, there is an implied dependence on the instructor—which works for *some* less mature students. For independent, non-conforming, and highly achieving students, however, this model is ineffective. They prefer, instead, a model of andragogy, which is a theory of adult learning that recognizes the psychological need of mature learners to be self-directive and independent. The CAP provides the flexibility for these learners to be accommodated. Thus, these students take responsibility for their own learning.

CAPs provide an engaging, useful alternative to the traditional college classroom, and can fulfill a variety of learning-style needs for the adult learner. CAPs can be used in myriad ways to offer maximum flexibility. Ultimately, the ways in which they can be used are limited only by our imaginations!

Chapter 21

How I Found Pedagogical Nirvana: Beware of the Law of Unintended Consequences!

E. L. Deckinger

A man lights a match for illumination in his home, and the whole house blows up.

Another man marries the girl of his dreams for bliss and contentment ever after and, instead, acquires a meddling mother-in-law.

A balding man buys a new product that is supposed to grow hair, but instead causes terrifying impotence.

Each of these scenarios illustrates the usually perverse Law of Unintended Consequences.

HOW I INITIATED THE LAW OF UNINTENDED CONSEQUENCES

I participated in the St. John's University Commencement exercises one fine day in the mid-1980s, as I always do. As usual, I thought it proper to honor our graduates. However, that time, perhaps for just once, the normally cantankerous Law of Unintended Consequences was not perverse. In fact, it was anything but problematic.

One unintended consequence of my attendance was a chance meeting with a distinguished fellow professor. That meeting resulted in a seismic conversion in how I went about the process of *teaching*: A conversion perhaps not of the scale of Saul's transformation into Paul on the Damascus road but, in its own way, of earthquake proportions! Attending that particular graduation rewarded me with an unexpected, but very welcome, dividend. So what *else* was learned from that experience—other than that we professors should *always* attend our college graduations?

Wise people have urged us to learn from mistakes; not just our own, but those of others too! There is a pretty good reason for the latter. We just cannot live long enough to make them all ourselves. I am confessing that I have made some mistakes—big ones—over many years while trying to hone my teaching. Only through that chance meeting at graduation did I find a way of dramatically improving how I teach.

CAN YOU TEACH BETTER THAN YOU DO? OF COURSE, IF YOU WANT TO!

While advertising for a weight-loss product, Tommy LaSorda, the legendary Los Angeles Dodgers' manager, said: "If *I* can do it, *you* can do it!" In effect, he was saying, "I used the product as directed and lost weight. If *I* can do it, *you can too!*" Let's call that statement the LaSorda If I Can Do It, You Can Do It Transformation Principle. And, let's face it, who doesn't want to lose weight?

I am writing this chapter to confirm the LaSorda Transformation Principle. He was right. I, too, used the product as directed. And I, too, lost weight. So as you see, dear reader, we're now on a winning streak of two. Accordingly, let's carry the LaSorda Transformation Principle one step further—to you.

The point is this. If I can adopt new methods and improve my work at the podium, then you can, too.[1] What turned my teaching around came from a chance meeting. Thus, you can turn yours around, too, through a chance reading of this chapter.

I SHOULDA, WOULDA, COULDA KNOWN; YEAH, BUT I DIDN'T!

Some will say that what I learned, I should have known anyway. Maybe *you* should know already, too.[2] Well:

> Little Red Riding Hood should have known that grandma didn't have such big teeth. But she didn't.
> General Custer should have known that the Indians knew how to handle rifles pretty well, too. But he didn't.
> Richard Nixon should have known that, unless he destroyed his tapes, they would come back and bite him. But he didn't.

Fact is, we don't always know what we should when we should. But what's done is done. What's gone is gone. Unhappily, the effects of behavioral changes are not retroactive. Never were. Never will be. However, at some point, we need to bite the bullet and make the proper adjustments for the future.

Kettering had it right. He said, "I am only interested in the future. I have the rest of my life to live there." Me, too. The worst reason in the world for doing anything in any one way is that *we've always done it that way*. Because maybe, just maybe, we've always been doing it wrong!

How did all this come about? What is it I want you to do in your classroom? Before I explain what I did, and what you can do too, I first need to take you back a few years.

IN THE BEGINNING (OF MY TEACHING HEGIRA)

I started teaching in the College of Business Administration at St. John's University in 1982, after a rewarding 45-year career in the *dream merchant* business—advertising. It had been a great ride. But, at the age of 65, I decided that it was time to try to touch a few young lives—hopefully, for the better.

I thought that I surely must have learned *something* from all those years on the firing line; the pressure-cooker world of business adventures (and misadventures) must have equipped me for something good. I hoped that it was to help a few young people find themselves a little faster, a little more surely, and a little more successfully.

I started out, I expect, as you did, very conscientiously. Like you, I wanted to be very good at my job. I had the enthusiasm. I enjoyed my students (still do). After 45 years in advertising, I knew my subject reasonably well. I was known as a reasonably good communicator. I had lectured widely. But how would I fare in a university lecture hall or classroom? Teaching couldn't be very difficult; or was it?

I really tried. I came to class prepared every day. I never missed a class. I never dismissed a class early.[3] I tried the latest teaching ideas that I read about, like Role Playing and Team Learning. My students will verify that I was *always* available to them—any time of day or night. Yes, I did all these things. But only with, at best, marginal success.

The record will show that I was a reasonably okay professor. Not the best. Not the worst. Just fair-to-middling. But nowhere as good as I wanted to be.

ENTER A BENIGN FATE

So, we now return to that fateful (for me) St. John's University graduation in the mid-1980s mentioned earlier. A benign fate placed me in line next to a remarkable fellow professor. This ball of fire turned out to be the eminent Dr. Rita Dunn.[4] This extraordinary lady, I learned, was the brilliant-but-unassuming female partner of the pioneering husband-wife research team. For years, it seems, they had been quietly breaking new ground, at what had to be breakneck speed, in the field of learning and teaching styles.

Up to that moment, I had never heard of the lady. (Not to my credit, but true!) But then, she had never heard of me, either.[5] She is in a different school at the same St John's University campus.[6]   At some point, I mentioned how hard I had tried to communicate with, stimulate, and bring out the best in my students—with considerably less-than-spectacular success. My reward: Professor Dunn told me a little about her work in teaching and learning styles. She touched more than a nerve. She touched my heart and soul. And that was the beginning of a beautiful friendship.

FINDING THE HOLY GRAIL OF PEDAGOGY AT COMMENCEMENT

I listened most cautiously as the good Dr. Dunn spoke so enchantingly. I'd been misled too many times before. Was what she was telling me about her work even mildly true? If it was, my (up to now futile) search was over! Here was a Holy Grail of teaching, one to which I had so long aspired, but never even came close!

And hear this! At the time, just about all the research in this fertile grassland had been conducted at education levels below that of higher learning. What an opportunity to ratchet things up a notch! So that's what we did. And, eventually, following the principles as best I could in the classroom, I became a markedly better teacher—and I can prove it. Several years later, the alumni of our College of Business Administration voted me "the teacher who most influenced my life." But first, we had to try out the principles.

MANNA FROM HEAVEN: A FORTUITOUS LABORATORY

It just happened that, the following semester, I was to teach two consecutive classes of an Advertising Principles Course (APC). What a fortuitous laboratory in which to put some of Dr. Dunn's theories to the test *at* the college level in a business school! So, then and there, we plotted our fateful experiment.

We developed a small, pilot research plan—just to see what would happen. I was to teach the two classes in my normal fashion. The only difference was to be the application of learning-style preferences for doing homework in one section of my advertising class, whereas the matter was never discussed in the other section. The first APC section served as a control group. We used:

• the same subject matter;

• the same professor;

• no exposure to learning style;

- virtually no opportunity for contagion with the second class; and

- a professor who was (a) only vaguely aware of learning-style particulars and (b) not involved in identification of style or its application to homework—*me*! I was neither involved with testing students nor explaining how they could use their strengths for studying.

The second section of APC provided us with both the experimental group and, in part, a second control group.

- Only part of the class participated and constituted the experimental group.

- The non-participants provided a second control group.

And, the Results? The Envelope, Please

The results were promulgated to a breathless world (Dunn, Deckinger, Withers, & Katzenstein, 1990). They are summarized in the tables that comprise Appendix I. As will be noted, significant differences in achievement in successive testing over the semester were established between those with the hope that springs eternal in the human breast and, thus, participated; and those too skeptical, cynical, lazy, or disinterested in our experiment to take a shot at it.

With Results Like That, What Would *You* Do?

The results of that experiment, as you can well imagine, had a profound effect on how I taught my classes. Thereafter, in my teaching style, I tried to cater, at the very least, to the dominant learning-style preferences of my students. At least I learned what their preferences were, made the students aware of them, suggested study strategies I thought might work for them, and adapted much of my teaching to the style of the largest cluster in each class. Unfortunately, at the end of a decade, my teaching activity declined with my own declining years. Accordingly, opportunities for me to experiment further have become limited. Although I since have cut back to adjunct status, I have continued to encourage my students to study according to their strengths—and am always surprised that many of them never realized that they *had* strengths! I also am surprised at their enthusiasm for learning styles.

For the most part, it is not difficult for students to study by using their styles. By the time college students achieve the exalted academic rank of senior, and just about all my students are seniors, most of them have a pretty good idea about what at least some of their learning strengths are. For example, they know whether they:

- like bright light or soft light;
- can concentrate better with background music or music;
- are night, morning, late morning, or afternoon high-energy persons or not;
- work best at a desk or in a lounge chair, and so on.

The problem is that they seldom make a conscious effort to correlate what they know about themselves with what they actually *do*. They just about never try to study to their strengths. That is, not without encouragement to do so. Not that they are stupid, of course. It just never enters their minds. So I entered it into their minds by encouraging them to do so.

To the extent that I can, I help them take advantage of their strengths while learning in our classroom. If they know they do better under bright light, I encourage them to sit near the window. If intake helps things sink in a little better, I encourage them to bring a soft drink to class. If they need to move about a bit, I encourage them to do that in class,[7] and so on.

With What Success, If Any?

How is this for evidence? In 1996, the CBA alumni voted me, "the professor who most influenced my life." (Some who "knew me when" might argue that the alumni had to have been overtaken by some manner of mass delusion. But, absent proof thereof, the voted mass opinion stands.)

Now, that happy outcome didn't just happen. It all came about from that chance meeting with the professor who "most influenced *my* life!" Will miracles never cease? Let's hope not. You're next! Step right up!

EXPANDING THE RESEARCH

After our beginning pilot study with my APC sections, we read that Clark-Thayer (1987) and Cook (1989) had obtained similarly good results when showing their college students how to study with learning-style strategies. In addition, Dr. Dunn and some of our colleagues at St. John's University expanded their research to experiment with teaching other college students to study that way. Their results documented statistically higher:

- across-the-board achievement and retention among community college freshmen (Nelson, Dunn, Griggs, Primavera, Fitzpatrick, Bacilious, & Miller, 1993);
- science achievement, grade-point averages, and curiosity about science, in addition to reduced anger and anxiety scores among undergraduates in a nursing program;
- unit test scores among students in an allied health program (Miller & Dunn, 1997); and
- unit test scores among law school students (Boyle & Dunn, 1998).

And Furthermore . . .

The good Dr. Dunn has given me further opportunity to expand my knowledge in this fascinating field. She invited me to participate as one of several advisors to some of her protégés—students for whom she served as doctoral dissertation mentor in the School of Education. In that capacity, I have been intrigued by the possibility of tangibly confirming claims by students that they have (or have not) made adjustments in their studying styles to conform to their learning styles. Some may regard that as unnecessary "make work." They may argue that what counts is the results. They view the issue in these terms:

1. Subjects claim to have made such adjustments.
2. They perform better than those who do not make such claims.
3. What could have made this happen, other than their actually having made changes in their study styles?
4. Ergo, Q.E.D., they must have done what they said they did.

However, the eternal search for rigor commands that we try to obtain objective evidence that samples really did what they said they would. Thus, I have enjoyed serving as part of a five-member supervisory committee involved in studies conducted with students examining the effects of learning-style strategies on business and mathematics students. Exciting endeavors in an already exiting life!

CONCLUSION

For now, please go to graduations at your institution! Who knows what unexpected[8] joyful consequences will be your reward?

NOTES

1. On the other hand, you already may have subscribed to the principles to be expounded here. In that case, you will be nodding throughout this opus—more and more emphatically as it unfurls. And you will serve as a corroborating witness, if needed by any hard-to-convince Ivory Tower types!

2. Maybe you actually do! If so, good for you! Go on to the next chapter, please!

3. Well, except once, on a major holiday eve. And perhaps you will forgive that one transgression—if that's what it was.

4. Had I not learned how to improve my teaching, or anything else, from this chance meeting, the meeting itself would have been reward enough. She is the most ebullient, effusive, energetic, prolific, learned (etc., etc., etc.,—you name it; if it is good, she's it) lady I have ever known. Or ever expect to meet.

5. For Dr. Dunn, that mutuality would fall into the "So what?" category of academic reciprocity. In my case, it was a monumental shortcoming.

6. Two different colleges in a university are often to each other like two different planets (an observation no doubt totally congruent with the reader's own.) My Alcazar at St, John's was, and is, the Business College; hers, the School of Education. Does Macy's, except rarely, talk to Gimbel's? Would you?

7. I know that can be distracting to others, but it is less distracting to them than it is beneficial to those who need to move.

8. Actually, a little less "unexpected" than before you will have read this chapter!

Chapter 22

Global Teaching in an Analytic Environment: Is There Madness in the Method?

Ralph A. Terregrossa and Valerie Englander

INTRODUCTION

Proficient teaching of college economics requires intensive training both in the principles of economics and in the principles of education. Although all economics professors receive rigorous training in economic theory, they receive virtually none in the principles of education. Consequently, their teaching methods are acquired mainly by trial and error, or by imitation of the styles of other adept economics instructors, perhaps including their shortcomings. In this regard, the *teaching* of economics fails to be guided by the *principles* of economics.

Meta-analytic research suggests the optimal method of teaching is congruent with students' learning styles (Dunn, Griggs, Olson, Gorman, & Beasley, 1995). According to the multidimensional Dunn and Dunn Learning-Style Model (1993), there is neither one right way to learn nor one right way to teach. Each person possesses an optimal, diversified learning style or way to concentrate on, process, absorb, and remember new and difficult information. Learning styles, which change with age, are determined by a combination of environmental, emotional, sociological, physiological, and psychological factors. What this means, for example, is that some students may prefer learning alone late at night while lying on the bed with low light and the radio playing. If they are taught in a more traditional way, such as during regular school hours while seated formally at a desk in a brightly lighted classroom by an authoritative teacher and without any background sound, then some of them may not live up to their potential.

Economists explain that to maximize output, resources must be optimally used so that the incremental cost of using them equals the benefit of the additional output attributable to their use. The economic cost to society of using any additional resource is the other output that may have been produced with the same resource. If resources are not so allocated, then actual output is less than potential output. It is our contention that, because of a lack of formal training in the principles of education, many college economics instructors may not be using their teaching resources optimally, and consequently may not be providing students with the best possible education. It also is our contention that by modifying their teaching style, instructors may realize substantial gains in the knowledge of economics learned and retained by their students.

What follows is a description of an experiment conducted by two professors at St. John's University, one in an undergraduate, and the other in a graduate, economics course. In this chapter, we: (a) review the literature that is concerned with teaching college economics and the issue of matching teaching styles with learning styles; (b) explain how traditional methods of teaching college economics may be biased; (c) suggest that using group learning may be a potential way to ameliorate the detrimental effects of this bias; (d) explain the method used to assess the outcome of utilizing group learning as an additional teaching resource; and (e) comment on the merit of this experiment and suggest other potentially interesting studies regarding the issue of matching instructors' teaching styles with students' learning styles in collegiate economics.

LITERATURE REVIEW

An increase in teaching efficiency associated with matching instructors' teaching styles with students' learning styles is not new to the field of economics. Charkins, O'Toole, and Wetzel (1985) conducted research on the relationships between learning styles and teaching styles and their impact on outcomes in the teaching of economics in 1982. Their results indicated that the less disparity between learning and teaching styles, the greater the students' *learning* of economics, as measured by test scores. The students also had a more positive attitude toward economics than with incongruent styles.

A conclusion one might draw from these results is that, if we could place students with a particular learning style in a class with a professor who utilizes a matching teaching style, the outcomes, as far as students' learning is concerned, would be positive. The same result would hold with respect to their attitudes toward economics, which could influence their interest in, and retention of, the material presented.

As Charkins and others mention, it would be difficult to change a professor's teaching style, but teaching-style differences already exist. All it would take would be to identify and match them to students' learning styles. This would not be that difficult, it would appear, in a small school or campus. And, perhaps, it would not be that much more cumbersome in larger schools if the commitment to better teaching outcomes exists.

Benzig and Christ (1997) conducted a survey of teaching methods among college economics teachers. Their findings showed a movement in the late 1980s toward more student participation and interaction and less straight-lecture teaching. There is more use of class discussion, multimedia technology, and student participation projects than ever before. They hope this trend will continue because they believe that more active instruction is associated with more learning. However, they conclude, "that lecture with the support of the blackboard, and classroom discussion is the dominant teaching method in undergraduate economics today" (p. 190).

Bartlett and King (1990) question whether economics professors are teaching our students how to think like economists. Their pessimism is prompted, in part, by a lack of understanding among economics instructors about how students learn. Therefore, the issue that we raise is not new; we simply shed new light on it. We suggest that current teaching methods predominantly used by college economics professors may be biased in that they simultaneously are favorable to one style of learning and unfavorable to another. As a result, we may be unintentionally discouraging certain students from majoring in economics.

IS TEACHING STYLE BIASED?

According to the highly researched Dunn and Dunn Learning-Style Model (1993, 1999), people process information analytically, globally, or by a combination of the two methods. Analytic learners process information by induction, reasoning from specific facts to a general conclusion. Global learners process information by deduction—reasoning from a general conclusion to specific facts. Approximately 50 percent of adults—a majority—are global learners, and 28 percent are analytic learners (Dunn, 1999). The remainder may be either global or analytic, depending on their interest in the particular subject, or they may use a combination of alternative processing styles.

Analytic learners and global learners also have different environmental, emotional, sociological, psychological, and physiological preferences. Analytics learn best in a quiet, brightly lighted and formal learning environment. They usually do not snack while working; they like to work alone, prefer to start and finish one project at a time, and generally are print oriented. Globals, on the other hand, learn best with background sound, soft light, and in a relaxed learning environment. They usually enjoy snacks while working, like to work with peers, take frequent breaks, and simultaneously work on several projects. Globals prefer that new and difficult information be introduced anecdotally, especially in a way that humorously explains how the lesson relates to them. They generally are picture and illustration oriented.

Whether students process knowledge analytically, globally, or in a combination of the two methods often can be determined from their preferences regarding sound, light, design, persistence, and intake.

It is our contention that conventional methods used to teach college economics may be biased in the sense that they favor analytic learners and not global learners with respect to the learning environment, teaching method, and approach to evaluating what students have learned. *With respect to the learning environment,* classes generally meet either three days per week for one hour per class, or two days per week for one and one-half hours per class, for thirteen weeks. Classes typically meet in the morning and early afternoon. Some undergraduate and graduate courses meet during the evening once a week for a three-hour class. Classrooms are brightly lit and formally designed, with students usually seated at desks while facing the front of the room where the professor lectures and writes supporting notes on a chalkboard. This conventional and formal learning environment is favorable to analytic learners and unfavorable to global learners.

With regard to teaching methods, students generally and predominantly spend their class time listening to, and taking notes about, the professor's lectures. Lectures are supported by written, graphical, and mathematical notes on the chalkboard. Some time occasionally is reserved for discussion, but usually only at the end of the class when questions are encouraged. This highly structured and authoritative method of teaching is more suitable for analytic learners and is less suitable for global learners.

With respect to teaching approaches, several are used by economics instructors, including the principles, problems, political, and institutional approaches. The principles approach focuses on sequentially teaching economics principles that ultimately lead to an understanding of the dynamic behavior of the economy. This approach is the predominant method currently used in teaching college economics (Benzig & Christ, 1997). The problems approach argues that, because economics was developed to understand and solve problems, economics principles should be taught in the context of solving real-world problems. The political approach focuses on the role of government in the economy. The institutional approach focuses on current economic institutions such as labor, banking, the firm, or the stock market, and can be either descriptive, historical, evolutionary, or comparative in nature. The principles, problems, and political approaches focus on teaching principles in different contexts and, as such, they are inductive in nature and suitable for analytic learners. Since the institutional approach usually is holistic in scope and deductive in nature, it is more suitable for global learners. Because the majority of economics courses use the *principles* approach, the teaching of economics may be biased in favor of analytic learners and against global learners.

In most economics courses, students are evaluated in terms of a grade that typically is determined by averaging the midterm and final examination scores. Objective tests predominantly are used for two compelling reasons. They (a) ascertain students' knowledge of a wide range of information and (b) are quickly and easily corrected. Because objective examinations encourage and focus on memorization of facts, they are more suitable for analytic learners. As average class size continues to increase, especially in the principles courses, and as other professional responsibilities compete for a professor's time, objective examinations are increasingly popular.

Essay examinations, the preferred way to more accurately test students' knowledge, are not commonly used (Becker & Watts, 1996), probably because of the relatively large amount of time required to read and correct them. To prepare for essay examinations, students must review with the aim of organizing information to develop a coherent written explanation of real economic events. In this way, essay examinations focus more on the dynamic functioning of the economy, and less on individual facts. In this sense, essay examinations are more suitable for global learners. Consequently, the trend toward *objective* exams used to evaluate students' knowledge of economics may be biased in favor of analytic learners and against global learners.

To the extent that the teaching style described above characterizes college economics teaching, and to the degree that it diverges from students' learning styles, our teaching may encourage analytic learners and discourage global learners from studying economics. To compensate for this potential bias, we need to modify our style of teaching economics so that it is more suitable for, and, perhaps, more interesting to, global learners, but without negatively affecting analytic learners.

As previously mentioned, the ideal way to accomplish this objective is to determine students' learning styles and then match them with a professor who uses that particular teaching style. However, data regarding individual teaching and learning styles is not readily available. According to learning-style principles, to accommodate global learners, teachers can utilize group learning as an additional teaching resource. With group learning, students take a more active role in, and enhance, their own knowledge of economics. Group learning, a peer-oriented teaching method, is a social characteristic of many global learners (Dunn & Dunn, 1993). For example, groups of students can work cooperatively on a research project, class presentation, or computer assignment, and learn from their social and academic interactions with one another. In this way, economics teachers can utilize a method that more closely matches the way that global students learn.

Because we teach in a college of business administration, we are responsible for preparing our students to be amenable to, and successful in, the competitive business environment. Many of our undergraduate students, and the majority of graduate students, work full- or part-time in the New York City financial district, where teams, committees, or groups commonly conduct and coordinate many business activities. To provide a learning environment that both encourages, and is consistent with, modern business methods is another compelling reason for utilizing group learning as a teaching resource.

ASSESSMENT OF GROUP LEARNING

In both the graduate and undergraduate courses, each class was randomly divided by students into groups of four to six members. Each group was responsible for appointing a chair and a recorder and assigning tasks to each member in whatever way they deemed appropriate. Each group was responsible for conducting tasks common to the class, including reading, discussing, and learning assigned material, and preparing written and oral reports of either computer projects or research papers. Some, but not all, class time was allocated for Team Learning (Dunn & Dunn, 1993, 1999). Students were encouraged to meet outside class to accomplish their assignments.

It is important to note that group learning does not necessarily prohibit analytic students from learning or completing assignments alone. However, it does impose certain costs on them, including, for example, decreased time available for lecture in the classroom, and decreased time available for independent studies outside of the classroom. To limit the potential negative impact of group learning on analytic learners, students were not *required* to participate, and all students were required to take the same examinations individually.

For reasons previously discussed, instead of using test scores to assess the outcome of our experiment, we relied mainly on students' responses to the following five questions regarding their inclination toward, and experience with, group learning:

- Do you prefer working or studying alone or with others?
- What are the advantages and disadvantages to group learning?
- Do you think that you learned more using this technique or a more traditional style of teaching, such as lecture?
- Did you enjoy the class more this way or with lectures?
- Did this teaching style resemble your work situation more than regular classroom teaching?

Graduate Students' Responses

In the graduate course, an economics forecasting course, virtually all 22 students worked full-time in the New York City financial district and, consequently, were studying on a part-time basis. The teaching method consisted mainly of lecture supported by notes on the chalkboard, combined with questions and answers, and discussion. Because of the applied nature of this course, students were required to show competence in using the computer to construct, estimate, and analyze mathematical models to make economic forecasts. One written summary of each computer project from each group was required. In this way, group learning was introduced as an additional teaching resource.

In response to whether they preferred working alone or with others, 46 percent, a majority, answered that they preferred working with others. Twenty-seven percent responded that they preferred to work alone, and the same percentage responded that *it depends.* Assuming that those students who prefer to work with others are global learners, and those who prefer to work alone are analytical learners, these results are consistent with the percentages reported by Milgram, Dunn, & Price (1993). According to the principles of learning styles, for those students who answered *it depends,* their inclination to utilize group learning depends on whether or not they were interested in the topic being learned. If so, then they prefer group learning, and if not, then they are indifferent.

The advantage cited by 82 percent of the class was that developing a mutual dependence on the group was an important and reliable source of information. Because of this mutual dependence, students said that they were more motivated to be better prepared in order to help one another learn the material. Many students mentioned that they learned the material better by teaching it to other members of the group. All students who preferred group learning emphasized that, in terms of quality and quantity, it was a much more efficient way to learn. Two main disadvantages reported by all students were (a) the difficulty of scheduling opportune times for meetings outside the classroom and (b) the free-rider problem: some students did not contribute their *fair share.*

Over 85 percent of the students said that they learned more in the group than during class lectures. Many students commented that the combination of group learning and lectures provided a practical way of teaching the material. Only one student responded that he learned more with the traditional style of teaching. Ninety-one percent said that they enjoyed the class more because of the utilization of group learning. A slightly higher percentage, 95 percent, answered that group learning very closely resembled their work situation.

Undergraduate Students' Responses

In the undergraduate course, an applied microeconomics course, many of the students also worked in the New York financial district, were part-time evening students, and were older than typical undergraduates. Similar to the graduate course, the teaching method consisted of lecture supported by notes on the chalkboard, with class input and discussion. A major part of their grades depend on a group research project. Each group was required to provide both a written and oral summary of its research project. In this way, group learning was introduced as an additional teaching resource.

Slightly over 50 percent responded that they preferred to work alone, and the remainder preferred to work with others. Again, assuming that those who preferred to work alone are analytic learners, and those who preferred to work with others are global learners, the percentage of analytic learners is much higher than the norm, 28. The percentage who preferred to work with others is consistent with both the graduate class and the norm for adults. Interestingly, no undergraduate reported being indifferent regarding working alone or with others.

Increased socialization among group members was the advantage unanimously cited by those who preferred to work with others. They stated that they enjoyed making new friends and opening their minds to other points of view. Two disadvantages reported by all students were the free-rider problem and the scheduling problem. Those who preferred to work alone did so due to scheduling problems and because sometimes they felt that there was more socialization than work that took place at group meetings. They seemed to be especially concerned with, and intolerant of, some students not contributing their *fair share*. However, 87 percent responded that they learned more with group learning, and all students reported that they enjoyed the class more this way. Sixty-seven percent responded that group learning resembled their work environment.

SUMMARY AND CONCLUSION

If the golden rule of teaching is to maximize the quality and depth and breadth of students' education, then instructors' teaching styles must complement their students' learning styles. Many college economics instructors receive virtually no training in how students actually learn. Consequently, educational economics researchers question whether we are actually teaching students how to think like economists. In this chapter, we suggest that economists may not be doing this because the teaching methods they predominantly use may be biased in the sense that they are favorable to inductive learners and unfavorable to deductive learners.

To ameliorate the detrimental effects of this potential bias, and, just as important, to provide a learning strategy that is more consistent with actual business practices, we utilized group learning as an additional teaching resource. Judged solely on the basis of students' responses to an open-ended questionnaire, we apparently achieved both goals. Almost all graduate and undergraduate students reported that group learning closely resembled their work situation. In this sense, we accomplished the goal of teaching in a way that was compatible with students' learning styles and work conditions. These findings are consistent with the results of previous economics research.

An unexpected and quite interesting finding is that, for those who preferred working with others, the graduate students' responses differed noticeably from the undergraduate students' regarding the main advantage of group learning. For the graduate students, the overriding response was that group learning enhanced the productive efficiency of the entire group. Not only were they able to learn more, but they were more motivated to do so. Conversely, the undergraduate students emphasized that increased socialization with group members was the major benefit gained from group learning. Perhaps this result indicates a relatively greater importance to undergraduate college students of learning the social skills that are necessary to be a more productive student and worker. Presumably, graduate students have acquired these social skills and are now putting them to good use both in the classroom and in the workplace.

To accommodate global learners, we utilized group learning intervention in conjunction with the lecture-discussion teaching method, which is traditionally associated with accommodating analytic learners. Therefore, two approaches were used for the entire class as opposed to designing two separate methods for accommodating and matching the styles of global versus analytic learners. However, the ideal is to accommodate a wide variety of differing learning-style preferences among students through the use of individually designed interventions or small-group work. Implementation of this optimal teaching strategy requires that college economics instructors become acquainted with each student's learning-style profile. The paramount challenge confronting college economics instructors is the identification of students' learning styles and designing corresponding teaching methods.

Epilogue

Three decades of experimenting with learning-styles instruction for elementary, secondary, and college students internationally have convinced hundreds of administrators and teachers of the effectiveness of teaching by first identifying, and then complementing, how *each* person begins to concentrate on, process, internalize, and retain new and difficult academic information and skills. Learning-style-responsive strategies also have evidenced effectiveness with adults in business, education, law, nursing, and the health-related professions. However, this is the *first* book in which professors of higher education share how they have been using learning-styles approaches in their college classrooms.

The contributors to this text are all at different stages of implementing learning-styles-based instruction. Some, like Rita and Ken Dunn, Shirley Griggs, Katy Lux, Sue Ellen Read, and Barbara Thomson, have been focusing on students' learning styles for decades. Others, including Ann Braio, Barbara Given, Joanne Ingham, and Joyce Miller, have been involved in research on learning styles for years. Several, namely Karen Burke, Heather Pfleger Dunham, Rose Lefkowitz, Barbara Lewthwaite, Bernadyn Suh, and Jodi Taylor, began incorporating style-responsive strategies for students four or more years ago, and a few have only begun during the past two or three years. Among the latter are Robin Boyle, Valerie Englander, Nancy Montgomery, Herbert Pierson, Laura Shea Doolan, and Ralph Terregrossa. Finally, E. L. Deckinger has essentially been an insightful observer and cheerleader for many of us who persist in refining learning-styles theory, practice, and research—with the full knowledge that there is a long road ahead.

The value of this book is that, for the *first* time, guidelines based on the multiple applications of learning styles are reported by practicing professors. This book is designed to help other professors who philosophically embrace the concept of individual differences but do not know how to translate that theory into practice.

As the new millennium begins, our contributors share with us the vision that higher education teaching *will* change to respond to the diverse ways in which college students learn. To these avant garde pioneers, we extend our heartfelt appreciation and respect!

Appendix A

Award-Winning Learning-Styles Research

Carbo, M. (1980). An analysis of the relationship between the modality preferences of kindergartners and selected reading treatments as they affect the learning of a basic sight-word vocabulary. Doctoral dissertation, St. John's University, New York. *Dissertation Abstracts International, 41*, 1389–04A. Recipient: Association for Supervision and Curriculum Development National Award for Best Doctoral Research, 1980.

White, R. (1980). An investigation of the relationship between selected instructional methods and selected elements of emotional learning style upon student achievement in seventh-grade social studies. Doctoral dissertation, St. John's University, New York. *Dissertation Abstracts International, 42*, 995–03A. Recipient: Delta Kappa Gamma International Award for Best Research Prospectus, 1980.

Lynch, P. K. (1981). An analysis of the relationships among academic achievement, attendance, and the learning-style time preferences of eleventh- and twelfth-grade students identified as initial or chronic truants in a suburban New York school district. Doctoral dissertation, St. John's University, New York. *Dissertation Abstracts International, 42*, 1980A. Recipient: Association for Supervision and Curriculum Development. National Recognition for Best Doctoral Research (Supervision), 1981.

Pizzo, J. (1981). An investigation of the relationships between selected acoustic environments and sound, an element of learning style, as they affect sixth-grade students' reading achievement and attitudes. Doctoral dissertation, St. John's University, New York. *Dissertation Abstracts International, 42*, 2475A. Recipient: Association for Supervision and Curriculum Development. National Recognition for Best Doctoral Research (Supervision), 1981.

Krimsky, J. (1982). A comparative analysis of the effects of matching and mismatching fourth-grade students with their learning-style preferences for the environmental element of light and their subsequent reading speed and accuracy scores. Doctoral dissertation, St. John's University, New York. *Dissertation Abstracts International, 43,* 66–01A. Recipient: Association for Supervision and Curriculum Development First Alternate. National Recognition for Best Doctoral Research (Curriculum), 1982.

Virostko, J. (1983). An analysis of the relationships among academic achievement in mathematics and reading, assigned instructional schedules, and the learning-style time preferences of third- , fourth- , fifth- , and sixth-grade students. Doctoral dissertation, St. John's University, New York. *Dissertation Abstracts International, 4,* 1683–06A. Recipient: Kappa Delta Pi International Award for Best Doctoral Research, 1983.

Shea, T. C. (1983). An investigation of the relationships among preferences for the learning-style elements of design, selected instructional environments, and reading achievement of ninth-grade students to improve administrative determinations concerning effective educational facilities. Doctoral dissertation, St. John's University, New York. *Dissertation Abstracts International, 44,* 2004–07A, Recipient: National Association of Secondary School Principals Middle School Research Finalist Citations, 1984.

Perrin, J. (1984). An experimental investigation of the relationships among the learning-style sociological preferences of gifted and non-gifted primary children, selected instructional strategies, attitudes, and achievement in problem solving and rote memorization. Doctoral dissertation, St. John's University, New York. *Dissertation Abstracts International, 46,* 342–02A. Recipient: American Association of School Administrators' (AASA) National Research Finalist Recognition, 1984.

Della Valle, J. (1984). An experimental investigation of the relationship(s) between preference for mobility and the word recognition scores of seventh-grade students to provide supervisory and administrative guidelines for the organization of effective instructional environments. Doctoral dissertation, St. John's University, New York. *Dissertation Abstracts International, 45,* 359–02A. Recipient: (a) Phi Delta Kappa National Award for Outstanding Doctoral Research, 1984; (b) National Association of Secondary School Principals Middle School Research Finalist Citation, 1984, and (c) Association of Supervision and Curriculum Development Finalist Award for Best National Research (Supervision), 1984.

Hodges, H. (1985). An analysis of the relationships among preferences for a formal/informal design, one element of learning style, academic achievement, and attitudes of seventh- and eighth-grade students in remedial mathematics classes in a New York City junior high school. Doctoral dissertation, St. John's University, New York. *Dissertation Abstracts International, 45,* 2791A. Recipient: Phi Delta Kappa National Finalist for Outstanding Doctoral Research, 1986.

Martini, M. (1986). An analysis of the relationships between and among computer-assisted instruction, learning-style perceptual preferences, attitudes, and the science achievement of seventh-grade students in a suburban New York school district. Doctoral dissertation, St. John's University, New York. *Dissertation Abstracts International, 47,* 877–03A. Recipient: American Association of School Administrators' (AASA) National Research Finalist, 1986; AASA First Prize National Award for Best Doctoral Research, 1987.

Miles, B. (1987). An investigation of the relationships among the learning style sociological preferences of fifth- and sixth-grade students, selected interactive classroom patterns, and achievement in career awareness and career decision-making concepts. Doctoral dissertation, St. John's University, New York. *Dissertation Abstracts International, 48*, 2527A. Recipient: Phi Delta Kappa Eastern Regional Research Award, 1988.

Ingham, J. (1989). An experimental investigation of the relationships among learning-style perceptual strengths, instructional strategies, training achievement, and attitudes of corporate employees. Doctoral dissertation, St. John's University, New York, 1989. Recipient: (a) American Society of Training and Development Donald Bullock Dissertation Award (1989), and (b) Phi Delta Kappa Eastern Regional Research Award, 1990.

Quinn, T. (1995). The relationship between situational leadership characteristics and productivity styles on the implementation of the Dunn and Dunn Learning-Style Model for educational administrators in the United States. Recipient: The American Association of School Administrators and Convention Exhibitors' Research Award (1994) for best doctoral proposal.

Callan, R. (1996). An experimental investigation of the relationships among the time-of-day preferences of students taking a comprehensive test in sequential I mathematics and achievement in the test. Recipient: The American Association of School Administrators and Convention Exhibitors' Research Award (1995) for best doctoral proposal (1996).

Listi, A. L. (1997). Effects of programmed learning sequences versus traditional instruction in the social studies achievement and attitudes among urban third graders. Recipient: Kappa Delta Pi International Award for the Best Doctoral Dissertation Proposal in the World, 1997.

Van Wynen, E. L. (1998). Analysis of the current and previous learning styles of older adults and the effects of congruent versus incongruent instruction on their achievement and attitudes. Recipient: Sigma Theta Tau International Honor Society of Nursing for best doctoral proposal, 1998.

Geiser, William P. (1998). Effects of learning-style awareness and responsive study strategies on achievement, incidence of study, and attitudes of suburban eighth-grade students. Recipient: (a) St. John's University's School of Education and Human Services Outstanding Graduate Award (Dean's Convocation, May 1998), and (b) Phi Delta Kappa Northeast Regional Award for "the best doctoral dissertation of 1998."

Hemispheric Preference Scale
(Zenhausern, 1988)

Name _____   Age _____

Grade _____   Sex _____

Instructions: This is a questionnaire designed to measure your consistent style of learning, thinking, and living. People differ and one style is not better than another. Some of the questions may seem similar. These are not trick questions, but involve subtle differences or different perspectives.

For each statement, circle the X that best describes the way you are.

	Never	Rarely	Sometimes	Mostly	Always
1. My decisions are based on objective facts rather than feelings.	X	X	X	X	X
2. I am psychic.	X	X	X	X	X
3. I use symbols and/or images in solving problems.	X	X	X	X	X
4. I am good at teaching and/or explaining by manipulating objects.	X	X	X	X	X
5. I am artistically or musically creative.	X	X	X	X	X
6. I am logical.	X	X	X	X	X
7. I am good at solving crossword puzzles.	X	X	X	X	X

	Never	Rarely	Sometimes	Mostly	Always
8. I can read quickly.	X	X	X	X	X
9. My daydreams are vivid.	X	X	X	X	X
10. I am good at thinking of synonyms for words.	X	X	X	X	X
11. I remember my dreams.	X	X	X	X	X
12. My dreams are vivid.	X	X	X	X	X
13. I am fluent in using words.	X	X	X	X	X
14. I use a playful approach to solving problems.	X	X	X	X	X
15. I use a businesslike approach to solving problems.	X	X	X	X	X
16. I like experiences to be planned and structured.	X	X	X	X	X
17. I like to think or read while sitting upright.	X	X	X	X	X
18. My thinking consists of using words.	X	X	X	X	X
19. My thinking consists of mental pictures or images.	X	X	X	X	X
20. I like teaching or explaining by visual presentations.	X	X	X	X	X

Hemispheric Preference Scale: Scoring Instructions

All 20 items are scored 1 (never) to 5 (always) from left to right. The key below indicates whether a question is to be scored as analytic or global. The averages of the 10 analytic questions and the 10 global questions are subtracted, and the difference score is a measure of preference.

Key

1. analytic	6. analytic	11. global	16. analytic
2. global	7. analytic	12. global	17. analytic
3. global	8. analytic	13. analytic	18. analytic
4. global	9. global	14. global	19. global
5. global	10. analytic	15. analytic	20. global

Norms

These norms are based on almost 800 undergraduate and graduate students and represent percentiles corresponding to mean differences between analytic and global mean scores for males and females. For example, a male who has a 1.23 difference in favor of analytic would be in the 70th percentile. The development of local norms for specific groups is suggested.

	Male		Female	
Percentile	Analytic	Global	Analytic	Global
10	.13	.25	.13	.16
20	.24	.45	.25	.30
30	.38	.65	.43	.44
40	.53	.74	.58	.66
50	.70	.94	.76	.92

	Male		Female	
Percentile	Analytic	Global	Analytic	Global
60	.90	1.17	.89	1.08
70	1.23	1.43	1.18	1.37
80	1.54	1.78	1.42	1.70
90	2.05	2.18	1.83	2.22
Number	156	168	168	245
Mean	.978	1.22	.98	1.07

Appendix D

Example of an Analytic-Format Syllabus

St. John's University
Division of Administrative and Instructional Leadership
Education 7120, Spring 1999
Learning-Styles Research, Theory, and Practical Applications

Professor Rita Dunn, Ed.D.
Office: 208 Marillac Hall
Jamaica, NY 11439
(718-990-6335/6)   Home: (914) 764-8266
e-mail: RDUNN241@ aol.com
web site: www.learningstyles.net

Objective 1: Knowledge of Various Learning-Style Models

1. Describe (a) at least five (5) learning-style models, (b) the pioneer(s) who developed each model, (c) at least two (2) biographical facts about each of the pioneers, (d) the major components of each model, (e) which models are "comprehensive" and which include only one or two variables on a bi-polar continuum, and (f) the ways in which the models are *similar* to and *different* from each other.

(Complete one Activity Alternative and its paired Reporting Alternative for the fourth class session.)

Activity Alternatives*

1. Develop PowerPoint slides or overhead transparencies that describe five (5) learning-style models, the

Reporting Alternatives

1. Present your resource to a small group of 3–4 in class during the fourth session. Request a four-

---

* All Activity Alternatives may be completed alone or in a pair.

Activity Alternatives

pioneers who developed them, the major components of each model, whether or not the model is comprehensive, and the ways in which the models are similar to and different from each other.

2. Develop a kinesthetic Floor Game that describes five (5) learning-style models, the pioneers who developed them, the major components of each model, whether or not the model is comprehensive, and the ways in which the models are similar to and different from each other.

Reporting Alternatives

sentence rhyming poem that evaluates your presentation.

Or

2. Have a small group of classmates play your Floor Game during the fourth session. Ask each person to write a one-sentence evaluation of your Floor Game.

Required Readings:

Miller, J., & Edgar, G. (1994). The *Learning Styles Inventory* and the *Learning Styles Profile*: Concurrent validity and the ability to discriminate among class rankings. *Illinois School of Research and Development, 31*(1), 14–18. [In *Articles & Books*]

Tendy, S. M., & Geiser, W. F. (1998/1999). The search for style: It all depends on where you look. *National Forum of Teacher Education Journal, 9*(1), 3–16. Los Angeles: California State University.

Optional Readings for Motivated Students:

Dunn, R., & Waggoner, B. (1995). Comparing three innovative instructional systems. *Emergency Librarian, 23*(1), 9–15.

LaMothe, J., Billings, D. M., Belcher, A., Cobb, K., Nice, A., & Richardson, V. (1991). Reliability and validity of the *Productivity Environmental Preference Survey*. *Nurse Educator, 16*(4), 30–34.

Consider (a) *why* and *how* current assessment instruments need to be improved and (b) the implications for achievement, intelligence assessments, and interest inventories. *You will be required to discuss your perceptions in class.*

Group Analysis:

1. _____   3. _____

2. _____   4. _____

   Recorder: _____

A. Explain *why* current testing instruments need to be improved and how that can be done.

B. Cite at least five (5) implications for achievement, intelligence, and interest assessments and inventories.

1. _____

2. _____

3. _____

4. _____

5. _____

Objective 2: Research on the Dunn and Dunn Model
(Complete any three (3) of the following five (5) objectives)

1. Synthesize the research supporting the impact of classroom *environments* on student achievement by referencing practitioners' reports and the findings of the major researchers in this area (DeGregoris, 1986; Della Valle, 1984; Dunn, 1987; Dunn, Della Valle, Dunn, Geisert, Sinatra, & Zenhausern, 1986; Dunn, Krimsky, Murray, & Quinn, 1985; Hodges, 1985; Krimsky, 1982; Miller, 1985; Murrain, 1983; Nganwa-Baguma, 1986; Nganwa-Baguma & Mwamwenda, 1991; Pizzo, 1981; Pizzo, Dunn, & Dunn, 1990; Shea, 1983). Name the practitioners and researchers, the date, and the institutions, and synthesize the treatments and results.

2. Synthesize the research supporting the impact of *emotionality* on student achievement by referencing practitioners' reports and the findings of Napolitano (1986), Sawyer (1995), White (1981), and Dunn, White, & Zenhausern (1982). Name the practitioners and researchers, the dates, and the institutions, and synthesize the treatments and results.

3. Synthesize the research supporting the impact of *sociological preferences* on student achievement by referencing practitioners' reports and the findings of DeBello (1985), Cholakis (1986), Dunn, Giannitti, Murray, Geisert, Rossi, and Quinn (1990), Giannitti (1988), Miles (1987), and Perrin (1984). Name the practitioners and researchers, the dates, and the institutions, and synthesize the treatments and results.

4. Synthesize the research supporting the impact of *perceptual preferences* on student achievement by referencing practitioners' reports and the findings of Bauer (1991), Dunn, Bauer, Gemake, Gregory, Primavera, and Signer (1994), Buell and Buell (1987), Carbo (1980), Drew (1991), Drew, Dunn, Sinatra, Quinn, and Spiridakis (1995), Dunn (1989), Garrett (1992), Hill (1987), Ingham (1989, 1991), Dunn, Ingham, Deckinger, and Geisert (1995), Jarsonbeck (1984), Kroon (1984), Martini (1986), Mitchell (1999), Roberts (1999), Urbschat (1977), Weinberg (1983), and Wheeler (1980, 1983). Name the practitioners and researchers, the dates, and the institutions, and synthesize the treatments and results.

5. Synthesize the research supporting the impact of chronobiology (*time-of-day*) preferences on student achievement by referencing practitioners' reports and the findings of Callan (1995, 1996, 1997, 1998, 1999), Dunn (1999), Dunn, Dunn, and

Freeley (1984), Dunn, Dunn, Primavera, Sinatra, and Virostko (1987), Lynch (1981), Freeley (1984), and Virostko (1983). Name the practitioners and researchers, the dates, and the institutions, and synthesize the treatments and results.

(Complete one Activity Alternative and its paired Reporting Alternative.)

Activity Alternatives

1. Design a kinesthetic Floor Game synthesizing the research supporting the impact of classroom environments on student achievement. Include at least three (3) of the five (5) stimuli and all of the elements in each strand.

Reporting Alternatives

1. Play your Floor Game with two (2) to three (3) classmates. Have each initial a card to verify the accuracy of its content.

Or

2. Develop a set of five- to six-part Task Cards on the research documenting the effectiveness of the elements.

2. Ask at least three (3) classmates to check the accuracy of your Task Cards.

Read:

Callan, R. J. (1997). Giving students the right time of day. *Educational Leadership*, *55*(4), 85–87.

Dunn, R. (1997–1998). How children learn: The impact of learning-style responsive instruction on student achievement, attitudes, and behavior. *National Forum of Applied Educational Research*, *11*(1), 4–9. [In *Articles & Books*]

Dunn, R., Della Valle, J., Dunn, K., Geisert, G., Sinatra, R., & Zenhausern, R. (1986). The effects of matching and mismatching students' mobility preferences on recognition and memory tasks. *Journal of Educational Research*, *79*(5), 267–272. [In *Articles & Books*]

Dunn, R., Dunn, K., Primavera, L., Sinatra, R., & Virostko, J. (1987). A timely solution: A review of research on the effects of chronobiology on children's achievement and behavior. *The Clearing House*, *61*(1), 5–8, 9. [In *Articles & Books*]

Dunn, R., White, R. M., & Zenhausern, R. (1982). An investigation of responsible versus less responsible students. *Illinois School Research and Development*, *19*(1), 19–24.

Roberts, A. (1998/1999). Effects of tactual and kinesthetic instructional methods on social studies achievement and attitude test scores of fifth-grade students. *National Forum of Teacher Education Journal*, *9*(1), 16–26. Los Angeles: California State University.

Objective 3: Information Processing Styles

1. Synthesize the research concerning *global versus analytic preferences* by referencing the studies and reports, naming the researchers or authors, citing the dates and the institutions or affiliations, and synthesizing the recommendations for classroom applications. Include: Dunn, Cavanaugh, Eberle, and Zenhausern (1982) and Dunn, Bruno, Sklar, and Beaudry (1990).

2. Describe the differences between *global* and *analytic* processing.

3. Describe the learning-style *characteristics* of extremely global versus extremely analytic students and the impact of conventional teaching on the former.

4. Identify your own processing style (in-class activity).

5. Both Thies (1979) and Restak (1979) concur concerning the *biological* basis of many learning-style elements. Consider their arguments and determine whether you agree or disagree with their basic premises (in-class activity).

6. Although Thies and Restak concur concerning the *biological* basis of many learning-style elements, neither they—nor any researcher other than Dunn—have reported what appears to be the relationship(s) between the element of Persistence and an individual's processing style. Hypothesize why no one else has perceived this relationship and argue the accuracy or inaccuracy of Dunn's belief.

(Complete one Activity Alternative and its paired Reporting Alternative.)

Required Activity	**Required Reporting**
1. Develop both an analytic and global single-paragraph introduction to the same article geared for a professional education journal. • *Due*: Fifth session.	1. Be prepared to distribute copies of the two paragraphs to all class members.

Read:

Burke, R., & McCaffery, C. (Fall 1988). A system to relieve the high anxiety of the global adult learner. *The Oregon Elementary Principals' Journal, 50*(1), 26–27.

Dunn, R., Bruno, J., Sklar, R. I., & Beaudry, J. (May/June 1990). Effects of matching and mismatching minority developmental college students' hemispheric preferences on mathematics scores. *Journal of Educational Research, 83*(5), 283–288. Washington, DC: Heldref Publications. [In *Articles & Books*]

Given, B. (1997–1998). Psychological and neurobiological support for learning-style instruction: Why it works. *National Forum of Applied Educational Research, 11*(1), 10–17.

Guastello, E. F., & Burke, K. (1998). Relationship(s) between the consistency scores of an analytic vs. global learning-style assessment for middle-school students (grades 6–8). *National Forum of Teacher Education Journal, 9*(1), 64–69. Los Angeles: California State University.

Objective 4: Teaching Students to Teach Themselves by Studying and Doing Homework Through Their Learning Styles

1. Describe the research concerned with teaching students to teach themselves.

2. Develop practical procedures for teaching students to teach themselves.

3. Identify your *teaching* style.

Activity Alternatives

1. Using the format employed by the *Learning Styles Network Newsletter* (pages 4, 5, and 8), develop a "Synthesis of the Research on Teaching Students to Teach Themselves."

2. Write a short article for a journal in *your* field synthesizing the research on teaching students to teach themselves and suggesting practical procedures for doing it. Introduce the article GLOBALLY.

Reporting Alternatives

1. Submit the material to Dr. Dunn.

Or

2. Submit the article to an editor and show Dr. Dunn the editor's response.

Read:

Callan, R. J. (February 1996). Learning styles in the high school: A novel approach. *NASSP Bulletin, 80*(577), 66–72. [In *Articles & Books*]

Dunn, R., & Geiser, W. F. (September 1998). Solving the homework problem: A heart-to-heart versus a tongue-in-cheek approach. *Michigan Principal, 74*(3), 7–10. East Lansing, MI: Elementary and Middle School Principals Association.

Geiser, W. F. (1998). Effects of learning-style awareness and responsive study strategies on achievement, incidence of study, and attitudes of suburban eighth-grade students. (Doctoral dissertation, St. John's University.)

Lenehan, M. C., Dunn, R., Ingham, J., Murray, W., & Signer, B. (November 1994). Learning styles: Necessary know-how for academic success in college. *Journal of College Student Development, 35,* 461–466. [In *Articles & Books*]

Marino, J. (1993). Homework: A fresh approach to a perennial problem. *Momentum, 24*(1), 69–71.

Nelson, B., Dunn, R., Griggs, S. A., Primavera, L., Fitzpatrick, M., Bacilious, Z., & Miller, R. (1993). Effects of learning style intervention on students' retention and achievement. *Journal of College Student Development, 34*(5), 364–369. [In *Articles & Books*]

Turner, N. D. (Summer 1993). Learning styles and metacognition. *Reading Improvement, 30*(2), 82–85.

Objective 5: Multiculturalism and Learning Styles

1. Describe the research concerned with cultural diversity and its implications for instruction.

2. Explain how various cultures, races, and religious groups are (a) similar to and (b) different from each other.

3. Identify your biases (if any) toward multicultural groups (in-class activity).

4. Determine the effectiveness of multicultural school programs given the research on learning styles and diversity.

5. To what degree does the political structure impact on multicultural school programs? Is its overall effect positive, negative, or neutral?

(Complete the following Activity Alternatives.)

Required Activity Alternative

1. Using the format employed by the
Learning Styles Network Newsletter,
develop an issue on a "Synthesis of
the Research on Multiculturalism and
Learning Styles."

Required Reporting Alternative

1. Submit the issue of the *Newsletter*
to Dr. Dunn.

• This Activity Alternative may be completed alone, in a pair, or in a small group of
three. However, you will need to put together a complete issue of the *Newsletter*. If
it is really good, our Center will publish it and the three can name themselves as
Editor, Assisting Editor, Contributor, and so forth. If accepted for publication, the
major contributors will be excused from the final examination in this course.

Read:

Dunn, R. (1997). Multicultural education: Its goals and track record. *ASCD Education Leadership*, 54(7), 74–77. Alexandria, VA.

Dunn, R., & Griggs, S. A. (1995). *Multiculturalism and learning styles: Teaching and
counseling adolescents*. Westport, CT: Praeger Publishers.

Milgram, R. M., Dunn, R., & Price, G. E. (Eds.). (1993). *Teaching and counseling
gifted and talented adolescents: An international learning styles perspective.*
Westport, CT: Praeger Publishers.

Objective 6: Implementation of Learning-Styles Programs

1. Name research studies directed toward implementation of learning-styles programs.

2. Describe practical steps for effective implementation of learning-styles programs.

3. Describe how learning styles change over time (in-class activity).

4. Develop three (3) alternatives for grouping students and teachers by matched styles.

Activity Alternative

1. Using the format employed by the
Learning Style Network Newsletter,
develop an issue of the *Newsletter* on
"Research on Implementing Learning-
Styles Programs."

Reporting Alternative

1. Submit the material to Dr. Dunn.

• All Activity Alternatives may be completed alone, in a pair, or by a small group of
three. However, you will need to put together a complete issue of the *Newsletter*. If
it is really good, our Center will publish it and the three can name themselves as
Editor, Assisting Editor, Contributor, and so forth. If accepted for publication, the
major contributors will be excused from the final examination in this course.

Read:

Braio, A., Beasley, M. T., Dunn, R., Quinn, P., & Buchanan, K. (1997). Effects of incremental implementation of learning-styles strategies among urban low-achievers' structural analysis and attitude test scores. *Journal of Educational Research, 91*(1), 15–25. Washington, DC: Heldref Publications.

Dunn, R., Given, B., Thomson, B. S., & Brunner, C. (1997–1998). The International Learning Styles Network: Who, when, what, where, and why? *National Forum of Applied Educational Research, 11*(1), 26–29.

Dunn, R., & Gremli, J. (1998/1999). Teaching urban students with Contract Activity Packages: Rap, rock, and ragtime—a rational approach. *National Forum of Teacher Education Journal, 9*(1), 27–41. Los Angeles: California State University.

Honigsfeld, A. (1998/1999). Teaching reading to English-as-a-second-language students with style. *National Forum of Teacher Education Journal, 9*(1), 42–49. Los Angeles: California State University.

Klavas, A. (1993). In Greensboro, North Carolina: Learning style program boosts achievement and test scores. *The Clearing House, 67*(3), 149–151.

Klavas, A., Dunn, R., Griggs, S. A., Gemake, J., Geisert, G., & Zenhausern, R. (1994). Factors that facilitated or impeded implementation of the Dunn and Dunn Learning-Style Model. *Illinois School Research and Development Journal, 31*(1), 19–23.

Montgomery, N. (1998/1999). An educated mind and a compassionate heart: respecting diverse urban cultures. *National Forum of Teacher Education Journal, 9*(1), 42–49. Los Angeles: California State University.

Objective 7: Emerging Research in Learning Styles

1. Collect at least eight (8) research studies (1997–2000 only) that used the Dunn and Dunn Learning-Style Model but were *not* included in *Research on the Dunn and Dunn Model* (2000).

2. Learning-styles research is branching out into fields other than education. Explain how it can and has been applied to business, law and court reporting, medicine, music, nursing, religion, sonography, and technology (any four of these fields).

Activity Alternatives

1. Read the following texts and any additional research sources available—but particularly those cited in *Research on the Dunn and Dunn Model*. Develop a *Network Newsletter* for publication, describing how learning-style research and applications are being expanded nationally and internationally.

Reporting Alternatives

1. Submit this issue of the *Newsletter*. You may work with one or two classmates and, if the issue is excellent, I will excuse you from the final examination.

Read:

Boyle, R., & Dunn, R. (1998). Teaching law students through their individual learning styles. *Albany Law Review*, 62(1), 213–255. Albany, NY: Albany Law School.

Dunn, R., & Griggs, S. A. (Eds.). (1998). *Learning styles and the nursing profession.* New York: National League of Nursing.

Dunn, R., Griggs, S. A., Olson, J., Gorman, B., & Beasley, M. (1995). A meta-analytic validation of the Dunn and Dunn Learning-Style Model. *Journal of Educational Research*, 88(6), 353–361.

Dunn, R., Ingham, J., & Deckinger, L. (1995). Effects of matching and mismatching corporate employees' perceptual preferences and instructional strategies on training achievement and attitudes. *Journal of Applied Business Research*, 11(3), 30–37.

Ingham, J. (1991). Matching instruction with employee perceptual preferences significantly increases training effectiveness. *Human Resource Development Quarterly*, 2(1), 53–64.

Miller, J., & Dunn, R. (1997). The use of learning styles in sonography education. *Journal of Diagnostic Medical Sonography*, 13(6), 304–308.

Resource Alternatives

Required Publications

(1) *Articles & Books* (2000). New York: St. John's University's Center for the Study of Learning and Teaching Styles. Cost: $50.00 (Two Volumes).

(2) *National Forum of Teacher Education Journal* (1998/1999). $5.00.

(3) *National Forum of Applied Educational Research* (1997/1998). $5.00.

(4) Current Issue of *Learning Style Network Newsletter* (Winter 1999/2000). $5.00.

Optional Publications

(5) Milgram, R. M., Dunn, R., & Price, G. E. (Eds.). (1993). *Teaching and counseling gifted and talented adolescents: An international learning styles perspective.* Westport, CT: Praeger Publishers. Cost: $60.00.

If you are interested in multiculturally diverse gifted and talented students and the concept of multi-intelligence, this book is unique. It describes the learning styles of such students in nine different cultures—Canada, Brazil, Egypt, Greece, Guatemala (Guatemalans and Mayans), Israel, Korea, the Philippines, and the United States—and demonstrates distinctive learning-style patterns among these adolescents that establish their uniqueness.

Or

(6) Dunn, R., & Griggs, S. A. (1995). *Multiculturalism and learning styles: Teaching and counseling adolescents.* Westport, CT: Greenwood Press.

This book provides extensive research documenting the differences in learning styles among African-American, Asian-American, European-American, and Hispanic-American students and provides support for the premise that the school-related underachievement among minority students is directly related to teaching analytically to many global, tactual, kinesthetic, in-need-of-mobility, and peer-interactive combinations of style.

Note: A book report on this publication that warrants an A will be sufficient to bypass the final examination.

(7) *Learning Styles Network Newsletters*. Cost: $3.00 each.

The *Learning Styles Network Newsletter* is published by St. John's University's Center for the Study of Learning and Teaching Styles and includes all but the most recent research that you will need. Request the specific issue(s) you wish in Room 208 Marillac Hall @ $3.00 per issue. Originals may be purchased by teams and shared.

- How to Get Started with Learning Styles. Spring 1988, *9*(2).
- Counseling Students Through Their Learning Styles. Autumn 1988, *9*(3).
- Are Schools Causing Academic Failure? Spring 1989, *10*(2).
- Each Classroom Environment Affects Individuals Differently. Winter 1991, *11*(3).
- Learning Styles and Cultural Differences. Winter 1989, *10*(1).
- Perceptual-Strength Sequencing Is Crucial to Achievement. Spring 1991, *12*(2).
- Data from College Campuses and the Corporate World. Summer 1992, *13*(2).
- Human Beings Affect Each Other Differently. Summer 1991, *12*(2).
- Time-of-Day Energy Levels Affect Achievement. Winter 1992, *12*(3).
- Learning Style and the Law. Spring 1993, *14*(1).
- Learning Styles and the Health Professions. Autumn 1993, *14*(2).
- Learning Styles and Special Education. Spring 1994, *15*(1).
- Learning Styles of Elementary School Students. Autumn 1994, *15*(3).
- How Learning Styles Change Over Time. Winter 1995, *16*(1).
- What Do We Know About Global and Analytic Processing? Autumn 1996, *16*(3).
- Why Do Many Multiculturally-Diverse Students Fail? Autumn 1996, *16*(3).
- How Learning Styles Differ Among Groups of Students. Winter 1996, *17*(1) (includes one new learning-style homework study and a student's report).

(8) Videotape:

Dunn, R. (1993). *Teaching multicultural students through their individual learning styles*. New York: Center for the Study of Learning and Teaching Styles (Videotape). Cost: $100.00 ($50.00 Reduction).

This videotape overviews learning styles and the implications for teaching multiculturally diverse students.

Grading Criteria:

- Reflection of readings and lectures in class discussions; includes attendance and punctuality: 10%.
- Originality, creativity, and knowledge of the research in learning styles as reflected in tests, quizzes, or their alternative: 35%.
- Creative application of knowledge as demonstrated in Activity Alternatives: 55%.

Time Allocations:

Course	Lecture	Supplemental Assignments
• In Class:		
Contact	15 Hours	30 Hours
Contact	15 Hours	30 Hours
• Out-of-Class		
Contact	0 Hours	90 Hours
	30 Hours	150 Hours

Example of a Global-Format Syllabus

Aquinas College
School of Education
EN 565: Learning-Styles Research and Development

Faculty: Katy Lux, Ph.D., Professor of Education, Director, Midwest
Regional Teaching/Learning Center
Phone: 616/459-8281 Ext. 5409 (Office)   616/245-1665 (Home)
e-mail: luxkat@aquinas.edu

SYLLABUS

Course Description:

This course focuses on how you—and everyone you know—learns and thinks. Of particular emphasis will be the issues of research in, diagnosis for, and applications to learning and teaching. In addition, the subsequent designing of instructional prescriptions will enable each class participant to transfer this information into practice.

Required Readings:

Caine, R. N., & Caine, G. (1994). *Making Connections: Teaching and the Human Brain*, 2nd ed. Rolling Meadows, IL: Addison Wesley.
Jensen, E. (1998). *Teaching with the Brain in Mind*. Alexandria, VA: ASCD. ISBN 0-87120-299-9 (pbk.).

and one (1) of the following books:

Dunn, R., & Dunn, K. (1992). *Teaching Elementary Students Through Their Individual Learning Styles: Practical Approaches for Grades 3–6*. Boston: Allyn & Bacon.

Dunn, R., & Dunn, K. (1993). *Teaching Secondary Students Through Their Individual Learning Styles: Preactical Approaches for Grades 7–12.* Boston: Allyn & Bacon.
Dunn, R., Dunn, K., & Perrin, J. (1994). *Teaching Young Children Through Their Individual Learning Styles.* Boston: Allyn & Bacon.

Course Objectives:

Emphasis is on the following objectives and will focus on the needs and backgrounds of the group participants to:

1. Understand and demonstrate the nature of the teaching methods required for a changing, diverse population.

2. Understand the multifaceted, complex interactions that learning and teaching involve and the impact such interactions have on academic achievement.

3. Identify and develop compatible learning situations and increase the effectiveness of both teacher and learner.

4. Assess and acknowledge personal styles, preferences, and strengths in teaching and/or administration.

5. Demonstrate knowledge of the processing differences that exist among students, staff, and administrators, and to facilitate change in instructional delivery.

6. Gain an awareness of current materials and resources available to assess learning preferences, and enhance the teaching and learning process.

7. Acquire knowledge of research findings and research opportunities in the fields of effective schools, learning styles, and brain-compatible approaches.

8. Enable the process of effective communication in the educational setting as well as in the public relations activities with school boards, volunteers, and parents.

Course Requirements:

1. Participation in all regularly scheduled class sessions. (Be there!)

2. Assigned readings and responses to journals as designated in class. (No Excuses!)

3. Chapter presentations as assigned. (You'll be a shining star!)

4. Identify your own learning and teaching styles. Determine the congruence between the two. (To thine own self be true!)

5. Design two of the following tactual/kinesthetic resources to teach one unit to your class: an Electroboard, a Flip Chute with cards, a Learning Circle, a set of 3-part Task Cards, a Pick-An-Answer, or a kinesthetic Floor Game (Dunn & Dunn, 1992, 1993). (Hands on and move with it!)

6. Set goals for the classroom, keeping learning styles and brain-compatible approaches as the focus. (Know where you want to go so that you get there!)

7. Describe and demonstrate a lesson plan to respond to diverse students' learning styles. Include matching perceptual strengths, processing style, and stating and teaching to the required standards. Include the assessment techniques you would use to correspond to the identified learning styles. (How will you know that you've done a good job?)

or

Redesign an instructional environment to respond to students' diversified styles, preferences, and learning needs, keeping students who are highly kinesthetic, in need of mobility, or an informal design in mind. (You need not necessarily apply for an interior-design license!)

or

Describe, or demonstrate how to work with non-conforming students and/or those who require a great deal of or little structure. (How will you know how to reach students?)

or

Describe what the research reports about the differences between how global and analytic students learn. Teach a global and an analytic lesson and report how different students react to clearly different cognitive strategies.

or

Contract for an individual project or idea that meets all the standards of graduate work and course objectives.

SCHEDULE OF CLASS MEETINGS

Session I: Monday, June 21

- Introduction, Course Overview, Structure, Expectations
- Determining Objectives
- Defining Style
- Learning to Learn
- Administration of PEPS
- Learning Style and Brain Behavior
- Global/Analytic Research and Practice
- Team Learning
- Assignment: Connections, Chapters 1, 2, 3, 4, 5, and 6

Session II: Tuesday, June 22

- Chapter Presentations (Chapters 1, 2, and 3)
- Discussion of Readings
- Individual Learning Characteristics (Dunn & Dunn)
- PEPS Interpretation
- Chapter Presentations (Chapters 4, 5, and 6)
- Discussion of Readings
- Analyzing Teaching Styles
- Circle of Knowledge
- Assignment: Connections, Chapters 7, 8, 9, 10, 11, and 12, and Dunn and Dunn to develop a Contract Activity Package (CAP)

Session III: Wednesday, June 23

- Chapter Presentations (Chapters 7, 8, and 9)

- Discussion of Readings
- Gardner's Perspective (Multiple Intelligences)
- Chapter Presentations (Chapters 10, 11, and 12)
- Discussion of Readings
- Dimensions and Types (Myers-Briggs)
- Contract Activity Packages (CAPs) Discoveries
- Assignment: Connections, Conclusion; Dunn and Dunn, Chapters 6–8
- Brain/Mind (Chapters 1, 2, 3, 4, 5, and 6)
- Programmed Learning Sequences (PLSs)

Sesssion IV: Thursday, June 24

- Chapter Presentations (Connections, Conclusion)
- Dunn and Dunn, Chapters 1–5, 9–10
- Discussion of Readings
- PLS Discoveries
- Accommodating Various Styles in One Room/Room Design
- Chapter Presentations (Brain/Mind, Chapters 4, 5, and 6)
- Discussion of Readings
- T/K Workshop
- Assignment: Brain/Mind (Chapters 7, 8, 9, 10, and 11)
- Provided Resources
- Projects

Session V: Friday, June 25

- Chapter Presentations (Brain/Mind, Chapters 7, 8, 9, 10, and 11)
- Resources and Materials Presentations/Sharing
- Mind-Body Connection
- Project Presentations/Sharing
- Evaluation
- Celebration!

Appendix F

Law School Quiz

Prof. Robin A. Boyle
St. John's University School of Law

LAW QUIZ
Point Headings, Persuasive Writing, Adverse Cases, and Citations

Work independently, with a partner, or in small groups, using your assigned texts to answer the following questions:

A. Point Headings
   1) What is a point heading?
   2) Where should point headings be located in the brief?
   3) What is the purpose of point headings?
   4) Do you move from general to specific headings or vice versa?
   5) Suppose you had a major heading, two subheadings, and three lesser subheadings. Which one would you put in:
      a) All capital letters, no underlining;
      b) No capital letters, with underlining;
      c) No capital letters, no underlining.
   6) What should your point headings contain?
      a) If you have only major headings, and no subheadings, what goes into the major heading?
      b) If you have major and minor headings, what goes into each?

B. Skim manual chapter, *Ten Tips for Writing a Persuasive Brief.* Then, close the manual. How many brief writing tips can you provide below and on the back of this page?

C. Adverse Cases
   1) When do you need to cite an adverse case?
   2) Where do you place adverse cases in the argument section of your brief?

3) How do you distinguish among adverse cases?

D. Citations

1) Do you use parallel cites for your appellate brief when you are citing to United States Supreme Court cases and to federal circuit courts?

2) Your full cite is: *United States v. Brown*, 43 F.3d 618, 623 (11th Cir.), *cert. denied*, 116 S.Ct. 309 (1995). You wish to again cite to *Brown*, but to page 631. There was an intervening cite. Your short form cite looks like:

3) There was no intervening cite, but you wish to again cite to *Brown*, this time for the material on page 633, running over in the same paragraph to page 634. Your short cite is:

4) You are reading a case with the following citation: *United States v. Doe*, 435 U.S. 222, 211 S.Ct. 333, 455 U.S.L.W. 333 (1987). How would you cite it for the first time?

5) You wish to cite to *Doe* again, when there was no intervening citation. However, there are two passages that pertain to your proposition. One passage begins and ends on page 224 of the *United States Reports*, and then another relevant passage begins and ends on page 226. How do you cite this?

Appendix G

Law School Quiz Answers

Prof. Robin A. Boyle
St. John's University School of Law

LAW QUIZ ANSWERS FOR
Point Headings, Persuasive Writing, Adverse Cases, and Citations

A. Point Headings
   1) A point heading is a statement of the legal conclusions the advocate is asking the court to adopt.
   2) They are located within the body of the Argument and in the Table of Contents or the Index.
   3) Point headings have two purposes: organization and advocacy.
   4) It is preferable to move from general to specific headings.
   5) Headings should be structured as:
      a) Major headings—all capital letters, no underlining;
      b) Subheadings—no capital letters, with underlining;
      c) Lesser subheadings—no capital letters, no underlining.
   6) What the headings should contain:
      a) The major heading should concisely contain the issue being discussed (including the relevant legal rule), your position on this issue, and the basic reasons for that position.
      b) When lesser headings are used, the larger heading should contain your issue and your position concerning the application of a particular legal rule. The lesser headings should provide the reasons for that position.

B. Ten tips for writing a persuasive brief are listed below:
   1) You do the work, not the reader.
   2) It is worth spending time to carefully craft the Question Presented, point headings, and subheadings.

3) Early in the brief, identify who is bringing the action against whom and the reasons why.
4) Use proper paragraph structure when writing the statement of the case.
5) Tell a story from your client's point of view in both the statement of the case as well as in the argument component.
6) Use placement and sentence structure to emphasize and de-emphasize facts.
7) In the argument component, move from general to specific topics.
8) Help draw the reader in your paragraph by stating, in the first or second sentence, the topic of the paragraph and your conclusion/position on that topic.
9) Avoid giving a history of the law; instead, synthesize the law.
10) Budget your time; proofread your brief several times, looking for one category of correction at a time.

C. Adverse Cases
   1) It is necessary to include cases in your brief when such cases are adverse to your position and they are:
      a) in the same jurisdiction as the case in your controversy; or
      b) otherwise relevant controlling precedent.
   2) It is advisable to bury the adverse case in the text of your argument, or at the end, but always place it in logical context. The most important rule to follow is to set forth your analysis before addressing the counterarguments (including distinguishing the adverse cases).
   3) Distinguish an adverse case by showing:
      a) how the facts of the adverse case differ from the facts in your case;
      b) that there are dissimilarities in the way in which the statute or law should be applied;
      c) jurisdictional diffferences indicating that the case is not controlling authority because it comes from a different state, circuit, or department;
      d) temporal differences because the adverse case was decided a long time ago;
      e) policy shifts when the policy that affected the outcome in the adverse case is no longer popular; or
      f) flaws in the reasoning or analysis of the adverse case that led to incorrect results.

D. Citations
   1) No. Do not use parallel cites for the United States Supreme Court cases and to the federal circuit courts in accordance with the proper citation rules in your citation book.
   2) *Brown,* 43 F.3d at 631.
   3) *Id.* at 633-34.
   4) *United States v. Doe,* 435 U.S. 222 (1987).
   5) *Id.* at 224, 226.

Alternative Instructional Methods Responsive to Diverse Learning-Style Characteristics

Alternative Methods	Responds to	
	Learning-Style Elements	Other Student Characteristics
Contract Activity Package	Environmental Preferences Sociological Preferences Perceptual Strengths Physiological Preferences Persistence Motivation Structure Analytic Processing Style	Self-pacing Independent Non-conforming Creative
Programmed Learning Sequence	Persistence Sociological Preferences Environmental Preferences Physiological Preferences Structure Visual/Tactual Strengths Global/Processing Style	Self-pacing Likes Variety Has Reading Difficulties Needs Feedback
Tactual Resources	Tactual Perceptual Strength Environmental Preferences Physiological Preferences	Keeps Hands Busy Likes to Touch
Kinesthetic Resources	Kinesthetic Perceptual Strength Environmental Preferences Physiological Preferences	Needs Mobility Is Restless Is Active
Small-Group Techniques	Peer-Oriented Preference	Tolerates Sound Conforming

Developed by Andrea Honigsfeld and Rita Dunn.

Appendix I

Research Concerned with College Students' Learning Styles

Researcher University	Date	Subject Examined	Aspect Examined
Clay, J. E. Alabama A & M University	1984	GPA	High vs. Low Achievers' Learning Styles

FINDINGS: Highly and poorly achieving freshmen revealed different learning-style characteristics. The lower the GPA, the more students preferred music, a variety of resources and methods, soft lighting, mobility, an informal environment, and studying with peers while learning difficult and new material. The higher the GPA, the more students wanted a quiet, conventional classroom environment. These findings tend to validate previous findings that differentiated between global and analytic individuals (Bruno, Dunn, Sklar, & Beaudry, 1990).

Researcher University	Date	Subject Examined	Aspect Examined
Vazquez Arce, W. The Union for Experimenting Colleges and Universities	1985	Various	Learning-Style Descriptions

FINDINGS: This study investigated the learning-style preferences of high-risk, non-traditional community college students in Puerto Rico. The purpose of the study was to make instructional recommendations on the basis of the identified learning-style characteristics of these particular students. They showed preferences for bright light, cool temperature, silence, formal seating arrangements, and studying in pairs, with an expert, or alone. They felt motivated but also expressed a need to be motivated by others. They viewed themselves as responsible, persistent, and in need of structure. They seemed to learn better by hearing and preferred kinesthetic experiences. Their preferred high-energy periods were early in the morning and in the evening.

Napolitano, R. A.   1986   Psychology   Structure
St. John's University

FINDINGS: This study investigated differences among traditionally, marginally, and underprepared college students' academic achievement and attitude scores when the degree of structure was either matched or mismatched with their learning-style preferences for structure. It revealed that students who needed a highly structured environment received significantly higher achievement and attitude test scores when their preference was accommodated. All students achieved higher test scores when the course was taught under highly structured conditions. However, students who did not prefer structure demonstrated lower attitudinal scores in the mismatched environment.

Lam-Phoon, S.   1986   N/A   Cultural + Gender
Andrews University   Differences

FINDINGS: This study compared the learning-style preferences of Southeast Asian and American caucasian college students. Asians' and caucasians' learning styles were statistically different from each other. Caucasians had a higher preference for warmth, intake, and mobility while learning; they were more conforming and remembered less well auditorily and visually. Males had a higher preference for noise, tactile learning experiences, intake, conformity, warmth, and patterns and routines rather than variety. They also were more persistent and preferred learning with peers more than females did. Caucasian males, as compared to Asian males, had stronger preferences for warmth, conformity, persistence, and intake, and a lower preference for learning auditorily or visually. Caucasian females were more conforming and preferred more warmth, mobility, intake, and morning learning than Asian females. They also had less preference for auditory and visual learning than Asian females.

Clark-Thayer, S.   1987   Mathematics   Achievement +
Boston University   Homework

FINDINGS: This study examined the relationships among freshmen's learning styles, study habits, and college achievement. Both study habits and learning styles correlated significantly with achievement. Successful students were motivated, responsible (conforming), preferred to learn alone, rather than with peers, and required varied instructional experiences rather than routines and patterns. They were not tactual learners. High achievers also engaged in specific study habits and had positive attitudes toward their educational experiences.

Bailey, G. K.   1988   N/A   Hemisphericity +
The University of   Environmental
Southern Mississippi   Preferences

FINDINGS: The study investigated the relationship between hemispheric-information processing and environmental preferences that influence learning styles. In addition, it also determined which of the PEPS variables in combination would successfully discriminate right, left, and integrated hemispheric preferences. The results of the study indicated that eight variables were related to left-hemispheric preference, five variables were related to right-hemispheric preference, and seven variables were related to an integrated processing style.

Dunn, R.,   1988   Business   Achievement
Deckinger, E. L.,
Withers, P.,
& Katzenstein, H.
St. John's University

FINDINGS: The learning-style preferences of college business students were identified. Students were taught how to study and complete assignments using their individual learning-style strengths. Students who applied the information about their learning styles to studying achieved significantly higher grades than those who did not. A comparison was made between the group that received exposure to learning styles and a control group that had not been introduced to learning styles previously. The learning-styles group performed better than the control group.

Reynolds, J.   1988   Decision Making   Learning-Style Traits of
Virginia Polytechnic   Dependent Learners
Institute and State
University

FINDINGS: Reynolds used identified characteristics and their associated instructional strategies to suggest interventions for dependent decision makers. Results indicated that any instructional model designed for dependent decision makers should consider four PEPS elements: sound, motivation, persistence, and responsibility.

Cook, L.   1989   General Education   Learning-Style
University of Florida   Awareness

FINDINGS: This study examined learning-style awareness and its effects on scholastic improvement and locus of control of community college students. The study also was designed to examine differences in areas of achievement and locus of control between typical college-age students (18–22) and older students (non-traditional community college age) following learning-style awareness treatment. There was a significant difference in academic achievement in favor of the learning-style awareness group ($p < .05$). In addition, the older group perceived that they had changed study patterns, improved their grades, and benefited from learning-style awareness more than the younger group.

Dunn, R., Bruno,   1990   Mathematics   Processing Style +
J., Sklar, R. I., &   Hemisphericity
Beaudry, J.
St. John's University

FINDINGS: This study identified the hemisphericity and processing-style preferences of community college students enrolled in remedial mathematics courses. All students were exposed to four lessons, two with a global approach and two with an analytic one. When these underachieving students were taught with instructional strategies that matched their processing style, their achievement scores were significantly higher, especially for the global learners.

Jenkins, C.   1991   Generic Freshman   Learning-Style
The University of   Studies   Preferences
Mississippi

FINDINGS: This study identified the relationships among selected demographic variables, such as entrance examination scores, gender, grade point average, major or
career choice, and the subset of environmental preferences favored by most freshman
students of Alcorn State University. Results indicated: (1) one out of the 20 elements
was significant (design) in discriminating among students' scores on the college entrance examination; (2) females' preferences were significantly different from males'
preferences in the areas of motivation, persistent, structure, authority orientation, and
kinesthetic preference; (3) males preferred peer and evening/morning learning more
than females; (4) students with a high rather than a low GPA preferred *tactile* instructional resources more; (5) there was no significant difference in the learning-style
preferences of freshman students based on their major or career choice; and (6) the
cluster of learning-style elements preferred by most freshman students included: afternoon, structure, authority figure present, and auditory perception.

Nelson, B., Dunn,   1993   Across-the board   Achievement +
R., Griggs, S. A.,   GPA   Retention
Primavera, L.,
Fitzpatrick, M.,
Bacilious, Z.,
& Miller, R.
St. John's University

FINDINGS: This study compared the GPA and retention rate for three groups of
freshmen in a Texas college. Members of the first group were introduced to learning
styles and had their PEPS Profiles interpreted. The second group was exposed to
learning styles and was also taught to study in congruence with each individual's learning-style strengths. The control group received no information about learning styles.
Students who received the most exposure to learning style and were instructed how to
study achieved significantly higher GPAs during the spring semester than those who
did not receive instruction. These students also demonstrated significantly higher retention rates than expected, whereas the retention rates of those having no or limited
exposure were significantly lower than expected.

Lenehan, M. C.,   1994   Anatomy   Nursing Students'
Dunn, R., Ingham,   Physiology   Achievement + Anger
J., Murray J. B.,   Bacteriology
& Signer, B.
St. John's University

FINDINGS: Nursing students in the Experimental Group were shown how to study
by capitalizing on their identified learning-style preferences. Control-group students
were shown how to study with conventional study-skill guidelines, tutoring, and advisement assistance. Students in the Experimental Group achieved statistically higher
science grades *and* grade point averages than students in the control group, suggesting that homework prescriptions for use in one subject affected grades in other subjects positively. In addition, the Experimental Group evidenced significantly lower

anxiety and anger scores, and significantly higher curiosity about science. The control group members were significantly more anxious about, and angry with, their science course(s) than the Experimental Group, and were less curious about science than when the term began.

Kennedy, M. D.   1995   Tennis   Matching and
Florida State University   Mismatching Teaching/
                                                               Learning Styles

FINDINGS: This study determined the effects of matching the teaching styles of professors with the learning styles of undergraduates enrolled in beginning tennis classes. The researcher concluded that when instructional strategies were developed, designed, and implemented in accordance with students' learning styles, all methods effectively enhanced tennis skills.

Miller, J.   1997   Diagnostic Medical   Programmed Learning
St. John's University   Sonography   Sequences (PLS) versus
                                                               Traditional Lessons

FINDINGS: Using a population of college juniors and seniors in a baccalaureate degree program in Diagnostic Medical Sonography, the researcher compared the effectiveness of PLSs in book versus computer versus CD-ROM formats with traditional lessons on student achievement and attitudes. Both classes involved in the study demonstrated significantly increased achievement scores and better attitudes when using PLSs, but the various strategies were differentially effective with students' diverse learning styles.

Tendy, S. M.   1998   Group Exercise   Perceptual and
St. John's University   Leadership   Sociological Preferences

FINDINGS: The effects of matching and mismatching instructional strategies on psychomotor achievement test scores of subjects classified according to a combination of perceptual and sociological learning-style strengths at a military college were analyzed. Data revealed no significant difference in psychomotor achievement scores between students whose combined perceptual and sociological learning-style preferences were matched as compared to those who were mismatched. However, positive trends indicated that future investigations utilizing larger sample sizes may lead to significant findings. Additionally, students evidencing a preference for instructional techniques employing visual strategies scored significantly higher ($p < .01$) than the visually non- or opposite-preferenced students.

Bovell, C.   2000   Non-traditional   Learning-Style
St. John's University   College Students   Preferences

FINDINGS: This study examined the learning styles of non-traditional students enrolled in a large, urban, Catholic university. Demographic data regarding gender, age, ethnicity, income, parenthood, previous educational background, or marital status were considered. Particular elements of the PEPS such as intake, time of day, learning in several ways, and responsible (conforming) demonstrated statistically significant differences among some demographic variables.

Dolle, Lynne	2000	Legal Research	Programmed Learning
St. John's University		and Writing	Sequences versus
			Traditional Lessons

FINDINGS: This study examined the effects of traditional and learning-styles-based instructional strategies on achievement and attitudes of first-year law school students in a legal research and writing class. The findings indicated significantly higher achievement test scores when the PLSs, rather than lectures, were used.

Created by Rita Dunn and Andrea Honigsfeld.

References

Acheson, K. (1992). *Techniques in the clinical supervision of teachers: Preservice and inservice applications.* White Plains, NY: Longman.

Alberg, J., Cook, L., Fiore, T., Friend, M., & Sano, S. et al. (1992). *Educational approaches and options for integrating students with disabilities: A decision tool.* Triangle Park, NC: Research Triangle Institute, P.O. Box 12194, Research Triangle Park, NC 27709.

Anderson, M. (1992). *Imposters in the temple: American intellectuals are destroying our universities and cheating our students of their future.* New York: Simon & Schuster.

Andrews, R. (1990). The development of a learning-styles program in a low socio-economic, underachieving, North Carolina elementary school. *Journal of Reading, Writing, and Learning Disabilities International, 6*(3), 307–314.

Andrews, R. (1997). Insights into education: An elementary principal's perspective. In R. Dunn (Ed.), *Hands-on approaches to learning styles: Practical approaches to successful schooling* (pp. 51–52). New Wilmington, PA: Association for the Advancement of International Education.

Arcieri, D. (1998). Informal forms of staff development: Cushion the task! In R. Dunn & K. Dunn (Eds.), *Practical approaches to individualizing staff development for adults* (pp. 33–40). Westport, CT: Praeger.

Astin, A. W. (1993). *What matters in college: Four critical years revisited.* San Francisco: Jossey-Bass.

Bailey, G. K. (1988). Examination of the relationship between hemispheric preferences and environmental characteristics of learning styles in college students. Doctoral dissertation, University of Southern Mississippi. *Dissertation Abstracts International, 49*(8), 2151A.

Bartlett, R. L., & King, P. G. (1990). Teaching economics as a laboratory science. *Journal of Economic Education, 21*(2), 181–193.

Becker, W. E., & Watts, M. (1996). Chalk and talk: A national survey on teaching undergraduate economics. *The American Economic Review, 86*(2), 448–453.

Benzig, C., & Christ, P. (1997). A survey of teaching methods among economics faculty. *Journal of Economic Education, 28*(2), 182–188.

Berliner, D., & Calfee, R. (Eds.). (1996). *Handbook of educational psychology.* New York: Macmillan.

Billings, D., & Cobb, K. (1992). Effects of learning style preference, attitude, and GPA on learner achievement using computer-assisted-interactive videodisc instruction. *Journal of Computer-Based Instruction, 19*(1), 12–16.

Bok, D. (1982). *Beyond the ivory tower: Social responsibilities of the modern university.* Cambridge, MA: Harvard University Press.

Bovell, C. (2000). Analysis of the learning styles of older adults enrolled in non-traditional university programs and recommendations for congruent homework prescriptions and teaching strategies. Doctoral dissertation, St. John's University.

Boyer, E. L. (1990). *Scholarship reconsidered: Priorities of the professorate.* New York: Special Report of the Carnegie Foundation for the Advancement of Teaching.

Boyle, R., & Dunn, R. (1998). Teaching law students through individual learning styles. *Albany Law Review, 62*(1), 213–255.

Braio, A. (1988). *Mission from no-style: Wonder and Joy meet the Space Children.* Jamaica, NY: St. John's University's Center for the Study of Learning and Teaching Styles.

Braio, A., Dunn, R., Beasley, M, T., Quinn, P., & Buchanan, K. (1997). Incremental implementation of learning-style strategies among urban low achievers. *Journal of Educational Research, 91,* 15–25.

Brand, E. (1999). Effects of learning-style based homework prescriptions on urban 11th-grade low-achieving students in vocabulary. Doctoral dissertation, St. John's University.

Braskamp, L., & Ory, J. (1994). *Assessing faculty work: Enhancing individual and institutional performance.* San Francisco: Jossey-Bass.

Brennan, P. K. (1984). An analysis of the relationships among hemispheric preference and analytic/global cognitive style, two elements of learning style, method of instruction, gender, and mathematics achievement of tenth-grade geometry students. Doctoral dissertation, St. John's University. *Dissertation Abstracts International, 45,* 3271A.

Brown, M. D. (1991). The relationship among traditional instructional methods, Contract Activity Packages, and mathematics achievement of fourth-grade gifted students. Doctoral dissertation, University of Southern Mississippi. *Dissertation Abstracts International, 52*(6), 1999A–2000A.

Brown, S. D., Lent, R. W., & Larkin, K. C. (1989). Self-efficacy as a moderator of scholastic aptitude-academic performance relationships. *Journal of Vocational Behavior, 35,* 64–75.

Brunner, C., & Dunn, R. (1996, Summer). Learning style in overseas schools. *International Education, 24*(1), 1, 9–11. In R. Dunn, *Everything you need to successfully implement a learning-styles program: Materials and methods* (pp. 78–81). New Wilmington, PA: Association for the Advancement of International Education.

Brunner, C., & Majewski, W. S. (1990). Mildly handicapped students can succeed with learning styles. *Educational Leadership, 48*(2), 21–23.

Buell, B. G., & Buell, N. A. (1987). Perceptual modality preference as a variable in the effectiveness of continuing education for professionals. Doctoral dissertation, University of Southern California. *Dissertation Abstracts International, 48*, 283A.

Buffalo Experience, The (videotape). (1993). New York: State Education Department and the Buffalo City Schools. Available from St. John's University's Center for the Study of Learning and Teaching Styles, 8000 Utopia Parkway, Jamaica, NY 11439.

Burke, K. (1998). Relationship(s) between the consistency scores of an analytic versus a global learning-styles assessment for middle-school students (grades 6–8). Doctoral dissertation, St. John's University.

Burke, K., Guastello, F., Dunn, R., Griggs, S. A., Beasley, M., Gemake, J., Sinatra, R., & Lewthwaite, B. (1999/2000). Relationship(s) between global-format and analytic-format learning-style assessments based on the Dunn and Dunn Model. *National Forum of Applied Educational Research Journal, 13*(1), 76–96.

Burton, E. H. (1980). An analysis of the interaction of field dependent/field independent styles and word type as they affect word recognition among kindergartners. Doctoral dissertation, St. John's University.

Canfield, A. A., & Lafferty, J. C. (1976). *Learning Style Inventory.* Detroit: Humanics Media.

Carter, D., & Wilson, R. (1992). *Minorities in higher education.* Washington, DC: American Council on Education.

Carver, D. S., & Smart, D. W. (1985). The effects of a career and self-exploration course for undecided freshmen. *Journal of College Student Personnel, 26*, 37–43.

Charkins, R. J., O'Toole, D. M., & Wetzel, J. N. (1985). Linking teacher and student learning styles with student achievement and attitudes. *Journal of Economic Education, 16*(2), 111–120.

Clark-Thayer, S. (1987). The relationship of the knowledge of student perceived learning style preferences, and study habits and attitudes to achievement of college freshmen in a small urban university. Doctoral dissertation, Boston University. *Dissertation Abstracts International, 48*, 872A.

Clark-Thayer, S. (1988). Designing study-skills programs based on individual learning styles. *Learning-Style Network Newsletter, 9*(3), 4. New York: St. John's University and the National Association of Secondary School Principals.

Claxton, C. S., & Murrell, P. H. (1987). *Learning styles: Implications for improving education practices* (ASHE-ERIC Higher Education Report No. 4). Washington, DC: Association for the Study of Higher Education.

Clay, J. E. (1984). A correlational analysis of the learning-style characteristics of highly achieving and poorly achieving freshmen at A & M University as revealed through performance on standardized tests. Normal, AL: Alabama A & M University.

Cody, C. (1983). Learning styles, including hemispheric dominance: A comparative study of average, gifted, and highly-gifted students in grades five through twelve. Doctoral dissertation, Temple University. *Dissertation Abstracts International, 44,* 163A.

Coleman, H. L., & Freedman, A. L. (1996). Effects of a structured group intervention on the achievement of academically at-risk undergraduates. *Journal of College Student Development, 37,* 631–636.

Cook, L. (1989). Relationships among learning style awareness, academic achievement, and locus of control among community college students. Doctoral dissertation, University of Florida. *Dissertation Abstracts International, 49*(3), 217A.

Cook. L. (1991). Learning style awareness and academic achievement among community college students. *Community Junior College Quarterly of Research and Practice, 15*(4), 419–425.

Cronbach, L. (1957). How can instruction be adapted to individual differences? In R. Gagne (Ed.), *Learning and individual differences.* Columbus, OH: Merrill.

Curry, L. (1987). *Integrating concepts of cognitive or learning styles: A review with attention to psychometric standards.* Ottawa: Canadian College of Health Services Executives.

DeBello, T. (1985). A critical analysis of the achievement and attitude effects of administrative assignments to social studies writing instruction based on identified, eighth grade students' learning style preferences for learning alone, with peers, or with teachers. Doctoral dissertation, St. John's University. *Dissertation Abstracts International, 47,* 68A.

DeBello, T. (1990, July–September). Comparison of eleven major learning styles models: Variables, appropriate populations, validity of instrumentation, and the research behind them. *Journal of Reading, Writing, and Learning Disabilities International, 6*(3), 203–222.

DeGregoris, C. N. (1986). Reading comprehension and the interaction of individual sound preferences and varied auditory distractions. Doctoral dissertation, Hofstra University. *Dissertation Abstracts International, 47,* 3380A.

Demitroff, J. (1974). Student persistence. *College and University, 49,* 553–557.

DiSebastian, J. (1994). Learning in style in Teguciagalpa, Honduras. *International Education, 21*(71), 11, 16.

Dolle, L. (2000). Effects of traditional versus learning style instructional strategies in legal research on the achievement and attitudes of first-year law students in a legal research and writing course. Doctoral dissertation, St. John's University.

Doolan, L. S. (1999). Teaching middle-school students to teach themselves: Life preservers. *Michigan Principal, 75*(1), 8–9.

Douglas, C. (1979). Making biology easier to understand. *American Biology Teacher, 41*(4), 277–299.

Duckwall, J., Arnold, L., & Hayes, J. (1991). Approaches to learning by undergraduate students: A longitudinal study. *Research in Higher Education, 32*(1), 1–13.

Dunham, H. P. (1999). Effects of sociological preferences and congruent versus incongruent instruction on college economic students' achievement and anxiety. Doctoral dissertation, St. John's University.

Dunn, R. (1987). Research on instructional environments: Implications for student achievement and results. *Professional School Psychology, 2*(1), 43–52.

Dunn, R. (1989). Individualizing instruction for mainstreamed gifted children. In R. R. Milgram (Ed.), *Teaching gifted and talented learners in regular classrooms* (pp. 63–111). Westport, CT: Greenwood.

Dunn, R. (1990, Fall). Teaching young children through their perceptual processing strengths, Part Two. *International Education, 17*(55), 5–7.

Dunn, R. (1990, October). Rita Dunn answers questions on learning styles. *Educational Leadership, 48*(15), 15–19.

Dunn, R. (1996a). *How to implement and supervise a learning-style program.* Alexandria, VA: Association for Supervision and Curriculum Development.

Dunn, R. (1996b). *Everything you need to successfully implement a learning-styles instructional program: Materials and methods.* New Wilmington, PA: Association for the Advancement of International Education.

Dunn, R. (1997). *Hands-on approaches to learning styles: Practical approaches to successful schooling.* New Wilmington, PA: Association for the Advancement of International Education.

Dunn, R., Bauer, E., Gemake, J., Gregory, J., Primavera, L., & Signer, B. (1994). Matching and mismatching junior high school learning disabled students' perceptual preferences on mathematics scores. *Teacher Education Journal, 5*(1), 3–13.

Dunn, R., & Brunner, C. (1997, June). International misconceptions about learning: Where did they begin? *International Education, 24*(1), 1, 9–11.

Dunn, R., Bruno, J., Sklar, R. I., & Beaudry, J. (1990, May/June). Effects of matching and mismatching minority developmental college students' hemispheric preferences on mathematics scores. *Journal of Educational Research, 83*(5), 283–288.

Dunn, R., Cavanaugh, D., Eberle, B., & Zenhausern, R. (1982). Hemispheric preference: The newest element of learning style. *The American Biology Teacher, 44*(5), 291–294.

Dunn, R., & DeBello, T. (1999). *Improved test scores, attitudes, and behaviors in America's schools: Supervisors' success stories.* Westport, CT: Bergin & Garvey.

Dunn, R., DeBello, T., Brennan, P., Krimsky, J., & Murrain, P. (1981). Learning style researchers define differences differently. *Educational Leadership, 38*(5), 382–392.

Dunn, R., Deckinger, E. L., Withers, P., & Katzenstein, H. (1990, Winter). Should college students be taught how to do homework? The effects of studying marketing through individual perceptual strengths. *Illinois School Research and Development Journal, 26*(3), 96–113.

Dunn, R., & Dunn, K. (1972). *Practical approaches to individualizing instruction: Contracts and other effective teaching strategies.* Nyack, NY: Parker Publishing Company.

Dunn, R., & Dunn, K. (1978). *Teaching students through their individual learning styles: A practical approach.* Reston, VA: Prentice-Hall Publishers.

Dunn, R., & Dunn, K. (1992). *Teaching elementary students through their individual learning styles: Practical approaches for grades 3–6.* Boston: Allyn & Bacon.

Dunn, R., & Dunn, K. (1993). *Teaching secondary students through their individual learning styles: Practical approaches for grades 7–12.* Boston: Allyn & Bacon.

Dunn, R., & Dunn, K. (1996). Teaching students through their individual learning styles: A practical approach. The 19th Annual Leadership Institute. New York: Learning Styles Network, St. John's University.

Dunn, R., & Dunn, K. (Eds.). (1998). *Practical approaches to individualizing staff development for adults*. Westport, CT: Praeger.

Dunn, R., & Dunn, K. (1999). *The complete guide to the learning-styles inservice system*. Needham Heights, MA: Allyn & Bacon.

Dunn, R., Dunn, K., & Freeley, M. E. (1985). Tips to improve your inservice training. *Early Years*, *15*(8), 43–45.

Dunn, R., Dunn, K., & Perrin, J. (1994). *Teaching young children through their individual learning styles: Practical approaches for grades K–2*. Boston: Allyn & Bacon.

Dunn, R., Dunn, K., & Price, G. (1974–1996a). *Learning Style Inventory* (LSI). Lawrence, KS: Price Systems.

Dunn, R., Dunn, K., & Price, G. (1974–1996b). *Productivity Environmental Preference Survey*. Lawrence, KS: Price Systems.

Dunn, R., & Geiser, W. P. (1998, Fall). Solving the homework problem: A heart-to-heart versus a tongue-in-cheek approach. *Michigan Principal*, *74*(3), 7–10.

Dunn, R., Given, B. K., Thomson, B. S., & Brunner, C. (1997). The international learning styles network: Who, when, what, where, why—and why not? *National Forum of Applied Educational Research Journal*, *11*(1), 24–27.

Dunn, R., & Gremli, J. (1998/1999). Teaching urban students with contract activity packages: Rap, rock, and ragtime—a rational approach. *National Forum of Teacher Education Journal*, *9*(1), 27–41.

Dunn, R., & Griggs, S. A. (1995). *Multiculturalism and learning style: Teaching and counseling adolescents*. Westport, CT: Praeger.

Dunn, R., & Griggs, S. A. (Eds.) (1998). *Learning styles and the nursing profession*. New York: National League for Nursing.

Dunn, R., Griggs, S. A., Olson, J., Gorman, B., & Beasley, M. (1995). A meta-analytic validation of the Dunn and Dunn Learning-Styles Model. *Journal of Educational Research*, *88*(6), 353–361.

Dunn, R., Ingham, J., & Deckinger, L. (1995). Effects of matching and mismatching corporate employees' perceptual preferences and instructional strategies on training achievement and attitudes. *Journal of Applied Business Research*, *11*(3), 30–37.

Dunn, R., & Klavas, A. (1990). Homework Disc. Jamaica, NY: St. John's University's Center for the Study of Learning and Teaching Styles.

Dunn, R., & Stevenson, J. M. (1997). Teaching diverse college students to study with a learning-styles prescription. *College Student Journal*, *31*(3), 333–339.

Dunn, R., White, R. M., & Zenhausern, R. (1982). An investigation of responsible versus less responsible students. *Illinois School Research and Development*, *19*(1), 19–24.

Egan, M., Welch, M., Sebastian, J., & Lacy, H. (1992). Distance education through television: Project RETOOL integrating special education technology into the higher education curriculum. University of Utah: Council for Exceptional Children.

Ellis, A. (1994). *Reason and emotion in psychotherapy revised*. New York: Carol Press.

Freeley, M. E. (1984). An experimental investigation of the relationships among teachers' individual time preferences, inservice workshop schedules, and instructional techniques and the subsequent implementation of learning style strategies in participants' classrooms. Doctoral dissertation, St. John's University. *Dissertation Abstracts International, 46,* 403–02A.

Freire, P. (1980). *Pedagogy of the oppressed* (Translated by M. B. Ramos). New York: Seabury.

Friedman, L. M. (1985). *A history of American law.* 2nd ed. New York: Simon and Schuster.

Giannitti, M. C. (1988). An experimental investigation of the relationships among the learning style sociological preferences of middle-school students (grades 6, 7, 8), their attitudes and achievement in social studies, and selected instructional strategies. Doctoral dissertation, St. John's University. *Dissertation Abstracts International, 49,* 2911A.

Glasser, R. (1966). Components of a psychological theory of instruction: Toward a science of design. *Review of Educational Research, 46,* 1–24.

GOALS 2000: A Progress Report (Table of Contents) [On-line]. http:// 165.224.220.253/19.

Greb, F. (1999). Learning-style preferences of fifth- through twelfth-grade students medically diagnosed with attention hyperactivity disorder. Doctoral dissertation, St. John's University.

Gregorc, A. F. (1982). Learning style/brain research: Harbinger of an emerging psychology. In *Student learning styles and brain behavior* (pp. 3–10). Reston, VA: National Association of Secondary School Principals.

Griggs, S. A. (1992). *Learning styles counseling.* Greensboro, NC: Educational Resource Information Center for Counseling and Student Services.

Griggs, S. A., Price, G. E., & Suh, B. (1997/1998). Freshmen students' level of satisfaction with roommates, residence, and college in relation to their learning-style preferences. *Applied Educational Research Journal, 11*(1), 30–36.

Guastello, E. F. (1998). Reliability and concurrent validity of a global learning-style assessment for elementary-school students (Grades 2–5). Doctoral dissertation, St. John's University.

Guastello, E. F., & Burke, K. (1998/1999). Relationships between the consistency scores of an analytic vs. a global learning-style assessment for elementary- and middle-school urban students. In R. Dunn & S. A. Griggs (Eds.), *Learning Styles and Urban Education. The National Forum of Teacher Education Journal, 9*(1), 68–74.

Guinier, L., Fine, M., Balin, J., Bartow, A., & Stachel, D. L. (1994). Becoming gentlemen: Women's experiences at one Ivy League law school. *University of Pennsylvania Law Review, 143*(1), 3–4, 63–65.

Hacket, G., Casas, J. M., Betz, N. E., & Rocha-Singh, I. A. (1992). Gender, ethnicity, and social cognitive factors predicting the academic achievement of students in engineering. *Journal of Counseling Psychology,* 39(4), 527–538.

Hill, J. (1971). *Personalized education programs utilizing cognitive style mapping.* Bloomfield Hills, MI: Oakland Community College.

Holmes Partnership. (1995). *The Holmes partnership network and goals.* Columbus: Ohio State University's College of Education.

Homework Disc. (1992). Jamaica, NY: St. John's University's Center for the Study of Learning and Teaching Styles.

Honigsfeld, A. (1999). Global warming: It's not cool. *Science and Children, 36*(6), 46–51.

House, J. D. (1993). The relationship between academic self-concept and school withdrawal. *Journal of Social Psychology, 133*(1), 125–127.

Hoy, W., & Forsyth, P. (1986). *Effective supervision: Theory into practice.* New York: Random House.

Hunt, D. E. (1982). The practical value of learning style ideas. In *Student learning styles and brain behavior* (pp. 87–91). Reston, VA: National Association of Secondary School Principals.

Ingham, J. (1991). Matching instruction with employee perceptual preferences significantly increases training effectiveness. *Human Resource Development Quarterly, 2*(1), 53–64.

Jadid, R. P. (1998). Analysis of the learning styles, gender, and creativity of Bruneian elite-, high performing-, and non-performing primary- (elementary) and secondary-school students and their teachers' teaching styles. Doctoral dissertation, St. John's University.

James, W., & Gardner, D. (1995) Learning styles: Implications for distance learning. In M. Rossman & M. Rossman (Eds.), *Facilitating distance education* (pp. 19–31). San Francisco: Jossey-Bass.

Jarsonbeck, S. (1984). The effects of a right-brain and mathematics curriculum on low achieving, fourth grade students. Doctoral dissertation, University of South Florida. *Dissertation Abstracts International, 45,* 2791A.

Jenkins, C. (1991). The relationship between selected demographic variables and learning environmental preferences of freshman students of Alcorn State University. Doctoral dissertation, The University of Mississippi. *Dissertation Abstracts International, 92,* 16065.

Jones, D., & Watson, B. (1991). *High-risk students in higher education* (ASHE-ERIC Higher Education Report No. 3). Washington, DC: Association for the Study of Higher Education.

Kauchek, D., & Eggen, P. (1989). *Learning and teaching: Research-based methods.* Needham Heights, MA: Allyn & Bacon.

Keefe, J. W. (1982). Foreword. In *Student learning styles and brain behavior: Programs, instrumentation, and research* (pp. i–v). Reston, VA: National Association of Secondary School Principals.

Keefe, J. W., Letteri, C., Languis, M., & Dunn, R. (1986). *Learning Style Profile.* Reston, VA: National Association of Secondary School Principals.

Kennedy, M. D. (1995). The effects of an individual's learning style preference on psychomotor achievement for college students. Doctoral dissertation, Florida State University College of Education. *Dissertation Abstracts International, 56*(04), A1286.

Kirby, P. (1979). *Cognitive style, learning style and transfer skill acquisition.* Columbus: National Center for Research in Vocational Education, Ohio State University.

Klavas, A. (1991). Implementation of the Dunn and Dunn Learning-Style Model in United States elementary schools: Principals' and teachers' perceptions of factors that facilitated or impeded the process. Doctoral dissertation, St. John's University.

Klavas, A. (1993). In Greensboro, North Carolina: Learning-style program boosts achievement and test scores. *The Clearing House, 67*(30), 149–151.

Kolb, D. A. (1976). *Learning Style Inventory.* Boston: McBer.

Kolb, D. A. (1979). *Student learning styles and disciplinary learning environments: Diverse pathways for growth.* San Francisco: Jossey-Bass.

Kristensen, E., & Moulton, D. (1993). Challenges for faculty developers and department chairs: When faculty arrive from professional settings. *To Improve the Academy: Resources for Faculty, Instructional, & Organizational Development, 12,* 39–52.

Lam-Phoon, S. (1986). A comparative study of the learning styles of southeast Asian and American Caucasian college students of two Seventh-Day Adventist campuses. Doctoral dissertation, Andrews University. *Dissertation Abstracts International, 48*(09), 2234A.

Lawrence, G. (1982). Personality structure and learning style: Use of the *Myers-Briggs Type Indicator.* In *Student learning styles and brain behavior* (pp. 92–105). Reston, VA: National Association of Secondary School Principals.

Lenehan, M. C., Dunn, R., Ingham, J., Murray, W., & Signer, B. (1994). Learning style: Necessary know-how for academic success in college. *Journal of College Student Development, 35,* 461–465.

Levy, J. (1982). Children think with whole brains. In *Student learning styles and brain behavior* (pp. 173–184). Reston, VA: National Association of Secondary School Principals.

Lewthwaite, B. (1999). The *Productivity Environmental Preference Survey* and *Building Excellence*: A statistical comparison of two adult learning-style diagnostic instruments applied to a college population. Doctoral dissertation, St. John's University.

Lipsky, S. A., & Ender, S. C. (1990). Impact of a study skills course on probationary students' academic performance. *Journal of the Freshman Year Experience, 2,* 7–15.

Luna, G., & Cullen, D. (1996). *Empowering the faculty: Mentoring redirected and renewed.* Washington, DC: ASHE-ERIC Higher Education Reports.

Luria, A. R. (1973). *The working brain: An introduction to neuropsychology.* New York: Basic Books.

Marcus, L. (1977). How teachers view learning styles. *NASSP Bulletin, 61*(408), 112–114.

Marland, P., & Store, R. (1993): Some instructional strategies for improved learning from distance teaching materials. In K. Harry, M. John, & D. Keegan (Eds.), *Distance education: New perspectives* (pp. 137–156). New York: Routledge.

Marsh, H. W. (1984). Self-concept, social comparison and ability grouping: A reply to Kulik and Kulik. *American Educational Research Journal, 21,* 799–806.

Marsh, H. W. (1991). The failure of high ability high schools to deliver academic benefits: The importance of academic self-concept and educational aspirations. *American Educational Research Journal, 28,* 445–480.

Marsh, H. W., & Craven, R. (1997). Academic self-concept: Beyond the dustbowl. In G. D. Phye (Ed.), *Handbook of classroom assessment: Learning, achievement, and adjustment.* New York: Academic Press.

McCarthy, B. (1990). *The 4MAT system: Teaching to learning styles with right/left mode techniques.* Barrington, IL: Excel, Inc.

McElheny, M. (1995). Learning styles differ among students. *The Hilliard High School Wildcat*. Hilliard, OH: Hilliard High School.

Mentzer, M. (1993). Minority representation in higher education. *Journal of Higher Education, 64*(4), 417–433.

Mickler, M. L., & Zippert, C. P. (1987). Teaching strategies based on learning styles of adult students. *Community/Junior College Quarterly, 11*, 33–37.

Milgram, R. M., Dunn, R., & Price, G. E. (Eds.). (1993). *Teaching and counseling gifted and talented adolescents for learning style: An international perspective*. Westport, CT: Greenwood.

Miller, C., Alway, M., & McKinley, S. (1987, September). Effects of learning styles' strategies on academic success. *Journal of College Student Personnel*, 399–404.

Miller, J., & Dunn, R. (1997, November/December). The use of learning styles in sonography education. *Journal of Diagnostic Medical Sonography, 13*(6), 304–308.

Miller, J., Dunn, R., Beasley, M., Ostrow, S., Geisert, G., & Nelson, B. (1999/2000). Effects of traditional versus learning-style presentations of course content in ultrasound and anatomy on the achievement of attitudes of allied health college students. *National Forum of Applied Educational Research Journal, 13*(1).

Miller, J. A. (1997). The effects of traditional versus learning-style presentations of course content in ultrasound and anatomy on the achievement and attitudes of college students. Doctoral dissertation, St. John's University.

Miller, J. A. (1998). Enhancement of achievement and attitudes through individualized learning-style presentations of two allied health courses. *Journal of Allied Health, 27*(3), 150–156.

Mintzberg, H. (1981). Organization design: Fashion or fit? *Harvard Business Review*, 1106, 103–116.

Mitchell, D., Dunn, R., Klavas, A., Lynch, V., Montgomery, N., & Murray, J. (in press). Effects of traditional versus tactual/kinesthetic instruction on the achievement, application to writing, and attitudes of junior high and high school learning-disabled students. *National Forum of Applied Educational Research Journal, 13*(2).

Murrain, P. G. (1983). Administrative determinations concerning facilities utilization and instructional grouping: An analysis of the relationships between selected thermal environments and preferences for temperature, an element of learning style, as they affect word recognition scores of secondary students. Doctoral dissertation, St. John's University. *Dissertation Abstracts International, 44*, 1749A.

Napolitano, R. (1986). An experimental investigation of the relationships among achievement, attitude scores, and traditionally, marginally, and under-prepared college students enrolled in an introductory psychology course when they are matched and mismatched with their learning style preferences for the element of structure. *Dissertation Abstracts International, 47*, 435A.

National Commission on Teaching and America's Future (NCTAF). (1996). *What matters most: Teaching for America's future*. New York: Teachers College, Columbia University Press.

Nelson, B., Dunn, R., Griggs, S. A., Primavera, L., Fitzpatrick, M., Bacilious, Z., &

Miller, R. (1993). Effects of learning style intervention on students' retention and achievement. *Journal of College Student Development, 34*(5), 364–369.

Newton, F. B. (1990). Academic support seminars: A program to assist students experiencing academic difficulty. *Journal of College Student Development, 31,* 183–186.

Oberer, J. J. (1999). Practical application of Thies' philosophical and theoretical interpretation of the biological basis of learning style and brain behavior and their effects on the academic achievement, attitudes, and behaviors of fourth-grade students in a suburban school district. Doctoral dissertation, St. John's University.

O'Brien, L. (1989). Learning-styles: Make the students aware. *National Association of Secondary School Principals Bulletin, 73,* 85–89.

Orazio, P. A. (1999). Effects of matching and mismatching global and analytic instructional resources on the achievement and attitudes of seventh-grade mathematics students. Doctoral dissertation, St. John's University.

Perrin, J. (1982). *Learning Style Inventory: Primary Version.* Jamaica, NY: St. John's University's Center for the Study of Learning and Teaching Styles.

Perrin, J., & Santore, S. (1982). *Elephant style.* Jamaica, NY: St. John's University's Center for the Study of Learning and Teaching Styles.

Pizzo, J., Dunn, R., & Dunn, K. (1990, July/September). A sound approach to reading: Responding to students' learning styles. *Journal of Reading, Writing, and Learning Disabilities International, 6*(3), 249–260.

Price, G. E. (1980). Which learning style elements are stable and which tend to change over time? *Learning Styles Network Newsletter, 1*(3), 1.

Quilter, S. M. (1995). Academic self-concept and the first-year college student: A snapshot. *Journal of the Freshman Year Experience, 7*(1), 39–52.

Ramirez, M., & Castenada, A. (1974). *Cultural democracy, bicognitive development, and education.* New York: Academic Press.

Raupers, P. M. (in press). Effects of accommodating learning-style preferences on long-term retention of technology training content. *National Forum of Applied Educational Research Journal, 13*(2).

Reid, J. (Ed.). (1995). *Learning-styles in the ESL/EFL classroom.* Boston: Heinle & Heinle Publishers.

Research on the Dunn and Dunn Model. (1999). Jamaica, NY: St. John's University's Center for the Study of Learning and Teaching Styles.

Restak, R. (1979). *The brain: The last frontier.* Garden City, NY: Doubleday.

Restak, R. (1991). *The mind has a brain of its own: Insights from a practicing neurologist.* New York: Crown Trade Paperbacks.

Reynolds, J. (1988). A study of the pattern of learning style characteristics for adult dependent decision-makers. Doctoral dissertation, Virginia Polytech Institute and State University. *Dissertation Abstracts International, 50/*04A, 854.

Roberts, A. V. (1998/1999). Effects of tactual and kinesthetic instructional methods on social-studies achievement and attitude test scores of fifth-grade students. *National Forum of Teacher Education Journal, 9*(1), 16–26.

Roberts, A. V., Dunn, R., Holtschneider, D., Klavas, A., Miles, B., & Quinn, P. (in press). Effects of tactual and kinesthetic instructional resources on the social-studies achievement, attitude test scores, and short- and long-term memory of fourth-grade students. *National Forum of Applied Educational Research Journal, 13*(2).

Roberts, P. H. (1999). Effects of multisensory resources on the achievement and science attitudes of seventh-grade suburban students taught on- and above-grade level. Doctoral dissertation, St. John's University.

Rogers, C. (1986). Carl Rogers on the development of the person-centered approach. *Person-Centered Review, 1*(3), 257–259.

Schiering, M. (1999). Effects of meta-cognition on fifth-grade, suburban students' achievement, attitudes, and ability to teach themselves: A comparison of traditional versus learning-style instruction. Doctoral dissertation, St. John's University.

Schmeck, R. R. (1977). *Inventory of Learning Processes.* Carbondale, IL: Department of Psychology, Southern Illinois University.

The Secretary's Commission on Achieving Necessary Skills (SCANS). (1991). *What work requires of schools: A SCANS report for AMERICA 2000.* Washington, DC: United States Department of Labor.

Senge, P. M. (1990). *The fifth discipline.* New York: Doubleday.

Shea, T. C. (1983). An investigation of the relationship among preferences for the learning style element of design, selected instructional environments, and reading achievement with ninth grade students to improve administrative determinations concerning effective educational facilities. Doctoral dissertation, St. John's University. *Dissertation Abstracts International, 44,* 2004A.

Simmons, G., Wallins, J., & George, A. (1995). The effects of a freshman seminar on at-risk under-, over- and low achievers. *Journal of the National Academic Advising Association, 15*(1), 8–14.

Skinner, B. F. (1983). The behavior of organisms. *Journal of Experimental Analysis.* New York: Appleton.

Somers, R. (1988). Working with the adult learner: Applied andragogy for development programs. *Review of Research in Developmental Education, 5*(5), 1–5.

Sperry, R. (1968). Hemisphere connection and unity in conscious awareness. *American Psychologist, 23,* 723–733.

State Board for Educator Certification. (1997). *Learning-centered schools for Texas: A vision of Texas educators.* Austin, TX: Author.

Studd, M. (1995). Learning style differences. *The Clearing House, 69*(1), 38–39.

Sullivan, M. (1993). A meta-analysis of experimental research studies based on the Dunn and Dunn Learning-Style Model and its relationship to academic achievement and performance. Doctoral dissertation, St. John's University. *Dissertation Abstracts International, 51,* 297A.

Tanenbaum, R. (1982). An investigation of the relationships between selected instructional techniques and identified field dependent and field independent cognitive styles as evidenced among high school students enrolled in studies of nutrition. Doctoral dissertation, St. John's University. *Dissertation Abstracts International, 43,* 68A.

Taylor, R. G., Dunn, R., Dunn, K. J., Klavas, A., & Montgomery, N. (1999/2000). Effects of learning-style responsive versus traditional staff development on the knowledge and attitudes of teachers. *National Forum of Applied Educational Research Journal, 13*(1), 63–75.

Teich, P. F. (1986). Research on American law teaching: Is there a case against the case system? *Journal of Legal Education, 36*, 167–187.

Tendy, S. (1998). Effects of matching and mismatching sociological and perceptual learning-style preferences on achievement of individuals in a group exercise leadership instructor training program. Doctoral dissertation, St. John's University.

Tendy, S., & Geiser, W. F. (1998/1999). The search for style: It all depends on where you look. *National Forum of Teacher Education Journal, 9*(1), 3–15.

Thies, A. P. (1979). A brain behavior analysis of learning style. In *Student learning styles: Diagnosing and prescribing programs* (pp. 55–61). Reston, VA: National Association of Secondary School Principals.

Thies, A. P. (1999/2000). The neuropsychology of learning styles. *National Forum of Applied Educational Research Journal, 13*(1), 50–62.

Tinto, V. (1993). *Leaving College: Rethinking the causes and cures of student attrition.* Chicago: University of Chicago Press.

Trautman, P. (1979). An investigation of the relationship between selected instructional techniques and identified cognitive style. Doctoral dissertation, St. John's University. *Dissertation Abstracts International, 40*, 1428A.

Urbschat, K. S. (1977). A study of preferred learning modes and their relationship to the amount of recall of CVC trigrams. Doctoral dissertation, Wayne State University. *Dissertation Abstracts International, 38*, 2536A.

Van Wynen, E. (1999). Analysis of current and previous learning styles of older adults in a residential setting and the effects of congruent and incongruent instruction on their achievement and attitudes. Doctoral dissertation, St. John's University.

Van Wynen, E. A. (1997, September/October). Information processing styles: One size doesn't fit all. *Nurse Educator, 22*(5), 44–50.

Vazquez, A. W. (1985). Description of learning styles of high risk adult students taking courses in urban community colleges in Puerto Rico. Doctoral dissertation, The Union for Experimenting Colleges and Universities, Puerto Rico. *Dissertation Abstracts International, 47*, 1157A.

Vertecchi, B. (1993). A two-level strategy for mastery learning. In K. Harry, M. John, & D. Keegan (Eds.), *Distance education: New perspectives* (pp. 126–136). New York: Routledge.

Wilhite, S. C. (1990). Self-efficacy, locus of control, self-assessment of memory ability, and study activities as predictors of college course achievement. *Journal of Educational Psychology, 82*(4), 696–700.

Williams, H. S. (1994). The differences in cumulative grade point averages among African-American freshman college learning styles: A preliminary investigation. *National Forum of Applied Educational Research Journal, 8*(1), 36–40.

Yin, R. (1984). *Case study: Design and Methods.* Beverly Hills, CA: Sage Publications.

Zenhausern, R. (1988). *Hemispheric Preference Scale.* Jamaica, NY: Department of Psychology, St. John's University.

Index

About the Editors and Contributors

ANN C. BRAIO is Director of Special Education, Yonkers Public Schools, New York, and Adjunct Assistant Professor of Education, Manhattan College, Riverdale, New York.

ROBIN A. BOYLE is Assistant Legal Writing Professor, St. John's University's School of Law, where she has been teaching Legal Research and Writing since 1994. She also is Adjunct Assistant Professor, Fordham University's College of Liberal Studies, where she has been teaching law-related courses in political science and English since 1993.

KAREN BURKE is Assistant Professor, Child Study Department, St. Joseph's College, Brooklyn, New York. She is the author of five chapters, six articles, and *Learning Style: The Clue to You!*—the first global-format learning-styles identification instrument for middle school students.

E. L. DECKINGER is Distinguished Visiting Professor, Department of Advertising and Marketing, College of Business Administration, St. John's University, New York. As noted in his chapter, he is a "fugitive from 45 years on Madison Avenue." Since 1982, he has been "seeking absolution by serving penance through teaching about advertising."

LAURA SHEA DOOLAN is a doctoral teaching assistant and candidate, Instructional Leadership Doctoral Program, Division of Administrative and Instructional Leadership, St. John's University, New York.

HEATHER PFLEGER DUNHAM is Professor of Business, Centenary College, Hackettstown, New Jersey. She has co-authored articles on learning-styles-based instruction in the *Journal of Staff, Program, and Organizational Development* and the *Journal of Staff Development*.

KENNETH J. DUNN is Professor and Coordinator, Administration and Supervision Programs, Queens College of the City University of New York. He is the author/co-author of 15 textbooks and 150 published articles and research papers. Dr. Dunn is the co-developer of the Dunn and Dunn Learning-Style Model and has been actively involved in its refinement, implementation, and research.

RITA DUNN is Professor, Division of Administrative and Instructional Leadership and Director, Center for the Study of Learning and Teaching Styles, St. John's University, New York. Dr. Dunn is the author/co-author of 22 textbooks and 300 published articles and research reports. She is the recipient of 25 national and international awards for the quality of her research and teaching. She is the founder of the International Learning Styles Network.

VALERIE ENGLANDER is Associate Professor of Economics, St. John's University, New York, with professional interests in the areas of economics, public policy, ethics, and the development and application of alternative teaching methods. Her publications include articles in the *American Economist*, the *Journal of Behavioral Economics*, *Policy Studies Review*, and the *Journal of Business Ethics*.

BARBARA K. GIVEN is Associate Professor, Graduate School of Education, and a member of the Research Faculty, Krasnow Institute for Advanced Study at George Mason University, Fairfax, Virginia. She also co-directs the Center for Honoring Individual Learning Diversity (CHILD), an affiliate of the International Learning Styles Network, and has authored one book and six articles.

SHIRLEY A. GRIGGS is Professor Emeritus, Division of Human Services and Counseling, St. John's University, New York. She has co-authored and co-edited four books with Professor Rita Dunn, and three books and 50 professional articles on learning-styles counseling, multiculturalism, at-risk students, and group counseling. She has received the Distinguished Service Award of the American Counseling Association and served as co-editor of the *School Counselor Journal* and as consulting editor of the *Journal of Counseling and Development*.

NORA HALL is a Ph.D. candidate at George Mason University and a curriculum specialist in mathematics in the Prince William County Public Schools.

JOANNE INGHAM is Director, Institutional Assessment and Retention, Polytech University, New York. She has authored many published manuscripts on learning styles, adult literacy, and multiculturalism.

WILLIAM JOHNSON is a Ph.D. candidate in American History in the Community College Doctoral Program at George Mason University.

ROSE F. LEFKOWITZ is Assistant Professor, Department of Health-Information Management, College of Health Related Professions, State University of New York Health Science Center, Brooklyn, New York. She has written extensively on information management and learning styles.

BARBARA-JAYNE LEWTHWAITE is Professor of Education, Centenary College, Hackettstown, New Jersey. She has co-authored articles on learning-styles-based instruction in the *Journal of Staff, Program, and Organizational Development* and the *Journal of Staff Development*.

PAM LITTLETON is Associate Professor, Department of Mathematics and Physics and Associate Dean, College of Arts and Sciences, Tarleton State University, Stephenville, Texas. She has taught at the university level for more than 10 years, is Co-Director of the Institute for Research on Teaching and Learning, and is a board member of the International Learning Styles Network.

KATY LUX has 25 years of public and private school experience. Prior to assuming her position as Professor of Education at Aquinas College in Grand Rapids, Michigan, she served as a teacher, reading consultant, staff developer, and adjunct university instructor. Dr. Lux has an extensive background in working with differential student needs and has received several awards and recognition for her work in this field. She is a board member of the International Learning Styles Network.

JOYCE A. MILLER is Professor and Chairperson, Department of Diagnostic Medical Imaging, College of Health Related Professions, State University of New York Health Science Center, Brooklyn, New York. She has written extensively on health-related issues.

NANCY MONTGOMERY is Associate Professor of Instructional Leadership in the School of Education and Human Services, St. John's University, New York. A professor in higher education for 18 years, she has authored

articles on the teaching of writing at the college level, computers and composition, Cooperative Learning, peer tutoring, developmental composition,
and networked electronic writing centers and classrooms.

HERBERT D. PIERSON is Assistant Professor, Institute of English as a
Second Language, St. John's University, New York. He is co-editor of the
Journal of Asian Pacific Communication, has written extensively on second-
language learning, and taught in higher education for 30 years.

SUE ELLEN READ is Professor of Education, Northeastern State University (NSU) in Tahlequah, Oklahoma, where she has taught for the past 10
years. Dr. Read chairs the Master's of Teaching Program and consults with
school districts and universities on learning styles. She has published a study
of Native American learning styles and is currently involved in two projects
to implement learning styles in schools with majority Cherokee populations.
She was recently named NSU Faculty of the Year in Teaching.

BERNADYN KIM SUH is Associate Professor of Education, Dowling College. Oakdale, New York, where she also co-directs the Center for Learning
and Teaching Strategies with Dr. Thomas C. DeBello and is a board member of the International Learning Styles Network.

JODY TAYLOR is an educational consultant who developed her chapter
during a five-year Virginia Department of Education Teacher-Training
Grant for Distance Learning.

RALPH A. TERREGROSSA is Associate Professor of Economics, St. John's
University, New York. His publications include articles in the *Quarterly Review of Economics and Finance*, the *Journal of Forensic Sciences*, and the
Journal of International Advances in Economic Research. His research focuses mainly on capital depreciation, investment behavior, and technical
change.

BARBARA S. THOMSON is Associate Professor of Science Education and
Director, Regional Center of Learning and Teaching Styles, Ohio State University, Columbus, Ohio. She is a board member of the International Learning Styles Network.

EDWARD P. TYLER is Senior Data Administrator, Fairfax County School
Division, and a student in the Doctor of Arts in Community College Education Program at George Mason University, Fairfax, Virginia.

JANET WHITLEY is Assistant Professor, Department of Curriculum and
Instruction, Tarleton State University, Stephenville, Texas. She is editor of

the *Journal for the Effective Schools Project* and has taught in higher education for more than 10 years. She is Co-Director of the Institute for Teaching and Learning and is a board member of the International Learning Styles Network.

MARGARET WOOD is a Ph.D. candidate in the Community College Doctoral Program at George Mason University and a consultant in Computer Engineering.

ISBN 0-89789-703-X

HARDCOVER BAR CODE

3